MW00915044

The Infinite Pool
of
Experience and Awareness

by Alexei Novitzky

"The Infinite Pool of Experience and Awareness"

"The Infinite Pool of Experience and Awareness" shows us that all manifestations, from matter to thoughts, are the result of a single motion through a primordial energy. We show that consciousness is like a gyroscope precessing through the fluid of time and design interdimensional technologies. Although we are all unique individuals, we harmonize as one.

"Your Influence in Space" shows us that our bodies light encompasses the entire Universe in at least one or more reference frames. We see that the speed of light is a limitation to human perception and not reality.

4-49

"The Liquid-Light State Universe" describes the Universe as if matter forms at nodes of overlapping EM. It also introduces the mind, body, and spirit diagrams.

50-115

"The Crystal of Time" shows that habitable zones for human consciousness exist where the acceleration of spacetime is equal to the speed of light.

116-148

In "Time Atom," we see there is a layering of conscious types that exist within time. We then relate conscious harmonics to flows of space and design an interdimensional telescope.

149-203

"The 5th Dimension" ties it all together and demonstrates that all experiences are the result of a single motion through a singular field of energy. We track our daily orbit through conscious density and see that consciousness is like a gyroscope precessing through the fluid of time.

204-257

"Looshes" is a book of 19 poems. Topics include spacetime, materialism, life & death

258-313

Philosophical Discussions include: Thinking with the Universe, A Shift in Natural Selection, Dreaming at Light Speed, & A Universal Goal

314-343

Your Influence In Space

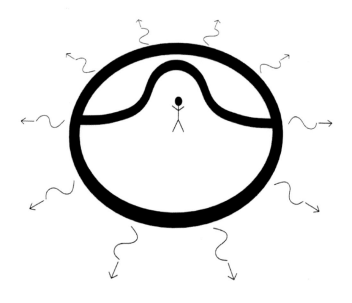

by Alexei Novitzky

Table of Contents

Introduction

"Your Influence in Space" primarily discusses the concept of Space Preparation. In short, your light extends to the edge of the Universe in at least one or more reference frames.

We begin our journey by looking at the evolution of the human senses. We see that some senses come from evolving on Earth and some come from evolving around the Sun.

The Doppler shift is examined and shows us how our light or influence can stretch and crunch depending on relative motions.

Our journey then takes another look at gravity. Perhaps the force of gravity comes from planets acting as shields blocking an interstellar star pressure rather than them being a source of attraction.

However, ultimately it is all waves and the nature of reality may be an overlapping of electromagnetic energies. We define the light-state of the Universe and introduce "The Liquid-Light State Universe."

The Senses

"Not only did we evolve on Earth which revolves around the Sun, but we also evolved in an expanding Universe, hence, our sense of time."

-Alexei Novitzky

Here we will take a look at the human senses. We will explore why we even have senses and where they came from. It is important to first explore these concepts because they are crucial for understanding our sense of space and time and the concept of Space Preparation.

Darwin's Theory of Evolution

Most of us are familiar with Darwin's Theory of Evolution. However, let's do a quick recap. It basically states that all life is related and extends from a common ancestor. Over long periods of time, these animals change to be better suited for their environment.

Sensory Evolution

First, it is important to discuss why beings even have senses, what they can sense with them, and why they may be considered beneficial for survival. We could go into much more detail on each topic, but considering this is simply a stepping stone for our understanding of Space Preparation, we will keep this simple.

While we discuss, keep in the back of your mind that physical existence is a combination of light and solid. More specifically, light creates the solids. Photons could be considered like electrons moving at the speed of light from atom to atom. However, different combinations of light create the physical world and these combinations may fabricate themselves to be any particle in existence. In short, matter is composed of light.

Evolving on Earth

Figure 1: shows a human evolving on Earth

Animals have been said to have evolved on Earth. This statement is a rather simple system when compared to the greater picture. Animals did evolve on Earth, yet they also evolved in a solar system. To take that one step further, evolution occurred within an expanding Universe.

For the senses of smell and taste we have organs that detect physical particles. The organs in this case would be the nose and tongue. They send electrical signals to our brain and let our bodies know if action is needed or not. They can tell us if something is edible or not. If something tastes or smells bad, it is most likely not edible. They can warn our bodies of approaching dangers like fire. The scent of smoke is strongly recognizable. You could say that these sensory organs are tuned to what would allow the species to survive and reproduce. The case for reproduction is clear with pheromones.

These senses have been designed through evolution on Earth to detect physical molecules. The nose and tongue are detecting molecules that are made of matter.

Now consider the sense of hearing. Again, you are detecting physical matter, but this time it is in the form of pressure waves. Pressure waves create the sounds you hear. The range of hearing is directly related to the frequency of a being's vocal cords. This is why we cannot perceive the highest pitches of a mouse and the lowest pitches of an elephant. Mice are tuned to a much higher frequency of sound and elephants are tuned to a much lower frequency. However, the main point is that this sense is also detecting physical matter.

The sense of touch is somewhat unique because it can detect molecules and light. Your sense of feeling comes from physically interacting with objects. You know that contact has been made because magnetic energy in your molecules is directly being interfered by the molecules of whatever you are touching. This is obvious. What might not be so obvious is that you can feel if something is hot or cold. The implications of this are much grander than you may think. Your sense of touch can actually sense temperature differences without contact.

You could say that human skin has the ability to detect infrared energy. It may be safe to assume that it may also be able to detect slightly shorter and slightly longer wavelengths. This means that you can essentially see with your sense of feeling. In the simplest terms, your skin can sense heat with no physical contact and only that of electromagnetic energy. The sense of sound, taste, and smell all come from directly evolving on Earth. Feel may be the first sense that gives us a clue of the Sun.

Evolving in a Solar System

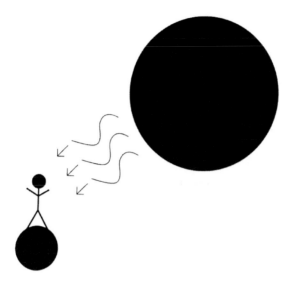

Figure 2: shows a human evolving in a solar system

Not only did we evolve on Earth, but we also evolved in a solar system.

For light, the organ would be the eyeball and it detects electromagnetism. Light comes in many wavelengths, and similar to sound, eyes are best tuned to the environment in which they live. Again, to keep this moving towards Space Preparation and not be to sidetracked, we will keep this section short.

The human vision is focused around the color yellow which is the maximum wavelength of output emitted by the Sun. The implications of this may be much grander than we realize.

The senses of sound, touch, taste, and smell all came from evolving on Earth. Here we see the first trace of a sensory organs evolutionary influence coming from space. Eyes detect electromagnetic waves that come from space. To keep it simple, the Sun's light hits the Earth and then bounces around in many visible wavelengths. Similar to the ear's form of acoustic wave detection, the eye has a limited range of electromagnetic frequencies in which it may gather information.

There are many wavelengths that the eye cannot sense. The eye cannot sense wavelengths that are shorter than blue or longer than red (some people have been known to see UV). Our eyes can only see an extremely small portion of the electromagnetic spectrum when compared to all the possibilities in existence.

The point, and I stress this point, is that light waves exist that we cannot detect and the ones we do are beneficial for surviving the current moment.

Evolving in an Expanding Universe

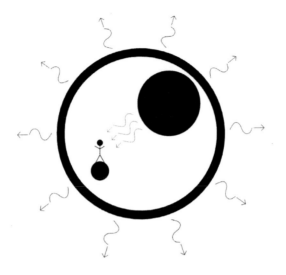

Figure 3: shows a human evolving in an expanding universe

The sense of time exists and is a result of evolving in an expanding Universe where light is able to move freely from atom to atom. The sense of time may be extremely hard to measure. Sure, you can measure how far light travels and use a pendulum but all that varies according to your relativistic velocity. It could be safe to say that similar waves like those from short to long of the electromagnetic and acoustic frequencies exist in time as well and we have the ability to detect the one that is most beneficial for surviving the current moment. Now for time, this may be an obvious statement, but it is most beneficial to sense the now and not the past or the future for your average animal. Every sense is ultimately filtered by your brain to give you a way to interact as best as possible with the environment.

The past is solid and exist yet we cannot physically see it. The present exist and we can see it. The future will be solid and it will exist. This implies that all future may be as solid as our past. Our sense of time is tuned to the now because it is what is most beneficial for surviving the current moment and producing offspring.

Limitations of Physical Medians

There are limitations to the medians in which our senses are tuned. We are now shifting over to talk about the accuracy of our senses to the physical environment. From the last section, we see that each sense has a threshold, a range of frequencies in which it may gather information. We also see that each sense is tuned to a certain substance or median.

For example, ears are tuned to acoustic waves which vibrate through physical matter. Typically, the median is air. However, you can put your ear on a desk and tap the desk and now you are listening through a desk which is made of a solid. Now the desk is the median. In both cases, the median determines the accuracy of your sense of choice. Accuracy, in this case, refers in your ability to locate the signal that you are searching for. In other words, where is the object you are listening for? For sound waves, the denser the median is the faster the wave will travel. The faster the wave travels, the more accurately you may predict the location of the source because there is less chance that it has moved. (Very quickly and for fun, could there exist a density to where the velocity of the sound wave is greater than the speed of light?)

It is important to recognize that sound has a maximum velocity which it can travel through any median and it is generally governed by the density of the material. The basic equation is as follows.

$$c = \sqrt{K/p}$$

c=speed of sound   K=Bulk's Modulus   p=density

Figure 4: The speed of sound is determined by the Bulk's modulus and the density of the material.

You can clearly see that the velocity of the speed of sounds varies through different medians. Let's do a quick thought experiment.

Imagine if we did not evolve with eyes and only had ears. Our entire world and understanding of space and time would be solely based off sounds. We might think that the speed of sound is the fastest speed available as far as communications are concerned. The perceived locations of objects would be directly related to the speed at which the sound takes to travel. Acoustic waves would be the source of information exchange within our known Universe.

We would not know of stars and light because we would not have evolved with the tools necessary to do so. However, as humans, and having evolved with electromagnetic detection abilities, we know that light travels much faster than sound. For example, we can see a lightning strike well before we hear the thunder. Knowing this, we think it's completely silly or even ridiculous to consider the speed of sound as the ultimate barrier as far as physical matter moving through space.

At Least we are Smarter than the Worms

Figure 5: shows a human has a much larger cognitive ability than a worm

Understanding our senses is crucial for understanding our Universe. Consider the earthworm and politics. The worm lives all day in the dirt and is extremely efficient at what it does. It eats and poops dirt. If you were to ask a worm about human politics it would be clueless. It would not know if it was a Democrat or a Republican. The worm would not have a clue. This is because of two main reasons. The first is quite obvious. The earthworm has a small brain. The second is that the earthworm does not need to understand human politics. For that reason, it did not evolve with the tool necessary to do so. Remember, senses help us live in the now and reproduce. Although human politics may influence a worm's habitat through farming and other secondary means, the worm will never be able to fully comprehend what is happening solely because it does not have the senses to be able to.

Will a worm ever truly understand human politics? The answer is no. Worms do not have the physical ability to comprehend such concepts. The worm is not physically or mentally evolved enough to understand with the same capability as a human as to what it means to be alive in the Universe. The worm has no knowledge of other planets, comets, black holes, and etc. Those parts of existence have no influence on the worm's day to day survival.

But we are not that Smart

Compare humans to the earthworm. We are bounds and leaps ahead of them as far as technological advancements and knowledge of the stars is concerned. We can make art, complicated communications, build telescopes, and decipher the stars, but how smart are we really when compared to the most advanced lifeforms in existence? The Earth has been around for about 4.5 billion years and humans roughly appeared 100,000 years ago. That's not really that much time when compared to the age of the Earth and especially when compared to the age of the Universe which is estimated to be around 18 billion years old. There could be lifeforms that have been around for 200,000 years or even a billion years. These lifeforms could potentially have much more developed senses than we do. Humans to these theoretical aliens, could be just as smart as earthworms are to us.

Light is the Source of Information Exchange

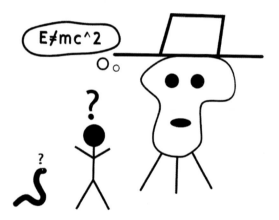

Figure 6: shows how a theoretical extraterrestrial may have a much larger cognitive ability than a human

The fastest source of information exchange when it comes to natural human evolutionary senses is electromagnetism. Electromagnetism is light. The speed of light may seem very fast. It may seem almost instant. You can have a conversation with someone on the other side of the planet with little to no delay.

This comes down to perception. Light appears to move fast to humans, but to the theoretical alien that may have more developed senses than we do, light may move extremely slow. The thought of communicating through electromagnetism may be equivalent to talking to someone with two cups tied together with a string. To give an extreme example for our humanly understanding, imagine that this being can see and travel through wormholes with their natural body and no technology just as easy as we can see the stars at night.

"The Universe's Greatest Magic Trick"

Matter can travel faster than light but it will not look like it. It is "The Universe's Greatest Magic Trick." Consider the magician. They use lights and trickery to create an illusion. The reason why the tricks work is because they make you believe something is happening when it is not. They will make a sound or show an image. People then think something is somewhere because they hear or see it. However, in reality, it is already in their back pocket. The same is true for light within the Universe.

The Doppler Effect

The Doppler shift can be seen in many different wave forms. Again, let's consider sound waves for this example. Imagine a simple tone. Let's say it's a generic 100 units in wavelength. Now take the source of sound and give it a velocity in a direction that is either moving towards or away from you. You will notice that the wavelength will change accordingly. When compared to a stationary object, objects traveling towards you will have a higher frequency and objects moving away from you will have a lower frequency. This is where things get a little tricky.

Figure 7: The person riding on the train does not notice any changes in sound.

Let's say the object is a train. When you are on the train you won't really notice anything. The sound will be a constant hum from the engine or wheels rolling on the tracks.

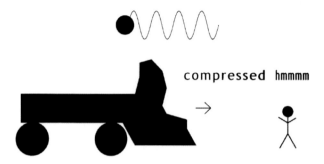

compressed hmmmm

Figure 8: Sound waves are compressed as the train approaches the observer.

stretched   h m m m m

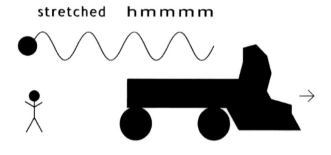

Figure 9: Sound waves are stretched as the train moves away from the observer.

Now let's say you are on the side of the tracks and the train comes racing by. The sound of the train will change as it passes. It will change from short waves while its coming towards you to then being shifted to long waves while it's moving away from you. This is an example of the Doppler shift that may be seen in our day-to-day life. All wave types undergo a Doppler shift.

The effect of the Doppler shift is directly related to the velocity and location of the wave source. In the previous example, the source would have been the train.

The Doppler effect is also true for electromagnetism. The electromagnetic spectrum may be broken down into many different wave types. However, for this section it is important to note that all waves, x-rays, visible light, radio waves, gamma waves, and etc. are all forms of electromagnetic waves.

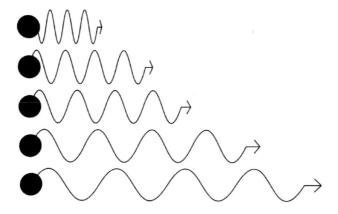

Figure 10: Shows how the same light or electromagnetic wave may look different depending on your relative motion.

They are all composed of the same forces that we physically see. The only difference is the frequency or wavelength. The appearance of an electromagnetic wave is directly related to the original source of the wave and its velocity when compared to the observer.

Let's now look at a simple example for light. Imagine a yellow light. It's sits somewhere stationary in space. Now the light decides to come racing towards you at speeds relative to the speed of light. As the object comes near, the light waves begin to crunch. The light therefor has a higher frequency and looks bluer. As the light passes, you notice that it turns from blue to yellow to red. The light is now traveling away from you so the wavelengths have been stretched. It now has a longer frequency because it is moving away.

Another important factor is that the speed of light is constant no matter how fast you are moving. This means that the apparent distances that the light has traveled may vary based on the observer.

Let's now imagine we have a UFO that can accelerate at infinite velocity. Imagine we shine a beam of light for one second. Let's now generalize on the relative distances the light has traveled based on the speed of the observer. For this, we'll need four observers. Observer 0 is stationary on Earth (0c). Observer 1 is flying at the speed of light(1c). Observer 2 is flying at two times the speed of light and Observer infinity is flying at infinite velocity.

A quick side, the theory of relativity says that nothing can travel faster than the speed of light. We are saying that is an illusion created by the permeation of light within space and human consciousness.

The Trick

Ask yourself, how can anything ever look like it's going faster than light if light is the most advanced source of information exchange for human consciousness? The relative time dilations are still of an important factor because that is how matter acts when it's in motion. However, what would two photons accelerating at light speed in the same direction look like to another? They may appear frozen in space, like matter.

Consider a particle accelerating at light speed. Try to imagine the light being emitted in front and behind. Here is a quick thought experiment to help you visualize the scenario. The force of gravity is 9.8 m/s^2 for Earth. In order to lift off with a rocket your acceleration needs to be greater than 9.8 m/s^2. If it is less, you wouldn't take off, but you would weigh less. However, at exactly 9.8 m/s^2 you will neither lift or have weight. That would be the same effect as a photon being emitted from a particle accelerating at light speed. They would either be stuck in the direction of travel and appear to be mass or emitted in the reverse direction. So, is there a difference between light and matter or is that just a result of your relative frame of motion? Is the matter we manifest with a result of light speed acceleration?

Let's go back to the example of the UFO and yellow light and while we are doing this relate the amount of energy the wave has with the distance it has traveled. We will now shine the light for 1 second of time.

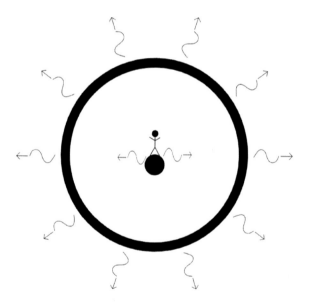

Figure 11: shows that for the person on Earth, the light has not been stretched

Observer 0, the person on earth not moving, experiences that the light has traveled 1c and looks yellow.

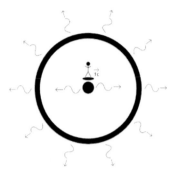

Figure 12: shows that the lights has been stretched by a distance of 1c

Observer 1, the person traveling at one time the speed of light, sees that the light has traveled 2c and looks redder. The wavelength is longer and the standing energy associated with frequency is less.

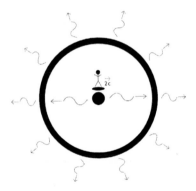

Figure 13: shows how the light has been stretched by 2c

Observer 2, the person traveling at two times the speed of light, sees that the light has traveled 3c and looks even more stretched. The light may now be in the radio wave form and its frequency even less.

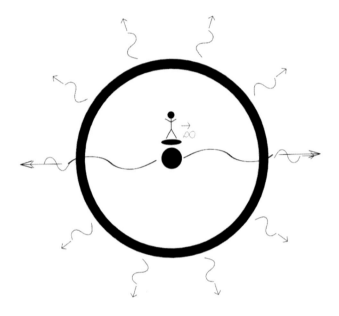

Figure 14: shows how the light has been stretched all the way to infinity

Observer 3, the person at infinite velocity, sees that the light has still traveled in front of them. It is at a distance of infinity+1c. However, the wave is so stretched that the energy associated is nearly equal to zero.

When you take the quick snapshot of this scenario, you see that an objects light encompasses the entire Universe in at least one or more reference frames. There is a bell curve associated with the energy and distance from material center.

It is interesting to compare this to Heisenberg's Uncertainty Principle because the bell curve shape associated with position and momentum seems to be related to this phenomenon. Our curve is directly relating the now standing energy with distance from center.

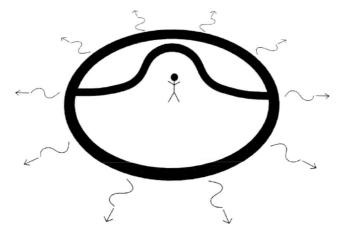

Figure 15: demonstrates that your light exists everywhere in the Universe in at least one or more reference frames. Your total influence in all frames added together resembles the bell shape.

This implies that your energy exists in all moments of space and time in at least one or more relative frames of motion. In other words, your light and therefor influence exist at the edge of the Universe but is most dominant and influential in your own relative frame of motion, in the physical space in which it resides.

Space Prepares Itself Before Matter Shines

Every particle or wave of light exists at all places and moments in time in at least one or more reference frames. In other words, everything is somewhat everywhere but your energy is strongest in your own frame. Now let's take another journey on a UFO. While doing so, we would be jumping from one relativistic frame to another. You would see the energy of an Earthly light beam slowly and slowly decrease as your velocity increased. You would reach a point to where the light is so stretched it becomes almost unnoticeable.

Now let's move backwards along this trip. Assume you are accelerating at light speed from infinite velocity, and instead of accelerating away from Earth you accelerate towards it. The wave of light you would originally see would be extended to infinity and then slowly and slowly the light would then fabricate into the light of the Earthly frame once the velocity of the bodies is the same. You never physically move towards the Earth. You simply accelerate towards it until the velocity differences are the same. What you would see is a shift from long waves to short.

What's interesting is that these particles already exist as long waves at the edge of the Universe and that it takes a certain amount of time for the particle of the sources frame to arrive.

When considering physical space now, it would take an infinite amount of time for the light as seen from the Earthly observer to arrive at the edge of the Universe. Whereas, in the subject moving at infinite velocity it is already there and takes no time. This shows potential for building a device that may be able to detect the future.

Space Preparation Conclusion

A particle or wave exists in all moments in space and time in at least one or more relativistic frames of motion. Space must first be prepared from long waves to short as particles or photons move through space or rather manifest. This Space Preparation can be sensed and therefor measured and computed.

Although current technology may not yet exist to capture this in motion, it is a real possibility and the concept of future imaging does exist.

Gravity from Above

One of the most fundamental forces in nature is gravity. It is the physical attraction of matter and its force may accurately be measured using a variety of equations. However, why are people so convinced that gravity pulls? Could there be a basic set of equations that considers gravity as a pushing force instead? Perhaps it is a force from Time itself?

Figure 16: Newton wonders why the fruit is falling from the tree.

Sir Isaac Newton

The story of Newton and the fruit tree is well known. He was sitting underneath and then saw a fruit fall. He wondered, "Why?" What he claimed was there was a force that attracted the fruit to the Earth. He then made equations.

Common Equations

Some of the most commonly used equations when calculating the force of gravity is $F=ma$ and $F=GMm/r^2$. $F=ma$ is good for when comparing a much smaller body to a larger body and the force of gravity is already well known. $F=GMm/r^2$ is great for celestial bodies within the galaxy. Very quickly, F is the force of gravity which is related to the masses of the objects and distances between them.

But the Universe is Expanding

That's simple enough. However, at extreme distances, say the length of the Universe, these laws aren't really applying. Intuition would tell us that the Universe should be contracting or at least slowing in its expansion. However, it is still expanding.

From this, it is obvious that something is missing or that it is being approached improperly. Consider now the source of gravity coming from an outside source instead of coming from the mass of the object.

Maybe it's from Above

Yes, let's pretend that gravity comes from above instead of the Earth. How could that work?

Electromagnetic waves carry momentum with them. You can physically move objects with lasers. A perfect example is getting a piece of lightweight tin foil and shining a powerful blue light at it. The tinfoil will jump. So, maybe the force of gravity comes from light. Even more added energy could be coming from particles or photons when you consider all the relative frames of motion. How could this work?

Imagine a free-floating body in space not near any planets or stars. The force of gravity is zero because there are no stars next to it. It is neither being pushed or pulled in one direction. This does not say anything about where the force of gravity is actually coming from. All it says is that the forces are balanced all adding to zero. This body could have billions and billions of tons acting on it but all the forces are canceling each other to make no motion.

All the Stars in the Universe

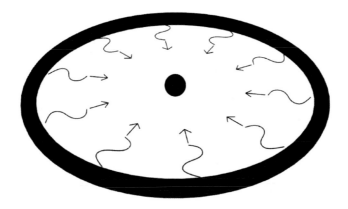

Figure 17: shows all the light in the Universe pushing on a body

Here is a case that has a free-floating body in space. There are still billions and billions of stars and a smooth cosmic background for this example. Either these stars have zero effect on the body or they have their natural effect. I would argue they have their natural effect. Each star in existence emits essentially every wavelength in existence from infinitely short to infinitely long. Each star pushes on the other and you could say that space and time is dense with electromagnetic waves. In any point in space there is essentially every wavelength of light coming in from all directions. There is a sort of universal mesh and the Universe is like liquid-light in that fashion.

Now let's add a massive planet to the scenario. What would a planet do to light coming in from all directions? The answer may be obvious. It would get in the way. So, you see a planet or any physical body is actually blocking light. The planets and other masses would be acting as shields.

A New Definition for Gravity

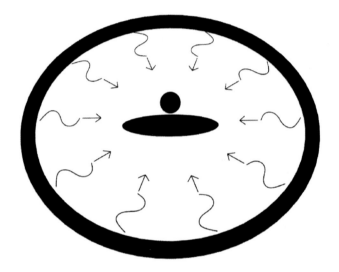

Figure 18: shows how two bodies that are close together have equal star pressure pushing on them causing them to come together

The force of gravity could then be equated as "interstellar star pressure (P)," minus "shielding (S)." The interstellar star pressure would be the force of natural light waves in any point in space time and would not be constant in the Universe. It would depend on the number of stars and varying wavelengths all creating a general light-state.

Your equation would then look like F=P-S. This is a very simple equation and works wonders in the Universe. Not only does F=P-S but F=GMm/r^2 for close ranges. So, you could assume that F=GMm/r^2=P-S. Remember, the answers are already there. The force of gravity will always be 9.8 m/s^2 for Earth. Therefore, P-S of Earth is equal to 9.8 m/s^2. All the answers are already out there and it may help to redefine our methods for some scenarios.

The Approach

The rate of expansion is known from observations. The force of gravity at relatively close distances is known. From this, we could find that the value of P at any point in space. P=F+S. So, what is S? Well, S is the "shielding force" which is created by any mass as it blocks or rather interacts with interstellar light pressure or energy.

By using many different examples of known gravitational forces we may approximate a reasonable interstellar pressure (P).

Just like the equations for gravity that exists, the amount of shielding pressure would be related to the amount of mass and the distance squared.

P would be the summation of energy of all light in space and time including those of different relativistic frames. This would give a vector account of star pressure and direction.

A simple example would be to say that P is at a maximum at the center of the Universe where it is being bombarded by light from all directions. The resulting energy is equal to zero because all the forces would cancel out. Then you could say at the edges of the Universe the total force would be due to P because there would not be any shielding sources.

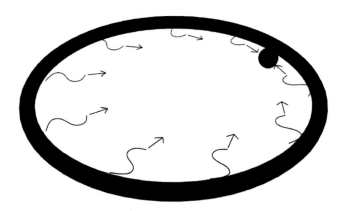

Figure 19: shows that near the edge the forces are solely due to interstellar star pressure

In short, you can say that shielding is equal to zero at the edges and the expansion is due to an interstellar star pressure of sorts.

Relationship to the Expanding Universe

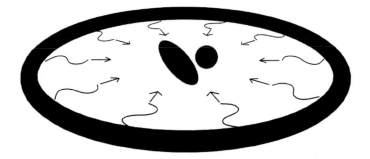

Figure 20: this simple model shows objects close to each other will be pushed together

Now to relate this to the expansion of matter at extremely large scales and the compression of matter at extremely close. Objects near one another are essentially pushed together. They have equal forces acting on them. However, objects near the edges would want to be pushed apart.

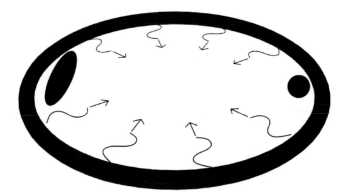

Figure 21: this simple model shows that objects far apart will be pushed apart

It's a very simple concept that explains how the Universe could be expanding yet matter is attracted to itself. Points where S is equal to P would be turning points of physical attraction or repulsion.

Walking Through Walls

Have you ever wondered if you can walk through walls? The idea may seem like fantasy. All evidence in your day-to-day life says if you walk into a wall, it will stop you. Well, that is not the case with particles such as photons and neutrinos. These objects have the ability to pass through objects without any interactions. Why then may a photon pass through a wall and not a person?

The main problem is interference of magnetic energies between the photon or particle and the electrons in the shell of the atom. Here is a theoretical solution.

Wave Nature of Light

1 wavelength

Figure 22: shows a wave with one wavelength

Light is a very tricky guy. It can be seen as a photon, which has mass, or a wave, which does not. Very quickly, a wave of light may be comparable to a wave of water at the beach. The wavelength of the wave is the distance from one wave to another. The frequency is the number of waves that would pass by a point in a second. There is a direct relationship between wavelength and frequency.

Building Waves

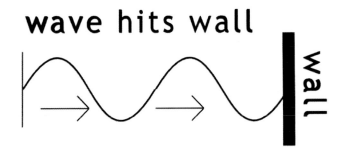

Figure 23: shows a wave that is about to bounce off a wall

Waves are awesome in many ways. One of the most interesting features is a waves ability to add and subtract from one another. If you were to have two waves of the same exact size but in opposite directions to where the top of one wave perfectly matches the bottom then the two waves would cancel out. Much energy could exist but there would be no physical indication because the two waves would be nullifying each other. However, after they pass, the two waves would return to their normal state and you'd see both of them traveling away as if nothing ever happened.

Bouncing Waves

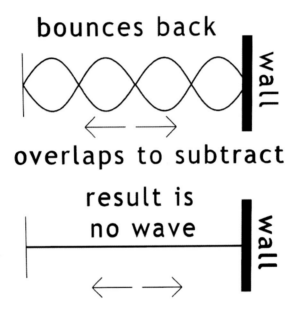

Figure 24: shows a wave that is interfering with itself causing moments when the energy is completely canceled out

Waves have many interesting properties. One of them is that they may bounce off of barriers or objects. Have you ever noticed an echo in a canyon? It is essentially your sound wave bouncing off of different objects. Light waves can bounce as well. However, for right now, we are speaking in terms of sound because it is the easiest to relate to in our day-to-day lives. Another easy example to see in nature is in water waves. You can see this as water waves bounce off of channel walls. Next time you see water bouncing off a channel wall watch as the bouncing waves overlap with the incoming and form nodes.

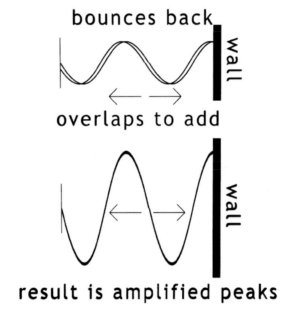

Figure 25: shows constructive interference. The wave peaks add to increase the power.

Standing Waves

By using the knowledge of how waves build and how they bounce, it is possible to create standing waves. A standing wave is a wave that appears to be frozen in time. It is the result of perfectly timed overlapping waves. Standing waves have many unique characteristics and may be used for many applications.

nodes of low pressure

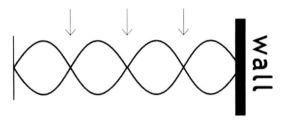

Figure 26: shows how nodes form on standing waves

One fun usage of standing waves is for the levitation of objects. Objects want to be in zones of low pressure. You can then control an object by controlling a node of low pressure. You can make the object go higher, lower, to the side, or whatever else you would want to do. It really just comes down to being able to control the node.

Standing waves can vary in length and size. The number of waves available for any system typically depends on the size of the container and what is in the container.

Let's say the container in this case is a swimming pool that is 10 feet long. We now create one wave that is ten feet in length. You will see you have created one standing wave with one node.

Now let's send a wave that is 5 feet long. You will see that we now have created two standing nodes. This trend continues for every common factor. If you want four nodes, then you just divide 10 by 4 and you get a wavelength of 2.5.

The point, and I stress this point, is that there are common wavelengths in which standing waves may form and those depend entirely on the size of the container and velocity of the wave. These common lengths could be considered factors of the total length of the container.

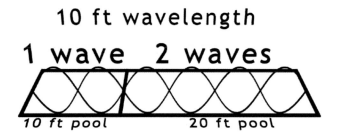

10 ft wavelength
1 wave   2 waves

Figure 27: shows how multiple pools may be tuned to the same wave

What's interesting about waves is that they are somewhat independent of the median. Yes, the median does control the speed at which the wave may travel, but the median does not control the source of the wave.

Imagine a pool of water. It has no waves. The water is just sitting still and being water. However, if we were to essentially massage the water in just the correct fashion, we could make a hole where someone could pass through without getting wet. We could potentially make a swimming pool that floats in midair.

The Elements

The elements are a creation of particles. Typically, there is a nucleus that contains protons and neutrons and then an electron shell that contains electrons. A simple example of an element is Hydrogen. Each element is characterized by the number of these particles. Hydrogen has one electron. Helium has two and so on. The number of electrons and protons determines the size of the atom. For our purposes, it would be directly related to the size of the swimming pools from the example before. By creating standing waves in the elements, it may be possible to change the phase of spin or magnetic energy associated with it. Similar to moving water up and down in a swimming pool, we could move electrons and protons around with electromagnetic waves.

A Common Factor

Just like swimming pools vary in size, so do the elements. Imagine you have two swimming pools but only one wave machine. How do you get the swimming pools in synch? You would have to find the common factor. This will allow the two different pools to carry the same standing wave energy. You can theoretically find the common factor of several pools to have them all in harmonic phase with one another.

This may also true for electromagnetic waves and elements. Each element has its own orientation and size. By finding the common factor of electromagnetic energy we may be able to tune them to one another. In other words, we can make a wall that has all the particles electromagnetically in phase with each other.

The easiest way would be to imagine if you have a wall composed of a solid element like gold or iron. The diameters of these metals are already well known. We could create a standing wave within the materials that compose the wall and then do the same with a rod. We would essentially have the rod and the wall tuned to the exact same phase and theoretically the rod may be able to pass through the wall with absolutely no interference.

Manipulating Gravity

Using our new theory in gravity along with the concept of Space Preparation we may now theorize on manipulating gravity. This would be our ability to create more or less gravity in a desired location.

Considering the force of gravity comes from an interstellar star pressure or overlapping of waves could there be a way to manipulate these waves? The answer is yes. Through our understanding of waves, we know that they will either add or subtract from each other.

The Light-State of the Universe

Consider the concept of a light-state within any physical spot in the Universe. Light-state could be considered that total amount of all the electromagnetic waves that is passing through that point. Light-state would vary at every point in the Universe because of relative shielding and pressure sources. It could be considered a sort of snapshot of the electromagnetic state.

The Liquid-Light State Universe

This really does lead to the question. Is matter just nodes of overlapping electromagnetism? Does it even make sense to say that gravity exist? Could it be a resultant illusion created by Space Preparation? All waves overlap and their energy adds and subtracts. Matter is always in a constant form of manifestation, blipping in and out of solidity.

Is it not just temporary waves passing through continuing onward? Are we not peaks of the same wave? Does the photon not only become matter to another photon when the conscious observer is accelerating at light speed in the same direction?

Let's continue on our conscious journey as "The Liquid-Light State Universe" examines the Universe as if it is all light. Matter forms at nodes of overlapping EM. We also discuss the conscious field and light-state harmony via the cartesian mind, body, and spirit diagrams.

Thanks for Reading
8/27/2014   revised: 3/4/2021
Leaders in Innovation   www.LooshesLabs.com

The Liquid-Light State Universe

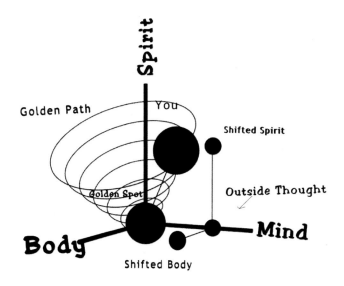

by Alexei Novitzky

Table of Contents

Introduction

The "Liquid-Light State Universe," discusses how the Universe is like a smooth pond of water. Overlapping waves add and subtract to create nodes of manifesting matter. As continued from "Your Influence in Space," the concept of a unique light-state for every point in the Universe is first reviewed. We see that space is dense with electromagnetic waves of all frequencies coming in from all directions. Just like water waves in an ocean, these waves add and subtract.

Scientifically, the physical experience an observer undergoes is directly related to its relative frame of three-dimensional motion. Objects can become time dilated, contracted, and etc. Science does a great job discussing the physical material environment but that is the limitation of science. Effects of relativity also occur in the mind and spirit. Mind and spirit also have direct effects on matter.

Where does consciousness exist and what creates it? Why is tomorrow not as easily predicted as one plus one equaling two? The answer would be in free will or choice. You could say we all have a "Golden Spot." It is the "you" in full confidence and awareness. It is the full you that exist without question or concern.

It is important to remember that almost 99% of everything you do is customary. You have been born into society and trained to think and act certain ways. Manmade infrastructures, ideologies, and customs are simply manmade and not natural to the Universe. All of those actions are done by choice.

This leads to a general programming of mental electromagnetic projections. Meaning, people generally walk with the same wants, don't wants, assumptions, and expectations, emulating from their bodies in the form of electromagnetic consciousness waves. All of these unnatural emanations physically alter your node of manifestation and the naturally occurring Universe.

Scientific applications of the Liquid-Light State Universe will yield technologies such as teleportation, levitation, canceling matter, manifesting matter from empty space, and consciousness-controlled devices. Applying Liquid-Light State principles into your daily routine will reduce anxious pacing, reaffirm personal confidence, and create a healthier manifested body.

"Your Influence in Space Recap"

I strongly urge you read "Your Influence in Space," before reading "The Liquid-Light State Universe." Many of the concepts are new to the scientific community and the terminology is first defined there.

Space Preparation

Empty space prepares itself before matter manifest. This can most easily be seen by looking at a single spot in the Universe from all relativistic frames of motion from zero to infinite velocity. What you will see is that for the stationary observer a yellow light will manifest as yellow. For the light speed traveler, it may be doppler shifted to red. However, for the traveler of infinite velocity, our yellow light manifest at a wavelength of infinity.

Relate that to distance after one second and you see the yellow light has traveled 1C. The red light has traveled maybe 2C. However, at the extreme, the infinitely long wave observed by the traveler of infinite velocity is already past the edge of the physical Universe.

Now relate the distances traveled or wavelength to energy density and you see the trend matches extremely well with Heisenberg's uncertainty principle about velocity and location. Velocity, for all in terms of purpose, for this example, relates directly to energy density. Here we have three wave examples. The total energy for the wave is the same for all observers. This implies that your light encompasses the entire universe but has most effect in the current relativistic frame and location. You have effect at the edge of space but your energy is strongest where you stand in place.

What you notice is that empty space prepares itself with infinitely long wavelengths then as the current now manifest the wave condenses into the current relativistic frame giving it a maximum energy.

Light-State

A single EM wave might or might not be enough to create matter. However, if you were to consider the light-state of any point in space and time you'd see that space is extremely dense with EM waves coming in from all directions. Light-state would be the current vector account of all EM waves within a certain volume. The smallest light-state that could exist would be that of a Plank Voxel. The biggest would be that of the Universe.

The Human Experience

Most likely any being reading this is a human. That being written and read, it is extremely important to understand that our day-to-day three-dimensional reality that you see is completely constructed in our brains. Our bodies have five major senses that we use to construct the physical reality. Not all animals/beings have the same senses. Some beings use sonar to see. Some don't even have eyes.

To go in the other direction, some beings may have senses that our brains cannot even comprehend. You could say, we measure intelligence by one's ability to express itself and solve problems. That is why we would say that an earthworm isn't that smart or advanced. You can literally just walk over and pick them up. Well, what does the worm think of the piles of dirt or amoeba? The worm probably thinks that they're not very smart.

Do your best to imagine being an earthworm and then being given the body and senses of a human. You would see a much grander picture than you could have ever possibly imagined. You would learn about stars and planets. You would learn how to construct telescopes, build and use computers. You would be an ascended worm master. So how smart or advanced are we as humans? Just imagine a being with the same gap in intelligence we have with worms but to us. Imagine they can open portals and travel light speed with no technology.

We live a very human experience and because of that we assume that all life must be made of matter. Matter is less than 1% of the entire construct of the Universe. There is a good chance that there are beings that exist without matter. Life, on Earth has filled every nook and cranny. Extremophiles inhabit the harshest regions and thrive. The further from earthly bodies we go, the less likely we will recognize life when we see it. At the same time, the human and many other earthly forms may be common across all planets.

Everywhere in the Universe hydrogen is hydrogen. Helium is helium, and so on. Why wouldn't the human form be common in other habitats that are similar to Earth? There is more chance that in liquid environments you'd have fishlike beings. In the atmosphere, you'd have birds and insects. In black holes, you might have natural time travelers.

The Easy-User Interface

When looking at reality with our bodies we are given a solid physical environment in which solids remain solids and fluids flow naturally with time. The act of picking something up with your hand is a solid-on-solid interaction. That is true, to you and to the earthworm. However, consider the human body to be an easy-user interface that allows our mind and spirit to easily interact with the Universe.

It is easiest to see when comparing the human body and physical experience within the Universe to a computer mouse and an operating system like Windows. On a computer, to open an application, all you need to do is grab the mouse and double click. Then to type words, you just push buttons on a keyboard. It is very simple to make amazing things happen on a computer even if you have absolutely no clue how the computer works.

All the programs that you've used your mouse for require hundreds if not thousands of lines of code to operate and function properly. Take it a step further, even the letters and symbols that construct the codes are made of simple on/off switches, the 1's and 0's of the matrix. Operating systems make using the computer more user friendly.

That is your body, the easy-user interface to the Universe. In order to move an object, you just reach out and move it.

The Electromagnetic Dance

What is really going on when you move? Is there not an electromagnetic light show going off in your brain? Is your body not massaging the Universe with EM? The thought alone, I want to move my arm, even subconsciously, may be the first physical hint. It is a spark, a pulse of EM emanating from your spiritual center that then overlaps with the current light-state of the Universe. The resultant summation is a new physical structure in the solid crystal of the Universe. Your arm has moved. The human body truly is the easy user interface to the Universe. Afterall, the body is the minds spaceship. The construct you have of reality in your head is a simplified user-friendly version. Senses filter, minds construct, and bodies pulsate all to make the Universe seem as if there are solid boundaries to different objects. It is true in mind, however in practice we are in a state of constant manifestation.

Manifesting Through Space

Time is relative to the mind experiencing it as well as the frames of physical motion in which it lives. The perception of time a being requires is related to surviving and being able to interact with the surrounding processes. You need time to act and react and so your perception of time is tuned to your environment and life cycle. It is a result of evolving on Earth, around the Sun, in an expanding Universe. This is why objects seem solid. Our perception of time is way too slow to see all of the underlying processes in the Universe. The hand is quicker than the eye. Well, the Planck second, is much quicker than that occurring at 10 ^-44 times a second. The Planck time is the amount of time it takes for a particle or wave traveling at the speed of light to travel one Planck length which equals 1.6 x 10 ^-35 meters. It is said that there are more units of Planck time in one second than there are seconds in the known Universe. This shows the amount of interaction required to simply move your arm is almost unfathomable and in a certain time scale, for that of a Planck consciousness, takes an eternity.

Wave Nature

Energies from all wave types overlap to create the experience manifested. Depending on how they add, two perfectly timed water waves traveling in opposite directions can make the appearance of no wave or timed a half wavelength from that would be a giant spike.

It is possible to have infinite energy in a system all adding to zero. Consider two sound speakers facing the same direction. They both play a constant and uniform tone but are placed physically a half wavelength away. The energy from the speakers in this case would be canceling each other producing absolutely no sound. You could turn the volume up on both of them but you still wouldn't hear a sound. It is only when you turn one speaker completely off that you can now hear the tone, or manifest the energy.

Figure 28: Two acoustic waves overlap to create no sound.

The Current Light-State

Detecting the current light-state can be done in many ways. Considering we are working in detecting and canceling wavelengths from the smallest in existence all the way to infinitely long, we would need to use a variety of systems.

Simple charged coupling devices are able to gather information on what type of wave or photon is incoming. These work great for visible light. Typical visible light laser and led systems can be used to cancel out incoming visible light.

Large radio antenna could be used to detect the incoming state of radio waves. Theses antenna would need to be on the size of the Very Large Array (VLA). Massive radio antenna would be required to cancel out the incoming radio source as well.

Effective Dish Diameter

├─────────────────────────────────────┤

Figure 29: An arrangement of radio antenna being used in combination to make a larger diameter.

For the super long radio form, we could construct something very similar to the VLA but using all the planets in the solar system. We would need to establish a virtual solar system sized antenna by combing all the signals of the individual antenna that have been placed on the individual planets or in orbit around the Sun.

The resulting area between the massive antenna on all the planets would become the effective surface area of your dish. You essentially would have a radio telescope with a diameter equal to that of our solar system. These same individual dishes can be choreographed in many different ways in order to measure the incoming light-state.

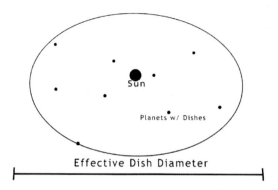

Figure 30: An arrangement of interplanetary antenna being used in combination to make an effective dish with the diameter of the solar system.

Once the incoming light-state is known, it is then possible to create nullifying waves. It is important to remember that the signal we are looking to cancel is not necessarily in the now or of a singular wave format.

Space preparation shows us that as matter manifest into three-dimensional space that it first prepares itself by coming in from infinitely long radio form and somewhat instantaneously that waveform transitions into a higher and higher frequency until it is in its solid form. This shows that in order to cancel the manifestation you would need to cancel the space preparation as well. It is all happening at once. Sure, you could just cancel the current manifesting frame, but the essence of the object being canceled would remain. It would appear half manifest like an out of focus picture on a camera.

This relates to how astronomers use sky flats in order to cancel out the noise of the object they are looking for. You don't completely cancel out the image but by taking a general sky flat you can dramatically reduce the background noise, in this case, the one without using shifting frequency waves, the object would probably be canceled enough to say it has been canceled but it would still have effect and produce localized photons.

A quick side: While studying astronomy in Boulder, Colorado, I once had a class on a very cloudy night. There was a full moon that night and the clouds were so thick you couldn't see anything. The professor was about to cancel the class and we were all going to go home.

That's when I suggested, "Couldn't we just take a random picture of the clouds not aiming at the moon? Then take a second photo aiming directly at the moon. Then by isolating the cloud CCD data subtract the clouds from the moon?" The professor looked at me and said, "hmmm, you know, that might work." We ended up slewing to an empty patch of stars so only cloud data was being received by the CCD. We then slewed over to the Moon and took a second photo. We subtracted the CCD data of the clouds from the Moon photo and to everyone's surprise, we had an incredible photo of the Moon. You could see every detail and crater. Just subtracting similar cloud CCD data was enough to clear up the sky for a great night of observation. This is an important point in the general canceling of matter.

Regular or Constant Waveform

Figure 31: A constant frequency will not fully cancel the manifestation of matter.

Back to the main point, by using regular or constant waves you may be able to somewhat cancel the object but it would still appear fuzzy and somewhat manifest.

Scaling Waveform

Figure 32: Scaling waveforms are required to fully cancel the manifestation of matter.

The ideal way to fully cancel an object from manifesting into the Universe is to use the changing wave form. This would require all of the varying telescopes, lasers, and dishes to work in harmony to create the effect of these rapidly scaling wave forms.

Going off the Boulder, Colorado example, it may be the case that incoming signals may be generalized for any particular area. Ideally, the light-state you would want to be detecting would be that of the now. Then you would cancel manifestation with waves directly related to the moment. However, when taking a crystal-clear image of the Moon through the clouds we didn't subtract the background light of the clouds directly in front of the Moon. We used sky that was next to it. It may have even been possible to use a picture that had been taken years prior. The important information and I stress this point, is that every object may have a manifest signature which could be recorded.

These signatures could then be used whenever by whomever to create effects of canceling and manifestation. It would almost be like the engineering books that exist today. Stress, strain, and material relationships have been developed for many years. The same would be the case for manifestation tables of the common particles. You could then document the frequencies, orientations of EM, scalar ratios, and any other properties that may become common place.

The Manifestation Tables

Particle	Time	Radio	Infrared	Visible	X-Ray	Pulse Rate
Higgs				∿		
Gauge	∿		～		∿	
Quark			∿			⌒
Lepton	∿					//
Neutrino				∧		⌒

Figure 33: A general concept for what a manifestation table may look like.

The use of a general particle manifestation table would also need to be accompanied with the local manifestation flats. A manifestation flat could be considered the equivalent of a sky flat. It is the localized incoming EM, but in this case, it would be that of a volumetric light-state. A fun side, not only is it possible to gather the manifestation properties of particles but it is also possible to record entire structures like homes and etc. Theoretically, and eventually a practicality, you could turn on and off your entire house with the flip of a switch. By turn off, I mean completely cancel from existence, and by turn on, I mean manifest from the emptiness of space.

A Fresh Start

Using the system of detectors and emitters discussed earlier you can make any matter you choose from the emptiness of space.

A less advanced way, yet a proper stepping stone in this achievement, would be to create a zone of absolute zero. I'm not familiar with any term for a completely empty environment except for vacuum, but I'm referring to a three-dimensional volume that has absolutely nothing inside of it.

It would not even let solar system sized EM waves pass through or neutrinos. This raw, pure empty space would be the perfect building block for all matter. Imagine if you could create this environment in a table sized box or storage closet. You could put whatever you wanted inside it. The box would then determine the light-state and cancel whatever you put inside. It would be a box that would always remain empty.

Similar to the two-speaker example earlier with both speakers playing at the highest volume setting, you would not hear a sound, see an image, or magnetically interfere with whatever is inside this box. You could say the box is completely empty. In order to retrieve items from the box, you just flip a switch that turns off the canceling wave energy. Your item now exists within the box and can be physically removed and used.

These same tables could then be used for transmutation as well. You would be able to see the differences in the light-states of each element. From that, you either add or subtract the necessary electromagnetic waves to create the desired results.

Teleportation and Levitation

It is even possible to use the knowledge and theoretical technologies to instantaneously teleport objects. Levitation could be considered localized teleportation so we will brush on that as well.

Considering that matter is essentially the current light-state of the Universe it may be possible to bend or alter the location at which the material focuses. This same concept can potentially be used for bi or multi locating depending on how much of the object is teleported and if you choose to only teleport to one spot per moment.

It is similar to how you can use a piece of glass to reflect an image on a wall. Yes, the light you are projecting passes directly through the glass. An image can clearly be seen. However, at the same time, part of the image is being reflected and appearing on the wall. This light or image is at two places at once. It is bilocating. You could then use three pieces or any number of pieces of glass to create the multi locating effect.

Apply the concepts of refracting and reflecting light to the manifestation of matter based on incoming scalar EM and light-state and you see that you can alter the location of natural nodes rather instantaneously. Earlier in the book we discussed the cancelation or manifestation of matter. Here we are talking about the shifting of nodes.

Shifting nodes occurs all the time every day. It is the act of matter moving through space. The manifestation rate could be considered timeless as it is related to the scales of Planck. Although, the flowing nature of our Liquid-Light Universe does not have intervals of nonexistence for it is an ever-existing flow of harmony, Planck scales are still a good way to equate. In a sort of fashion, to give a measurement of time it would take to teleport, levitate, bilocate, or etc. just really doesn't make any sense. It is instantaneous. It is now. To not be too sidetracked, man created measurements of time and the concept of a second. It is one of the daily happenings that subconsciously emanate from your electromagnetic center. We will talk about how underlying conscious assumptions affect the natural state of the Universe on our mind, body, and spirit graph later. For now, let's stay focused, no pun intended, on focusing or reflecting the natural nodes of manifestation.

How can you alter the location of nodes? The easiest way may be through gravitational lensing. Gravitational lensing can be seen occurring naturally in the Universe. Physically, it is the act of large bodies having so much gravity that they are able to bend light as it passes by. It is most easily seen when looking for black holes. The bending of a star's light as it passes by a large gravitational force will alter the apparent location of the star. We would want to bend the sphere of light that surrounds the body being teleported.

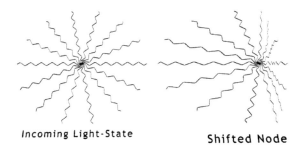

Incoming Light-State   Shifted Node

Figure 34: Demonstrates the changes in electromagnetic waveform required to alter a node of manifestation.

Depending on the direction of travel relative to the starting point is how you would want to bend the light. Light coming from behind you would need to be accelerated. Light coming from in front of you would need to be slowed. Light coming from the sides would just need to be moved while staying in the same vibrational state. The electromagnetic alteration required would resemble the picture above.

It may also be possible to achieve this alteration of the liquid-light state by use of permanent magnets, electromagnets, and potentially geometric shapes of dense material.

Harmony of Zero

There are many options or ways to create an offset yet harmonious relationship within the Universe.

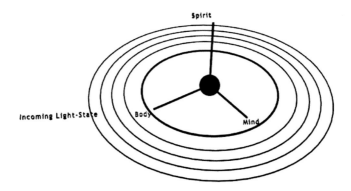

Figure 35: Demonstrates a general incoming light-state.

Here is a very simple diagram to show an incoming light-state for the volume of space. This volume may or may not have a conscious entity within it. However, for this example, let's say it is a uniform light-state.

It is possible to create harmonious motions within this space. Technologically, these internal never-ending motions may be used to generate great power in mind, body, and spirit, and potentially even used as a never-ending supply of electricity.

Let's Be Square for a Minute

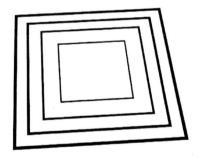

Figure 36: The squares represent an incoming light-state.

For this next section, we have turned the incoming shape of the Universe into a square. We are simply altering the way we are demonstrating the wave nature of the Universe. Now let's add a generic light-state value to the square. For this case, the value is x.

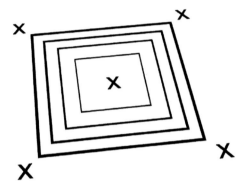

Figure 37: Demonstrates a light-state of value X.

This wave is in perfect harmony. It will continue to act as X inside and outside the interior square. In other words, this system is equal to zero. It is in a Golden Spot of neverending existence.

What if we were to somehow able to "trick" the light-state to think inside the square is "X" when it really is not? The answer comes in the form of magic squares.

Magic Squares

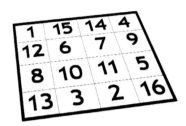

Figure 38: Represents a 4x4 magic square.

Magic squares come in all size grids. 3x3, 4x4, 5x5, and so on. Numbers are layed out onto a grid and no matter which way the numbers are added together they will equal the same value on the outside.

For example, in the above magic square, all verticles, horizonals, diagnols, and corner sets are equal to the value of 34.

1	15	14	4	34
12	6	7	9	34
8	10	11	5	34
13	3	2	16	34
34	34	34	34	

34	34	34 / 34
34	34	34 / 34
34 34 34 34		

Figure 39: Shows how all sets of 4 numbers add up to 34. In this magic square, even the middle four numbers equal 34.

This arrangement has profound implications for creating structures that are harmonious with the light-state. These structures may be designed such that the uniformity only exist when in motion or harnessing energy. For example, if the 16 were a 17, the system would not be in harmony. However, if you have a device drawing an energy of 1 from the 17 with a wire then you have a virtual 16. This structure would be able to theoretically remain in motion while generating an energetic work output of 1.

Magic Sphere

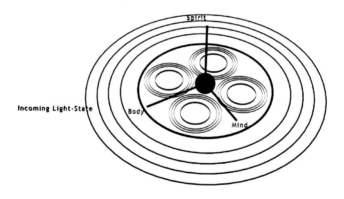

Figure 40 : Demonstrates how a magic square can be turned into a ring and even a sphere.

Here we see how the inside and outside of the magic ring or sphere are in perfect harmony. This is a state of being where the body is perfectly sustainable with its environment. The smaller circles on the inside are nodes that have been created by the individual. Here you see that the four interior nodes are in perfect vibrational harmony with the Universe.

Imagine now that the large circles above depict one of the smaller four circles. You can see how these individual nodes, which represent thoughts or physical creations, may continue in this fashion inward creating an infinite number of potential creations while maintaining perfect harmony with the Universe.

An entity in this state of being is in a state of infinite and instantaneous manifestation of all thought forms projected. Meaning, their thoughts and visions will become their reality.

Personal Implications

There are many implications that arise from looking at the Universe in such a fashion. You see that your body exist in all of space and time. It becomes apparent that your thoughts and vibrational harmony alone affect the solid or manifested state of the Universe.

The Golden Spot

Considering your mind, body, and spirit are part of the Universe, it is important to understand that there is a Golden Spot where you will fully manifest. This is the place in the Universe where you are happiest, healthiest, most confident and therefor most creative.

Earlier, we mentioned how the overlapping electromagnetic waves of the Universe add and subtract which forms nodes of manifestation. We also discussed how the human body is an easy-user interface to the Universe.

Other than the original primordial thought, Big Bang, or naturally occurring Universe, you could say there are also the minds of the beings that inhabit it.

A Smooth Pond with Falling Pebbles

Consider the Universe with no mind. It is a perfect smooth pond of water. Then, a thought arises as if someone were to have tossed in a stone. The ripples emulate outward causing distortions in the surface of the pond. Then, another thought, another stone. The pond becomes filled with rings of waves all heading towards each other. Then, they overlap. Nodes are created. Each additional stone that gets tossed in creates more rings and more nodes. As the stones change shape so do the nodes. Eventually, the stones stop being tossed. The pond becomes still again and returns to its natural state.

The same is true for the Liquid-Light State Universe. All subconscious and conscious thoughts are constantly in vibration emulating out from your electromagnetic center. The wants, don't wants, assumptions, and expectations you hold true in your gut becomes the vibrational output you are sending into this pond. They are the "shape" of the stone you are tossing into the pond.

All these internally and externally flowing ripples create a distortion within your manifestation which translates into a pacing of your mind, body, or spirit. They can create a partially manifested body similar to the bilocating examples mentioned earlier.

Mind, Body, and Spirit Diagram

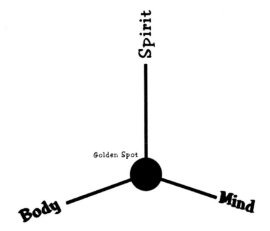

Figure 41 : Mind, Body, and Spirit Diagram designed to depict pacing about the Golden Spot.

Here is a cartesian mind, body, and spirit coordinate system to help explain the pacing nature thoughts, experiences, and energetic fields have about the Golden Spot for any matter or energy within the Liquid-Light State Universe.

It is first important to define the terms mind, body, and spirit. Although, no real definition exists, for purposes of these diagrams this is what we will be referring to.

Mind would be the field of consciousness. It is your thoughts, and those that effect you, both consciously and subconsciously.

Body would be anything in your physical reality. This would be from your personal body to the trees on the other side of the planet. Anything physical is considered part of the body.

Spirit would be your overall vibrational state. This can be in or against harmony with the Universe.

All three, mind, body, and spirit may be controlled by the individual. You can take posture in body, mind, and spirit. You can develop and strengthen each one independently although it is important, they rise together.

This first example shows a body with no outside influences. The being is at its Golden Point in mind, body, and spirit. It is likely this state of health does not degrade. It could continue onward for eternity. At the same time however, it may or may not experience anything, similar to existing within a magic sphere.

The Outside Thought

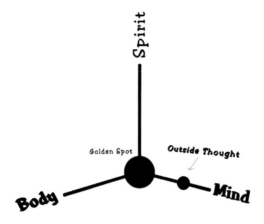

Figure 42 : An outside thought is introduced into the system.

Now here comes an outside thought. It could be anything from your friend suggesting a different color paint for a home project to the media telling you what you think you should be spending your money on. What does this outside incoming electromagnetic consciousness wave do to our mind? Well, it occupies it. It harmonizes with it. It influences the sitting state by overlapping with the existing. It has influence and creates change. These changes create a shift first in mind. It has become your thought. This translates to a shifted body, which in turn demands a shifted spirit while your new body harmonizes with the already existing light-state of the Universe.

Shifted Bodies

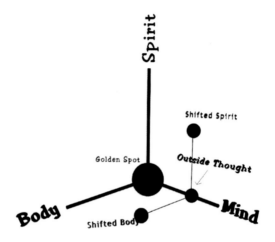

Figure 43 : Demonstrates how an outside thought will cause a shift in the body and spirit of the being in review.

This graph is a simple visual representation of how the outside thought has created shifts in body and in spirit. It creates a shift in spirit because the new thought harmonizes with your existing electromagnetic field. Therefor in order to harmonize with the Universe the body must move or it will undergo stress and strain. In engineering terms, stress is the amount of force being applied, and strain is the amount of bending occurring.

When your body is fixed in the Universe and the mind and spirit harmonize with external factors it creates a potential energy between where you currently exist and where you are harmonizing to.

New Node of Manifestation

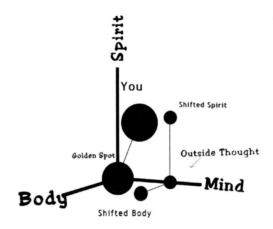

Figure 44 : Shows that a new node of manifestation has been created due to the changing light-state of the body or being.

The figure above is a simple visual demonstration of your physical essence existing off centered from its golden point. The shifted body represents the change in physical location. The outside thought would be the change of mind. The shifted spirit represents the change in vibrational light-state harmony.

The stress would be that driving force. The strain would be the resulting distortions or microscopic changes to the solid structure as a whole. Strain would be the malformity or fuzziness created due to physically not existing in the Golden Spot.

The total change would be the location labeled "You," which is the combination of mind, body, and spirit. It is the new node of manifestation based off of the pebble that has been tossed into the pond. It is a temporary and distorted existence.

The Path to and from the Golden Spot

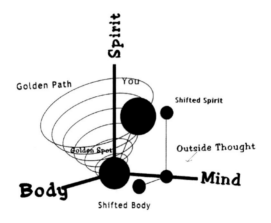

Figure 45 : This figure represents the Golden Path of returning to zero.

On the journey back to zero, or your Golden Spot, you will notice that you may pace or rather spiral inward about the major shifted axis. The pacing inward will typically pass the zero point then accelerate back towards it again. Mapping the trajectory resembles orbital motion or rather a spiral represented by the Fibonacci sequence.

To quickly relate that spiraling trajectory to energy, you could say that your driving force for motion or oneness would be directly related to the difference in your current part of the spiral relative to the center. Let's call this value manifestation potential or gravity of all three mind, body, and spirit.

It is as if all creations strive for that divine ratio and that we too experience it in mind, body, and spirit, when moving toward and away from our Golden Spot. When moving toward the golden spot the energy drive becomes minute. When moving away, is when you have the ability to create great energies however it is not sustainable.

A Thought from Your Center

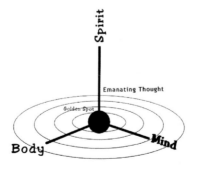

Figure 46 : Is a simple representation of a thought emanating from your center.

Now imagine you are as close to zero or your Golden Spot as possible and you have a thought. Your thought then ripples outwards overlapping with the naturally occurring Universe. You are in perfect harmony. Then, a second person has a thought. The two thoughts collide.

More than one body at play

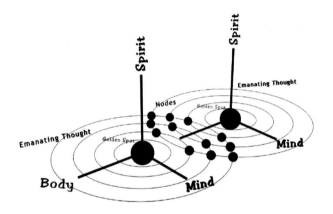

Figure 47 : This figure shows two thoughts colliding in the conscious field.

As the thoughts collide, they add and subtract creating distortions in the mind or conscious field. If the waves are of similar nature, they may harmonize creating standing waves which result in more complex shapes or thought. Perhaps a successful brainstorming session would be a good example of that. At the same sense, if the thoughts are of a half step or polar orientation then they may be nullifying to one another and nothing may transpire.

The saying, "Let me bounce some thoughts off you," is quite literal in this sense. Although, a more accurate saying may be, "Let me overlap some waves with you and see what nodes come up."

Timed Dampeners

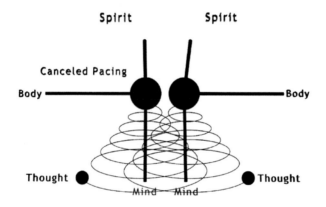

Figure 48 : This figure shows how it is possible to dampen pacing by creating nullifying waves.

It is possible to dampen the amount of pacing a mind, body, or spirit undergoes by interfering with the process. One perfectly timed wave will send you straight back to your Golden Spot.

Timed Amplifiers

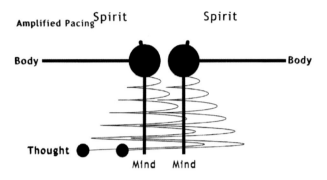

Figure 49 : Shows two waves in perfect harmony.

The reverse is also possible. Two waves in perfect harmony will amplify the entire mind, body, or spirit connection. The resultant wave is the addition of energies. This example shows two bodies that excite one another overlapping to create a zone of harmony.

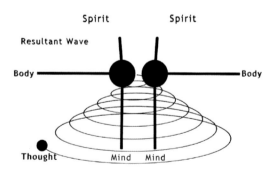

Figure 50 : Shows how waves in harmony add to create a bigger unified wave.

Emitters and Receivers

All thoughts overlap in the Liquid-Light State Universe which creates a sort of superconscious. It is easy to see the mesh of projections created by all the minds in existence. They all overlap and influence the natural light-state.

A being which has quieted the inputs of its own body and quieted the chatter of its mind is in the proper state to receive thought form vibrations projected by others. Consider your consciousness to be like a guitar. Each string or note is an associated thought.

Here you have two guitars tuned the same. One is sitting in the corner of the room. The other is being played by someone. Every time the playing guitar plays a string it causes a ringing in the exact strings of the guitar in the corner. This is because the acoustic wave generated by the playing guitar matches the vibrational frequency of the one resting in the corner. However, if instead of sitting quietly in the corner someone was playing a different song the guitar would not resonate as well as the previous example. This is because it too is sending out waves which interfere with the vibrations of the first guitar.

Minds have the ability to communicate directly through the conscious field by use of harmonic resonances. A loud mind emits and a quiet mind receives.

Manifestation Potential and Gravity

When we think about the motions of physical objects in the Universe one extremely important factor is gravity. We are rather familiar with the equations for material gravity. The force and translated accelerations are related to the gravitational constant times the mass divided by the distance squared. However, what factors drive the motions of objects with mind, spirit, free will, and choice?

Using the mind, body, and spirit diagram we can see that manifestation potentials or mental and spiritual gravities emerge. The displacement about the shifted major axis relative to the Golden Spot and location of current shifted body give clues on methods to calculate force.

Potential energy typically is related to distance from rest, the amount of mass, and a form of constant. The positive and negative directions are somewhat arbitrary. Let us speculate on a spring system (kr) for thought and a radiated system (km/r^2) for spirit.

There are two important major differences between the two. In a spring system, the general force becomes greater as the distance increases. In a radiated system, the general force becomes smaller as the distance increases.

You could say the driving force is a somewhat disharmony with the current light-state and that bodies in general want to move towards more of a harmonious synchronicity.

In the diagram, you can see how your conscious and subconscious field emulate outwards. As they do, they overlap with the natural state of the Universe as well as other minds. You could say animals or beings take the path of least resistance and so it is almost like a walking trail in the woods.

The stress fields create barriers and a path of least resistance is formed. That becomes the direction of the force.

In the physical world, there is the scale of matter. A gram has a certain weight and a kilogram is 1000 times that. The force of gravity is directly related to the amount of body.

Calculating Conscious Gravity

Let us say the same for the conscious field. Each thought contains a certain amount of mass to it. In a social sense, you could call it the importance.

One way it may be possible to equate is to consider the ratio of thoughts. For example, how many times does a certain thought comes up in the conscious mind over a certain amount of time? How does that compare to all other thoughts?

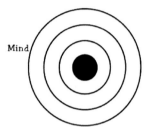

Figure 51: Depicts an empty mind. There are no thoughts or preconceived notions.

The diagram above depicts a mind in harmony. It has no reason to do anything. It is sitting. Then a thought arises and the mind distorts.

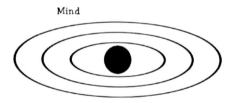

Figure 52: Is a representation of a mind that has a thought in it.

This new shape of individual consciousness adds and subtracts to the superconscious of all beings in existence. It adds to the overall light-state of the

Universe and creates distortions in the minds around it. These distortions could be called mental strains. It is the resultant difference in a state of no mind versus one in thought.

There are many minds in the Universe as well as naturally occurring nodes. Let us look at a theoretical example of a conscious field which contains assumptions and expectations. The thoughts that make the mind take shape literally alter the conscious field. In this example, the conscious field lines act as walls of barriers that require additional energy to spatially maintain a body within.

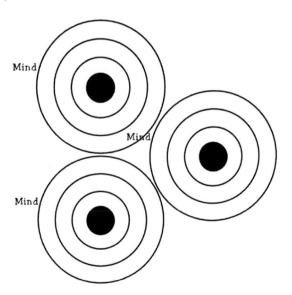

Figure 53: Shows three empty minds in harmony.

The first drawing shows three people in harmony. All the people are at rest. Then, one of them has an assumption or sends out a relating thought that has much mental mass or importance.

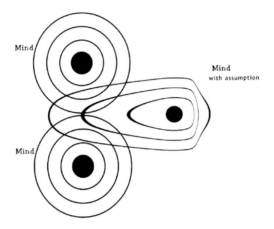

Figure 54: Shows two empty minds and one that has an assumption or thought.

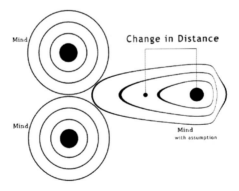

Figure 55: Represents the total change in distance associated with the new thought. This change in distance is your change in x.

A new conscious field now takes shape. This new conscious field thrives for harmony within the Universe and natural light-state. The result is a force towards this new harmony and away from conscious interference. It is typically in a direction away from the Golden Spot and shifted body which creates a spring like pacing or spiraling inward relative to the Golden Spot.

Equating Conscious Force

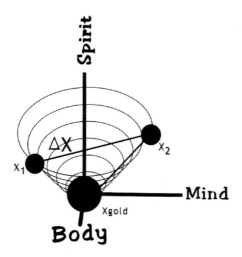

Figure 56: Shows how the Golden Spot is labeled Xgold, the location of your body prior to the incoming thought is X1 and the location during maximum displacement is X2.

Like all springs, there is a thought coefficient and distance associated with the force and potential energy of the new conscious vibration. The thought coefficient ranges between 0 and 1. 1 would be maximum importance and 0 would be of little importance. This varies depending on the individual experiencing the thought. It is up to them to decide how important an idea is on a range of 0 to 1.

The distance (X) would be more related to a vibrational harmony within the Universe versus a physical distance. How "close" are you to being in harmony with your new thought? From the diagram above you can see three positions. You have the X_{gold}, X_1, and X_2. X_{gold} is your mind at the Golden Spot. X_1 is the location of your shifted body prior to the new thought. X_2 is the location of your shifted body after you have fulfilled the duty associated.

K = Thought Constant (N/m)   X = Distance (m)

Force = $(K)(x_2-x_1)$

Energy = $\frac{1}{2}(K)x^2$

Difference = $\frac{1}{2}(K)(x_2^2-x_1^2)$

$Energy_{(golden\ spot)}= \frac{1}{2}(K)(x_2^2-x_{Gold}^2)$

The values obtained by these equations may or may not make sense at first. However, after cataloguing many thoughts and actions we may find a common factor that relates them to the equations of our physical Universe, call it a consciousness to manifested force and energy ratio. After all, what did a Newton first mean when it was invented? How did it relate to reality? It took time to understand the values obtained from the equations. Similarly, it will take time to fully understand what a Newton of thought is. However, it is not a Newton, it is a conscious force. The N will remain.

Amplitude and Frequency of Thought Forms

There are many types of thought forms and for reasons here we will break it down to wants, don't wants, assumptions, and expectations. The "in the moment" short pacing, for example, getting a glass of water, a kind of "I'll just do this real quick," kind of thought would have a higher frequency when compared to a subconscious thought form relating to assumption and expectation about the general nature of reality.

This is easiest to see by looking at the theory or concept of Space Preparation. As the now manifest from the light-state, there is the crunching effect of the electromagnetic wave. It shows that the future of the light-state exists in extremely long wave form. The now exist in the state of matter. The light-state just before the now is composed of very short waves but not yet manifested.

The easy-user interface of the mind, body, and spirit is the shifter or reorganizer of nodes. The wants of the now work with the waves that are closer to being manifest. These would be of a very high frequency almost that of matter. The assumptions and expectations of a lifetime work in the longest of wavelengths. They start reorganizing the light-state from the greatest reaches of our consciousness.

Size of Consciousness

It is said that your minds light encompasses the entire Universe when considering all relativistic frames of motion. However, how much does it encompass in the now? What is the longest wave we can sense and how does that translate into seeing into or rather modifying the future with thought form?

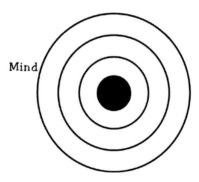

Figure 57: A depiction of a mind field.

Figure 58: The minds light travels 1x10^7 meters per conscious snapshot.

Humans, on average take a snap shot of existence 60 times a second with electromagnetism. That becomes 1/60 of a second. The speed of light is $3x10^8$ m/s. This means that light from your physical body travels $5x10^6$ m per conscious snapshot. Let's call that the radius of the conscious now. The diameter would be twice of that.

Figure 59: The longest wave that can fully exist in the conscious now is 1x10^7 meters. This length varies on the time of your conscious snapshot.

This implies that the longest standing wave that can exist in your conscious field is 1×10^7 meters. Of our natural senses, the fastest form of communication or perception is electromagnetism. It is our source of information exchange in our day-to-day life that seems instantaneous to us. It determines our perception of time and what is waking reality. The smallest wavelength we can see is around 350 nm.

Figure 60: Depicts the smallest naturally observable wavelength by the human eye.

Now let us compare the relative crunching of our longest wave we have ability to influence and that of the shortest wave we can detect. Let us compare the relativistic velocity and therefor time dilation associated with the two. Are there any profound implications that arise from this conscious ratio? The ratio of wavelength is $(1x10^7m)/(350x10^{-9}m) = 3.5x10^{14}$ (conscious field / conscious ability). The crunching of the now is done naturally by the Universe. The Preparation of the Future is done by the conscious mind.

This now becomes our multiplying factor or distortion ratio. Conscious perception has been stretched.

Figure 61: Depicts how incoming light waves crunch as matter manifest.

Figure 62: Depicts how outgoing conscious waves expand to match the frequency of incoming waves.

The overlapping of both universal crunching and conscious preparation adds and subtracts from the light-state. The now manifested result is a relationship between the two.

So how far can our conscious mind prepare into the future? General insight may be obtained by looking at the Conscious Ratio described earlier. This is the size of the conscious snapshot divided by the size of conscious perception. It is important to remember that we derived this from our perception of the now based off of how many visual frames per second our minds perceive in electromagnetism. This number varies between individuals and species of animals. It may or may not be the best way to equate but it is a good starting point. (The "greatest errors" potentially would be coming from our method of determining the length of the conscious snapshot.)

Our calculated conscious ratio is 3.5×10^{14}. Our time interval is 1/60 of a second. Let us now use our ratio in combination with our time to see how far into the future our consciousness has effect.

Time = **(Conscious Ratio) x (Conscious Snapshot (s))** of Conscious influence
   = 2.1×10^{16} seconds = 6.6×10^{8} years

this is roughly 700 million years

Figure 63: A simple calculation to determine how far in the future human conscious has effect on space preparation.

From the numbers used in this example you see that consciousness has effect for 700 million years into the future. Although we may influence that far in advance, most minds are operating on the assumptions and expectations more related to a lifetime in today's pacing monetary society. Remember, our thoughts are somewhat products of culture and society, therefor we have been trained to think in smaller and smaller waveforms. This relates to one's sense of self confidence and general well-being.

Calculating Spirit Gravity

Let's introduce the concept of spirit fields and how they may relate to multiple realities or rather potentialities. Spirit fields exist naturally as the Universe passes through a median, potentially orbiting a solid crystal of time. The timeline experienced is directly related to the vibrational harmony of the being. Harmony may be the deciding factor as to which "direction" the being will go. It is almost like an electron orbiting an atom. The electron may jump up a shell, down a shell, or stay the same. However, it still orbits in the same direction around the same atomic center through the same median without interference.

In our multiple reality or potentiality system, you see that all options overlap each other but do not physically interfere. They all travel in the same direction, which is forward in time and through the same median, which is the crystal of time. Our standing energy state may be the key factor as to which shell we are following along our orbit.

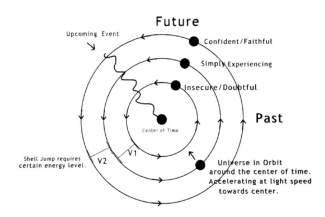

Figure 64: This image depicts the theoretical Crystal of Time

The spirit may act more like a light bulb rather than a spring and so for calculating the force associated with spirit gravity it is more reasonable to use a (km)/r^2 approach. Your coefficient of spirit, k, would be related to the percentage of body and mind in harmony with the location of light-state in question. A negative k value would imply repulsion and a positive k value would imply attraction.

Considering the entire body as a collection of vibrations it is easy to see why not all parts will vibrate in unison. For example, imagine being perfectly in harmony and you are at a k of 1. Then, anxiety before an event. This will send the vibrational state of your body out of sync. Your K value as a percentage has dropped from 100% to 95%. This is just a generic example to help you visualize the light-state harmony your body has within the light-state of the Universe.

Smooth Spirit Field

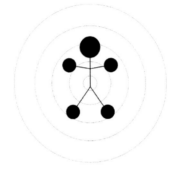

Figure 65: This image depicts a smooth spirit field.

Disrupted Spirit Field

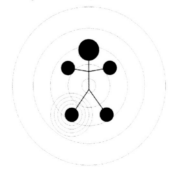

Figure 66: This image depicts a disrupted spirit field.

What actions have altered? Remember, there is no mind associated with this. It is almost 100% related to instinctual motions. Do you pace for a little bit, react harshly unprovoked? Either way, the change in vibrational harmony associated with body creates a force for motion.

This force may be calculated as such, $F=(km)/r^2$. For spirit, using the physical mass of the object may properly quantify the force. The distance, r, would be directly related to the manifested distance of body in question and the most appropriate preexisting light-state of harmony.

In the figure below, you can see a state of spirit of the being and also the liquid-light state potentials based on mind preparation and body crunching before the event. Then a new state after. The new spirit state or rather disharmony with the location of current manifestation within the light-state creates a force towards a harmonious manifestation.

Figure 67: A Spirit in harmony with the current shell.

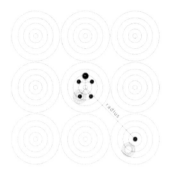

Figure 68: A person who is disharmonizing with the current shell.

After the event takes place, the body has a new vibration. The new "ideal spot" for manifestation creates a pull.

In a sort of fashion, each one of the circles represents a potential timeline of manifestation. The deciding factor on what physical probability manifest is directly related to your spirit vibration and that of the surrounding light-state. There may be many more than just three lines of orbit as depicted in the crystal of time depiction.

Just like with the conscious force, there may be a common factor which can then be used to relate this to a traditional Newton. Overtime, experimental data will be collected and this new (N) may become a common unit of spirit force.

Mind, Body, and Spirit Technologies

Through the use the mind, body, and spirt connections we are able to theorize and develop consciously controlled devices. Let us now speculate on how this may be possible.

The spirit fields and conscious preparations of the future light-state may be the key. By creating a near instability in physical manifestations the potential energies of mind and spirit may create physical changes in structures alone. These on/off switches will guide technology. It is all chance in a way, which light-state will manifest. But chance can be diminished when you increase the total number of "correct" spirit fields and conscious preparations in accordance with properly placed amplifiers. It is also important to diminish outside sources of vibration which may cause interference.

In general, an amplifier increases the energy in the wave by overlapping the wave with itself. With small amounts of input and properly bounced waves, great energy can be achieved. It does not change the frequency. It merely increases the effective power behind the wave.

Theoretically, you could use solid structures of dense materials and/or electromagnets to reflect and refract your consciousness and spirit field on to itself. The overlapping of your own fields would amplify and your conscious preparations become the most likely spirit field or direct line of path. Remember, from the spirit fields we see an almost infinite number of potentialities of light-states that we may be drawn to. The one that pulls or is most likely to manifest is the one with the greatest potential energy which relates directly to physical distance and the percentage of your body at which you harmonize to that field.

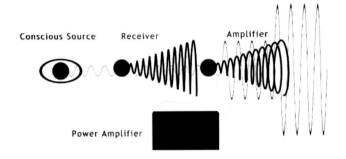

Figure 69: A system used to amplify the conscious preparations of the user.

Amplification of the consciousness will most likely need to be done by use of electromagnetic coils with many numbers of turns that are in the shape of cones. The cone or always changing diameter will allow for signals of varying wavelengths to be perceived. This would take the shape of a sphere around the conscious entity. At the same time the coiled cones would need to be connected directly into a type of electronic amplification circuit where sufficient electrical energy could be then routed to a secondary set of cones. This secondary set of cones would be the emitting station and would exactly match the wave emitted by the user. You would have an effective amplification of an individual's conscious field which relates directly to an amplification of their conscious preparations.

Now to create the correct spirit field and you are golden. Remember that conscious preparations are mindful and thoughtful, but they are not the same as the bodies vibrational state. A general harmonistic vibrational state is most easily achieved through the use of acoustic waves. They create a back-and-forth motion in all matter that they touch which creates a somewhat harmonious unity to the particles. All matter has spirit and is harmonious with the Universe. Create discord through tone and you will change the spirit of the matter. It will then harmonize into a new location in the Universe.

An Exercise in Harmony

A body not in its Golden Spot in mind, body, and sprit will degrade. Consider the Universe to be a river for this example. A node that has been shifted could be like an ant swimming on the surface. The want, don't want, assumption, or expectation you hold true is where you want to be, swimming against the current of a flowing river.

The want or need to fulfill underlying conscious projections (assumptions and expectations) that have been instilled throughout life create all the pacing about our Golden Spot.

It is not natural by any means to spend eight hours in a day working for paper, meaning money, so that you can go buy food. It is not natural by any means to strive to become a named title created by mankind. Within todays' society, there are many, infinite, underlying customary teachings that make it virtually impossible to simply exist in a Golden Spot as such.

To live by your heart or intuitive notion alone would be to be insane in modern society. Values are determined by monetary wealth, marketed looks, and nonsensical ideologies. That translates directly into a lifelong journey of anxious pacing and nonfulfillment.

The answer to harmony and a life of fulfillment may be found in the form of the magic square. Sit quiet and explore the wants, don't wants, expectations, and assumptions that shape the pacing or motions of your reality. Have they been created by another being? Are they natural to the true you? Where is your Golden Spot? Where are you most confident and in love with yourself?

As shown by the infinite creative ability of the magic square, harmonize with the Universe and your dreams may become reality.

A Slip in Time

From our perspective in the light-state, we may see a new picture. There was once a moment when the Earth was flat. The Sun went around the Earth and that's what was. Then an awakening of sorts. We saw the moons of Jupiter and realized we may be the ones circling the Sun. Our perception was backwards.

We looked at the stars with our own eyes and we thought we saw all. Then a solar transit, other solar systems became reality. The Hubble telescope then led to new foundations as millions upon millions of galaxies emerged into existence. We saw a smooth cosmic background. We saw evidence of a big bang. We are one grain of sand, one galaxy in the vast ocean of space.

Now, we see evidence of conscious preparations as space constantly crunches fluid waves into solid existence. What could that mean? In a fashion of sorts, are we not back on Earth again, saying the Sun travels around us? Is this still not just another perspective in which there is a bigger picture? Does the Earth not orbit the Sun?

We see space preparing in our direction. However, it is all in motion. The Earth around the Sun, the Sun around the galaxy, the galaxy around the Big Bang, and the Big Bang around what?

Is the Big Bang not traveling and accelerating through a median? Is there not another underlying motion that would cause the appearance of light crunching?

There is another way to have the effect of space and conscious preparations and that would be if we are all in a constant state of light speed acceleration through the "Crystal of Time."

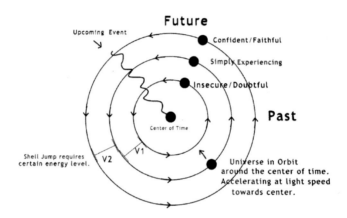

The Crystal of Time

From the Author:

Mankind has recently just begun to scratch the surface of the physical Universe, the human consciousness, and the human spirit. This is an attempt to quantify values and put practical use to them.

Light-state technology has the ability to take mankind to the stars and beyond.

Consciousness-controlled devices will be the future of technology. We may one day steer our vehicles, explore the web, and perform our task for the day, all through thought.

Spirit field technology will have much application in the health industry, body manifestation, and even time travel applications.

We do have a long way to go before we truly understand our place in existence and all that is possible.

"Matter is just the surface of the ocean."

-Alexei Novitzky

Leaders in Education, Innovation, and Sustainability
www.LooshesLabs.com   2021

The Crystal of Time

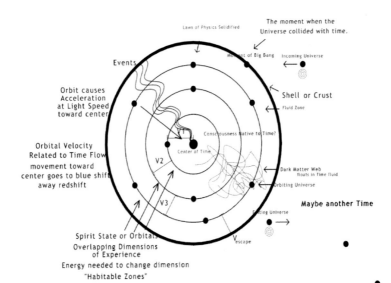

The moment when the
Universe collided with time.

Laws of Physics Solidified

Moment of Big Bang   Incoming Universe

Events

Shell or Crust

Orbit causes
Acceleration
at Light Speed
toward center

Fluid Zone

Consciousness Native to Time?

Orbital Velocity
Related to Time Flow
movement toward
center goes to blue shift
away redshift

Center of Time

V2

Dark Matter Web
floats in Time fluid

Orbiting Universe

Maybe another Time

V3

Exiting Universe

Spirit State or Orbitals
Overlapping Dimensions
of Experience
Energy needed to change dimension
"Habitable Zones"

V escape

by Alexei Novitzky

Table of Contents

Introduction

"The Crystal of Time," explores thought experiments relating to the nature of space preparation and "The Liquid-Light State Universe."

From "Your Influence in Space," we see that our body's light encompasses the entire Universe. We also see that space must prepare itself before matter can manifest into reality.

As seen in "The Liquid-Light State Universe," along with space preparation comes conscious preparations. Conscious preparations project outward while space preparations contract inward towards the observer or experiencer. The summation of both waves creates nodes where matter manifest.

However, what does it mean to have constant space preparation and conscious crunching? What could that imply? Could we not be missing a much grander picture? Did we not once believe the Sun orbited the Earth?

"Your Influence in Space" gives us the first glance at a solution when it asks, "What do two particles accelerating at the speed of light and traveling in the same direction look like to another?" It may appear as a solid particle frozen in space.

Through the use of the spirit fields described in "The Liquid-Light State Universe," we see that vibrational harmony may be the deciding factor to your solidification and your journey through existence.

The Human Body

The human body is one amazing piece of equipment. It has the ability to sense, make educated decisions, and ponder questions such as the nature of reality. It is our easy-user interface that allows our bodies to electromagnetically dance with the light-state of the Universe. It is our minds spaceship that glues us to our dimension of reality as we are in a state of constant manifestation.

The Experience

It is extremely important to understand that all beings gather information differently. Humans primary source of information exchange is electromagnetism centered around the color yellow. It is the fastest sense humans have and it seems instantaneous. Using EM, you can talk to someone on the other side of the planet with little to no delay. However, to a theoretically advanced being, the concept of communicating through electromagnetism could be equivalent to talking to someone with two plastic cups tied to a string. Our five humanly senses would be primitive to a being that has six senses or more. They could be just as smart to us as we are to earthworms. With roughly only 4.5 billion years of Earthly existence, it is unfathomable to consider the amount of intelligence and technology that may exist after 18 billion years of conscious evolution. To think we are the most advanced species, is a very Earthly and human thing. It is important that we learn our place in reality. We are one intelligence, on one tiny island, in the infinite pool of awareness and experience.

Perspectives Grow with Senses

Every sense is used to construct a mental environment that allows the user to interact and survive.

Sit quiet and explore your senses. What is it to feel, to hear, to taste, to smell, and to see? What is it to have an experience in time? What is it to be aware? What is this thing we call consciousness?

Each sense adds to the users experience within reality and stems from a grander and grander picture of existence. Each one comes from revolving around or being inside of something greater.

Let us be the most primitive being you can imagine, completely senseless. We would think reality didn't exist. Now let us scale this up in an educated fashion. Let us compare the range of senses in physical distance and the median it is tuned to with the greater picture involved.

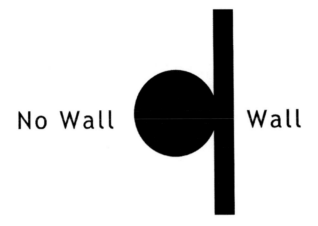

No Wall   Wall

Figure 70: Is a simple illustration of a being experiencing either wall or no wall. All beings strive towards harmony.

You could say the most primitive sense is our ability to feel. Single celled organisms have cell walls that allow for endocytosis. It is our most primitive awareness when it comes to how we describe traditional life. This sense is literally within the global realm of physical contact. You could say the distance is 0 meters for ability to communicate and understand existence. What does a sense of 0 meters in ability do for us? It lets us know we are touching something. It lets us know that something exists beside us. The best mental image we could have is either wall or no wall.

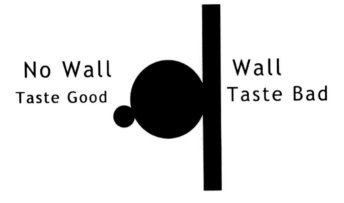

No Wall
Taste Good

Wall
Taste Bad

Figure 71: Shows a being that has the ability to taste and/or smell. In a way, this is just an advanced version of wall or no wall.

Let us now combine smell and taste into one category. They are essentially sensing the same thing anyway which would be the structure of molecules and if they will be harmful or helpful to bring into the body. This lets us know that different types of structures exist. The range again is directly associated with touch. You must physically interact with the molecule in order to perceive a mental stimulus of some sort. You could say the distance for this sense ranges from 0 meters to many kilometers. The kilometer distance would come from molecules being carried by wind but from the perspective of the being they would not be aware of the origin. The effective distance is 0.

Sound could be considered our first awakening. It gives us the feeling of vibration and allows us to be able to detect direction.

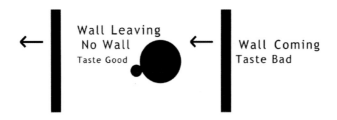

Figure 72: A yet even more advanced version of wall or no wall for the being with the ability to hear and see. Reactions are limited to harmonistic potentials.

Sound or primitive feeling, may be the first hint that there is motion. The mind or consciousness would be able to detect the doppler shifts in vibratory frequency. It is the first hint towards varying velocities of matter, and distance. Sound will not travel from beyond the Earth. All four, feeling, smell, taste, and sound, let us know we are on something bigger. There is an environment in which to grow, the Earth.

Our next sense would be vision which is centered around the color yellow. The concept of seeing through visible yellow light is a very Earthly thing. It is directly related to the Sun's maximum wave of output which is the color yellow. In other words, we most likely would not be tuned to yellow, or even have eyes if the Sun didn't exist. This ability to see through electromagnetism would be our next big jump in self-awareness and conscious evolution. We can now see. There is color to the noises we heard and felt. We have a new sense of awareness. We can see to the edge of the Universe and to the illusionary beginning of time. Similarly, to how we can see to the source of sound and to the illusionary locations of manifested objects. Our awareness has now shifted to encompass the entire Universe or at least to the smooth cosmic microwave background. Our environment in which to grow has increased to the entirety of the known Universe or rather limitations of aided visual perception. However, to say that is all, would be to not understand how our senses have been developing. We are all one awareness, coming from the more primitive single cell. In a fashion, we are one being, becoming more aware.

Now, let us explore our sense of time and compare the now to the visual spectrum. Could not the past and the future physically still exist just like longer and short wavelengths of sound and light than our now may perceive? Either way, one thing is for certain. We do see and experience time. We are in time, just like the Universe, just like the solar system, just like the planet Earth. We are in or on time. We revolve around the center of Time. The flowing nature of past, present, and future, is a limitation to our perception and cognitive ability. We are however, orbiting and flowing through, the Crystal of Time.

The Crystal of Time

Let us now examine existence as if we are in a Universe that orbits through the crystal of time.

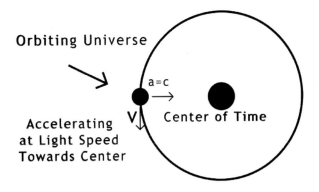

Figure 73: Is a simple depiction of a universe orbiting time with a constant acceleration equal to the speed of light.

Our physical experience gives us that of space and conscious preparations, a constant crunching of electromagnetism to matters manifestation. One way that is achieved by "stationary motion" would be by the body being at constant acceleration at light speed through an ocean of infinitely long scaled waveforms.

There are two basic motions associated with a never-ending smooth constant acceleration. One would be to have a continuous force from behind and the other is to be in constant velocity while changing directions around a circular path or arc.

The Big Bang

Let us quickly cover what is currently accepted. From the evidence, there was a Big Bang followed by subatomic lava. The subatomic particles then coalesced and formed elements and so on. There is much evidence to suggest this is the case. However, what was the source of the Big Bang? Why did it take time for subatomic particles to come into existence? Why is the Universe expanding now? Where is it going? There are many questions left unanswered.

With every new sense of awareness comes a new sense to question and a new realm to explore. With our new model, The Crystal of Time, let us see if we can answer some of the questions associated with the Big Bang theory.

The Moment when the Universe Collided with Time

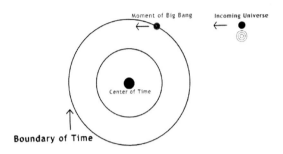

Figure 74: Depicts the moment when the Universe collided with Time. This event is known as the Big Bang.

Consider our single celled organism with its single sense of wall or no wall. The sense let us know of a physical body, the Earth. The sense of light let us know of physical bodies, the Sun and Universe. Here too, we will say that our sense of time, our clock, lets us know that there is a physical structure. It is the Crystal of Time. The Big Bang was when our Universe collided with the Crystal of Time.

At that initial moment, science argues that particles did not exist and time did not yet exist. Here we say, time existed before our Universe entered.

Let us take a look at a Universe that is on a collision course with the center of Time. The very first event would be the Universe would collide with the barrier of the crystal. This event is known to modern science as the Big Bang.

Immediately after the Big Bang you could say that the Universe was too hot for particles to solidify. It was in a state of subatomic lava. Maybe it was too hot, or was it too cold? Was the soup not the right temperature or nature to solidify? Is that a fundamental property of the Universe or Time?

Subatomic Goldilocks

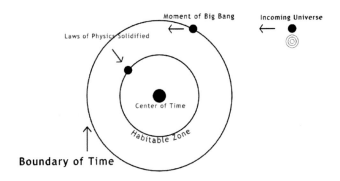

Figure 75: Depicts the distance from the center of Time where/when the laws of physics solidified.

Let us consider the concept of the Goldilocks paradox for the planets within our Solar System. It was said that Venus was too hot for life. Mars was too cold. However, Earth was just right for life to flourish. Earth is in what we call the habitable zone around the Sun. It is a distance from the star that allows for water to be in all three phases, solid, liquid, and gas.

When the Universe first entered Time, it does not seem to have been in a favorable location for subatomic particles to form. You could say that Time was too hot and dense there. There was a sort of thick crust of time as the Universe collided breaking through then sinking deep.

Subatomic particles started to solidify as the Universe found a more favorable position in the orbit of Time, one where matter could exist and light could travel.

What is that boundary distance from the center of Time where matter exist? What could potentially create this subatomic Goldilocks zone? Perhaps, it is the moment, or place of conscious crunching, it is where the acceleration toward center is equal to the speed of light. It is where matter is in constant manifestation.

What does that mean? What could that imply? Could there be other distances from the center of Time where matter may manifest and therefor physical reality? Is there another distance from center to where peaks of manifestation may overlap? Let us logically think of how waves overlap to create nodes of manifestations. It may be logical to think that for every common factor of event distance from center a reality may be habitable.

Event Distance from Center

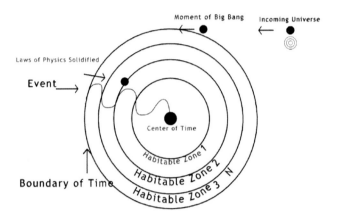

Figure 76: Depicts a Time that contains several habitable zones for matter to manifest in relationship to human consciousness. The distance of each zone from center is related to a harmonic of 1 MU.

The wave in the image depicts an event. Consider the multiple habitable zones as depicted in the image above. Each one of these zones is at a harmonic distance from the center. There would be zones between where our ability of conscious crunching would not overlap properly with the space preparations to create a constant and steady state of manifested reality. In these "fluid zones" of Time, realities as we know it would not make much sense because our bodies would not be able to manifest. We, and all matter would be solely mind and spirit.

You could imagine the first distance of habitability would be that of one wavelength from center. The next distance would be that 2 wavelengths and so on. As we approach the habitable zones from the fluid, we would see matter begin to coalesce and universes filled with galaxies emerging. The same event may be experienced completely different depending on which habitable zone you are in. The zone of residence may be determined by the original amount of energy the Universe had when it first entered Time and potentially how long it has been orbiting or existing within Time.

What would be the difference between Habitable Zones? You can imagine that your centripetal acceleration is equal to velocity squared divided by the radius. By examining the relationship between acceleration and radius a velocity may be equated. For example, our acceleration must be equal to the speed of light, therefor $a=3x10^8$ m/s^2. This leaves two variables which may decide the locations of safe habitable zones for human consciousness, velocity and radius.

A Spiral of Perception

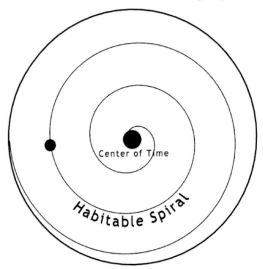

spiral of a=c
associated with changing v

Center of Time

Habitable Spiral

Figure 77: Depicts the spiral of perception related to the velocity of the traveling Universe. For V slowing the spiral travels inward and for V increasing the position of manifestation travels outwards.

For example, if a=c and you have a radius of 1 m, then your velocity squared must be equal to c in order for human consciousness to perceive manifested reality. Let us look at an example that shows only variations of velocity and distance. We will keep our centrally directed acceleration equal to the speed of light. We will be using generic Manifestation Units (MU) as our distance from center.

What you see is as the distance from center increases, the tangential velocity needed to maintain light speed acceleration towards center increases as well. In the simplest words, the further from the center you are, the faster you need to go to perceive reality, or a multiple of the proper wavelength. The feeling of constant acceleration is directly related to the constant change in velocity while maintaining a constant speed tangent to the center.

What you notice is that the combination of velocity and radius makes a spiral pattern of where your acceleration towards center is equal to the speed of light.

Let's Assume Constant Velocity

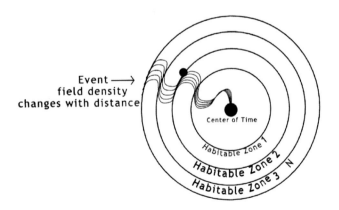

Figure 78: Shows how a single event can cross over multiple Habitable zones.

It is always dangerous to make assumptions, however, for this model we will assume a constant velocity through Time, as in, the flow of Time is uniform. The velocity of the Universe around the center of Time relates directly to how quickly events would be experienced. Therefore, you are left with a series of rings in which matter may be perceived by human consciousness. There would be time dilations associated with the angular velocity differences between events. In other words, consciously experiencing an event on an outer ring would take more time than experiencing an event in one of the inner rings. You could say that everything is happening all at once in the center of time, a sort of time singularity where all events overlap. Near the outer rings, events seem to take longer however the clocks would tick the same rate as an event in an inner ring. The main difference is the perceived length of the experience.

The easiest way to see this is to look at what we will call the "event density". It is the arc length divided by the number of field lines.

The number of cognitive snapshots a user undergoes per event traveled is related to the arc length and velocity. You can see that at the center all the lines converge and form a singularity. Events would all be happening simultaneously. If you were to extend this ring outward, events at infinity would take an eternity to unfold in mind and there would be no overlap.

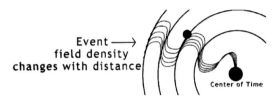

Figure 79: Event density is defined by the number of event lines per arc. The denser the event, the less separated they are in conscious time. Physical clocks will tick the same rate.

Dark Matter and Energy

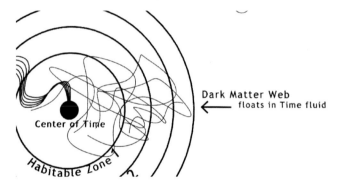

Figure 80: Depicts dark matter and energy as a web-like structure that is native to time. The Universe then collides and bounces off of dark matter and energy as it revolves around the center of Time.

What is dark matter? The easiest way to describe it would be that it is a superstructure that guides the shape of our expanding Universe. It is only detectable by the gravitational effects it has on matter. It has not been directly observed. When it is mapped across the Universe it makes a sort of highway network similar to the nervous system of a human body or to the mineral veins of mountains.

In the Crystal of Time theory, dark matter is native to Time and not the Universe. The Universe is bumping into and colliding with dark matter as it orbits the singularity of all moments. It would be very similar to water in a river flowing around rocks. Manifesting matter bumps into and flows around dark matter. Dark matter is part of the raw crystalline structure of Time itself.

Dark Matter Disturbances

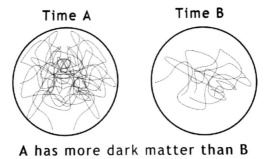

Time A   **Time B**

A has more dark matter than B

Figure 81: Shows that not all Crystals of Time have the same amount of dark matter. Theoretically, there could be a Time with no dark matter and also one that is entirely dark matter or energy.

Looking at this model, you could say that dark matter and energy would be one of the fundamental differences between habitable zones of conscious experience. It may also be the fundamental differences when considering the concept of multiple atoms of Time and universe hopping. One Time may be dense with dark matter and one may be completely empty.

Looking at the simple depiction, you can see that dark matter is not uniform by any means. It could be considered an impurity in the system of Time. In some places it's thick and runs parallel with itself and in others it intersects. Perhaps, it is a fundamental part of Time, or it to, has collided with time. Could it be an overlapping universe that does not manifest in our conscious spiral of light speed acceleration? It is most probable that it is what holds the Crystal of Time together, a sort of glue. Or perhaps, similar to a living being, it is used to transfer energy like the cardiovascular system of reality. Either way, it is as if matter is attracted to and forms around dark matter.

Dark Matter Disturbances and Event Density

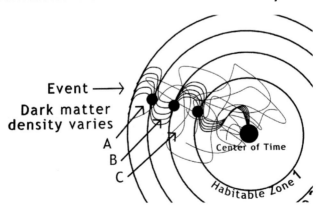

Figure 82: Shows that dark matter density varies greatly throughout the structure of Time.

The varying nature of dark matter in the Time fluid causes slight changes in the unfolding of events in different habitable zones or densities. The experience perceived by consciousness is directly related to spirit harmony. We will return to this.

Expansion of the Universe

Let's continue to solve or explain some of the riddles we see in our Universe today. One of the most puzzling questions we come across is: "Why is the Universe expanding when the force of gravity should be causing it to contract?"

In "Your Influence in Space," we discover that there is a sort of interstellar star pressure that may be observed. We saw that matter acts as shields. The force of gravity was equated to being interstellar star pressure minus shielding from mass. It is as if objects near each other are pushed together and stars far apart are pushed apart. What is being shielded? Could it be consciousness?

We see that matter is a result of space preparations and conscious crunching. We see matter drifting further and further away. Is there a sort of drag on our Universe being caused by the fluid of Time itself? Is the expansion of the Universe a result of a boundary condition between the natural rotational velocity of the fluid of time, the initial velocity or energy state of the incoming Universe, and the consciousness that resides inside?

Like any mass-on-mass interaction there will be a drag or friction of some sort. As the Universe rotates or moves through Time, the fluid would naturally want to reshape the Universe. For typical fluids, at the boundary, the velocity of the fluids will be the same. Which implies, for this example, that the velocity at the edge of the Universe would strive for balance with the general motion of the Time Fluid.

The maximum motion in our Universe would naturally be towards the edges because the rate of Time Fluid flow is greatest. One could also imagine vortexes forming on the trailing end of our Universe as it orbited through Time displacing the fluid in a turbulent fashion.

The Rotation of Time Fluid

There are no stationary bodies in the Universe. Again, making an assumption, however somewhat safer this instance, you could say that the fluid of time itself is in a state of rotation about the center of time regardless of any intruding universes.

Remember the spiral of perception earlier? The location of matters manifestation is directly related to the balance between conscious crunching and space preparation which occurs when you are accelerating at light speed. This means that as the fluid of time either rotates faster or slower, the "Habitable Zones" will change accordingly.

Another factor to the fluid dynamics associated with the Time fluid and our Universe would be the initial velocity or energy at which the Universe entered time. Motion of balance is caused by the degree of imbalance. As the initial velocity differences between the Time fluid and incoming Universe increases so does the expansion rate.

Nowhere here does this imply that the Universe will one day crunch back into a singularity. Nowhere here does this imply that the Universe will end as a frozen land of absolute zero.

This implies that the Universe will continue to cool and expand until it reaches an energetic balance with the Time Fluid. At that point, the Universe would no longer be expanding or contracting. The second fate described by this model would be an energetic exiting of the Universe from Time.

Shielding

Back to the example of gravity being a result of interstellar light pressure minus shielding from mass, and you see that perhaps it is consciousness that is being shielded creating wells of perception which translates into gravity.

Conscious Preparations, Space Crunching, Shell Jumping

Using the techniques explored in "The Liquid-Light State Universe," we may see how our conscious experience guided by spirt potential may travel from one habitable zone of experience into another. This relates directly to spirit fields, events, and dark matter density.

Magic Sphere

Let us now go back and examine the Magic Sphere in slightly more detail.

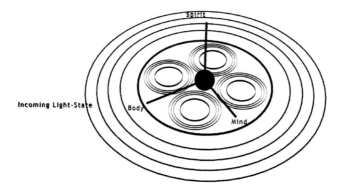

Figure 83: Depicts a magic sphere that is originally and more fully explained in "The Liquid-Light State Universe."

Here is a magic sphere of mind, body, and spirit, as derived from the magic square. This pattern is one that does not interfere with the light-state of the Universe. It almost tricks the light-state into thinking it does not exist meanwhile allowing for infinite energy to be created inside.

1	15	14	4	34
12	6	7	9	34
8	10	11	5	34
13	3	2	16	34
34	34	34	34	

		34
34	34	34
34	34	34
34	34	34
34	34	34

34 34 34 34

Figure 84: Depicts a magic square where all the solutions are equal to thirty-four. It is easy to see the harmony created by disharmony within this square. The center four squares also add to thirty-four which would make an energetic spike.

In this special example, even the middle four numbers (6, 7, 10, and 11) add to equal 34. Each one of the smaller rings may be represented by the original bigger picture. Each one would contain a spike in the middle. As you can see, the height of the spike may become infinite as the number of rings increases towards center. Consider this spiking height to be your antenna which connects you to the varying densities of your conscious perception and therefor waking reality.

The density of reality, the thickness and fullness of time you experience, is directly related to which habitable zone your consciousness resides in. Remember, the Universe is existing and having experiences at each of the habitable zones simultaneously. There are almost infinite numbers of habitable zones as they are related to the whole number ratios of our space preparations and conscious crunching ability to accelerate towards center at light speed.

Conscious Preparations and Spirit Harmony Relation

The Universe has nodes of manifestation which stem from the natural overlapping of EM. Our consciousness waves add and subtract to create potentialities across all habitable zones or spirit fields in unison. The physical experience one undergoes is a result of the vibrational harmony in accordance with the potentialities that exist. It is the spirit potential described in "The Liquid-Light-State Universe." Your consciousness is tuned to the "best light-state of coherence" in relation to your spirit vibration and that is where you feel as if you have physically manifested.

For a quick simple explanation, you could go out on a date. Plan everything perfectly (conscious preparations). It was the best date of your life and both of you are about to kiss (space preparations).

Then, anxiety….. fear…. Or perhaps overconfidence…. It creates a shift in your body's vibration or spirit state. You now, through use of shell jumping, have jumped into a physical existence or mental construct of that vibration. You have effectively changed energetic densities which coincides with a different array of dark matter influences and event paths. The event now literally manifest differently than if you were to have just stayed cool and calm. He or she now flees in fear because of the anxiety. The love is gone, but both regret it. It was all doubt in the mind and they will eventually pace back towards "no wall," because there is either "wall" or "no wall" in our primitive understandings. We will pace back to this.

Exiting Universe

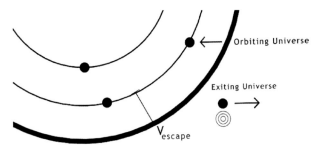

Figure 85: Depicts a universe being ejected from Time.

What happens when and if a universe comes near another universe? Is there and does it even make sense to consider the possibility of interference with one another.

Let's consider a universe in a couple ways. We could say it's a solid, a liquid, or a gas. For the example, let's use an electric liquid model with high viscosity. This means our universes are "sticky" to themselves and have an electric charge.

The electric charge would be related to the spin state of the entire structure. It may be reasonable to think of it like an electron. Any matter that spins creates a magnetic field. When you have something the size of the Universe, you end up making a pretty big magnet.

In our simple model, if a universe collides with another one, then they will either bounce off each other or stick to each other depending on the direction of the magnetic field. It may be possible for enough energy to be gathered during one of these collisions for an entire universe to escape through crust or mantle of Time.

Where would it go? In our crystalline structure of Time, we see the Universe orbits towards center at light speed. It somewhat mimics the behavior of an electron around an atomic center. Could it be that the "Time Molecules" or atoms also have a positive and negative charge based on the electric charge of the universes within? Could the "Crystal of Time" we speak of be similar to one single atom of time in a yet bigger structure? Will our electron Universe travel to another atom of Time? If so, what might we experience?

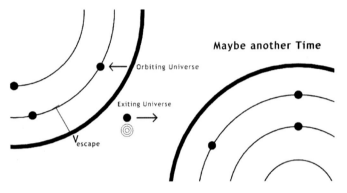

Figure 86: Will the Universe enter another time?

Consciousness Native to Time?

This leads to the ultimate question. Is the consciousness that's been evolving in our Universe native to the Universe or to the Crystal of Time itself? What is the order of operations as far as events? Was it Time, Consciousness, then Universe, or do we really think it went, Universe, Time, then Consciousness?

Cleaning out the Inside Through Harmony

Circling back to "Your Influence in Space," we see that the answer may be that the order of operations is Time, Consciousness, and then Universe.

Let's look at our Crystal of Time as if it were a living being. What would the goal of our lives in relation to this much greater picture be?

We all seem to strive for love and harmony with our environment. People fear death and pain. It is that easy to understand. There is either love and harmony or struggle and discord.

Let us go back to the single celled organism with the simple ability to detect wall or no wall. The wall distorts the organism. It favors no wall. It favors freedom and potentiality. Although our senses have evolved to detect more complicated structures, they basically still say the same thing. The translation to the mental projection is now "love" or "no love."

All beings in Time strive towards natural harmony. When looking at the light-state of the matter, it is smooth, calm, and everlasting. The Universe may be a distortion of sorts in a smooth fabric of Time and Consciousness. Conscious agents could be the harmonizers of Time with the goal of being to remove discord created by entering bodies (Universes).

Afterall, all there is, is love.

Spirit Potenial

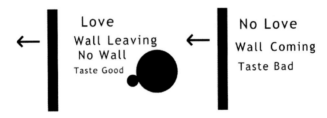

Love
Wall Leaving
No Wall
Taste Good

No Love
Wall Coming
Taste Bad

Thanks for Reading

Leaders in Innovation   2:21 am 2/21/2021   www.LooshesLabs.com

Time Atom

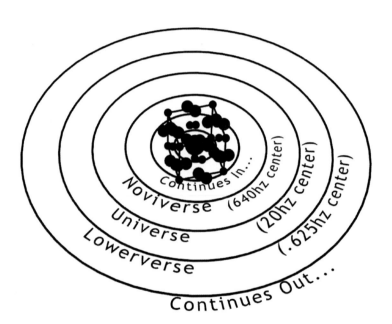

by Alexei Novitzky

Table of Contents

Introduction

The concept of multiple dimensions within reality may seem like science fiction. However, what is it that determines our reality in the first place?

From "The Crystal of Time," we see that spirit harmonics or state may be the deciding factor of which event line you fall into when orbiting the center of Time.

We see that habitable zones exist at places where our acceleration towards the center of Time is equal to the speed of light.

However, could we once again be missing a greater and greater picture? Is it not wheels within wheels as described by ancient text? Do we really think we are currently at our most advanced state of technological, mental, and spiritual development when compared to life in the past?

"Time Atom" explores existence in a fascinating new way. Imagine you are a single atom in the much larger Crystal of Time. Our cocreated conscious reality is constructed by passing universes back and forth to each other. A universe enters a habitable shell, we gather information, add to it, and then pass it off.

But what if we could fall into another consciousness? What if our Universe is the layering of a multiverse of some sort? What if we could alter our minds standing harmonics to accept new universes that we normally would not. Would we not see, feel, and experience a completely new realm?

For every action desired there is the most appropriate physics. Here we will develop a new technique for body manifestation within an alternate dimension of space, time, and consciousness.

We will say that our conscious manifestation is a direct result of conscious harmonics and spirit state. Conscious harmonics determine which universes are captured. Spirit state would determine the location in Time and how reality would unfold.

Crystal of Time

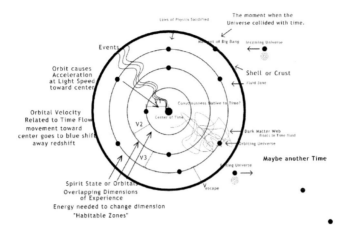

Figure 87: The Crystal of Time demonstrates the concept that our Universe may be orbiting Time.

"The Crystal of Time" shows that your spirit or orbital state alone may determine your physical manifestation through our Universe.

The spirit state is your motion through time. Let me explain. In order for a human to perceive conscious reality you would need to be accelerating at the speed of light towards the Center of Time.

The rings depicted and used in "The Crystal of Time," consider a constant velocity around the center, which creates an acceleration towards center at light speed. But just like any object orbiting and falling, if your velocity decreases your radius needs to decrease in order to stay in orbit. This is what creates the spiral of perception.

spiral of a=c
associated with changing v

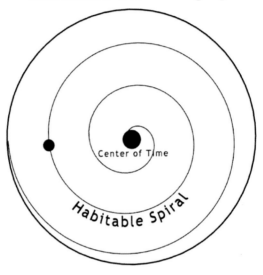

Figure 88: The spiral of perception is formed by the connection between human consciousness and the expansion of our Universe.

This spiral represents the habitable locations for a universe with slowing time flow.

This leads to the question. How many universes may occupy Time at once? Is it possible to have particles flowing through Time that are unobservable to our consciousness? What if we are the consciousness of a single Time Atom in a much larger crystal?

In a way, are we not here, in Time, saying reality circles us, just like we once believed the Sun circled the Earth? Would we not get the same effect from having multiple universes orbiting and layering upon us? Let us take a step back and look at another picture.

Time Atoms

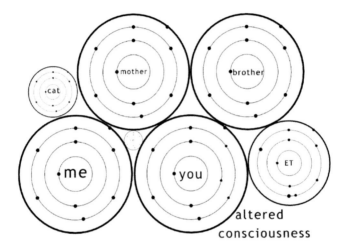

Figure 89: Represents a cluster of Time Atoms making a crystal. Common universe types are exchanged because the atoms are of similar nature.

What we see from "The Crystal of Time" is that our known Universe orbits the center of Time. We see that our position in 3D space-time is directly related to orbital distance and velocity. We see multiple universes with the same energy and velocity circling Time. We see dark matter interfering with the flow of matter through Time. We see events playing out differently as dark matter varies across Time. We see drag from the Time Fluid causing the expansion of the universes as they orbit. We see our ability to perceive these universes relates to the acceleration towards center at light speed. We see the exiting of universes from Time itself.

The Table of Universes

It is possible that there are multiple universe types that exist in nature. Each one of these universe types varies based on its fundamental properties. They might have a certain spin, electric charge, size, viscosity, and etc. The ability for a universe to be perceived by a consciousness is directly related to the "acceptability" of the universe to the Time Atom under review.

With this in mind, it may be reasonable to create a Table of Universes. From this, we will be able to compare it with acceptable universe types with human consciousness.

Types of Time Atoms

When considering the concept of Time Atoms, it makes sense that there would be several different types. Some would have more stable universe shells than others. The rotation rate of the Time Fluid might be faster, slower, or spin in the opposite direction. The total diameter may vary as well. So, you could see the potential in creating a table of Time Atoms.

What does that even mean? Each Time Atom would be its own set of consciousness that may perceive or accept similar universe types. For example, human, dog, and cat all have the ability to interact in our modern construct of reality. You could say we all have the ability to experience a common universe. Although our physical universal experience may overlap, they are not the same. Humans, dogs, and cats have different consciousnesses and bodies. Therefore, they are of a different Time Atom experiencing the same universe. Perhaps they have fewer number of stable orbital shells.

Some beings or rather Time Atoms may have the ability to naturally interact with universe types that we cannot. This may be why animals for an easy way of putting it... do weird things sometimes.

In a way, you could also say that this phenomenon would translate directly into the type of mental construct the being has.

Dimensions of Perception

It is always important to go back in our time and look at our senses and our ability to perceive when attempting to explain the mysteries of reality.

For this example, let's consider the number of shells a Time Atom may contain, as well as the potential number of universes within each shell.

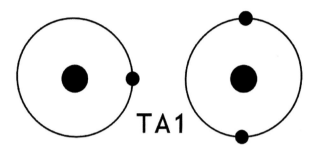

Figure 90: Is a representation of a type 1 Time Atom. In our Universe, this may resemble a stone or a particle.

Let us go back to the senseless being, as in a being that does not have any senses. It would most likely think that reality did not exist. It would probably not know it was even alive. It, at the very best, is simply existing in our reality. This being or stone for all we know, would most likely only have one shell with one or two universes orbiting. It merely has the ability to exist. Its mental construct is one dimension. "I." For this case, let's call this a TA1 (Time Atom 1).

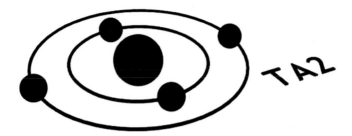

Figure 91: This image represents a type 2 Time Atom. The being here has one physical sense.

Our next being on the list would have the simplest ability of feel. It would have wall or no wall. Its mental construct would be that of two dimensions. It can either perceive away from the wall or towards the wall. This being may have two shells of universes orbiting it. Its mental construct or consciousness is more advanced than the previous case. "I exist. There is a wall." Let's call this being a TA2. The universes inside would pack or orbit in a way that preserves balance. It is possible that the shells do not need to be completely filled. You could imagine beings that fall into the category of a TA2 similar to flowing mater, a magnet, or archeobacteria.

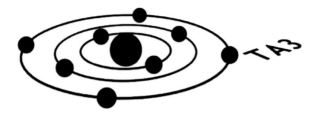

Figure 92: This image represents a type 3 Time Atom. There are now three shells in which to capture universes.

The next being on the list would have the ability to feel and to taste/smell. This would give it the impression of wall or no wall, and taste good or taste bad. You could say that this being has a greater sense of self awareness for survival. It could be considered the first form of passion. It has purpose. "I exist, I want that molecule." Perhaps this being has another shell in its Time Atom than the previous example. Let's call a being with the ability to smell and taste a TA3.

As the beings become more conscious you can see the number of available universe particles increases dramatically. A being in the TA3 category is one that has the ability to taste and smell. An example of a TA3 being would be an amoeba. There are easily eight space holders for potential universes available.

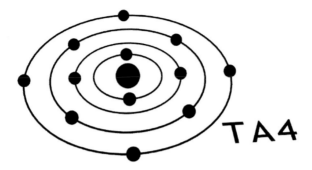

Figure 93: This image represents a type 4 Time Atom. This includes starfish and other "simple" animals. This may include some plants as well.

All of the previous examples still only give the being a conscious perspective of a distance of 0. Sound or advanced feeling is the first sense that allows us detect velocity and location. It is our first ability of precognition. You could imagine a being with a consciousness like this to have more shells than the previous one. "I exist, I want to go there for that molecule, but I need to time my approach." Let's call this being a TA4.

A being of TA4 has the ability to hear sounds. This translates into the ability to construct a three-dimensional environment in which there is motion. Again, the number of universe particles increases dramatically as the circle or spherical shape grows in size. This example shows a being with 12 universe particles orbiting its center. An example of this would be a blind animal found in a cave.

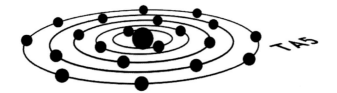

Figure 94: This image represents a type 5 Time Atom. Humans would be in this category.

Now here on Earth, this is where things get a little tricky. Some animals, like us humans, developed the ability to detect electromagnetism centered around the color yellow. Some animals, like dolphins and bats, developed a sonar system. However, all those animals also have the ability to see with eyes. For our next grouping, we will only consider animals that have the ability to see in electromagnetism with eyes. Their mental construct is now, "I exist. That looks good! I want to go there for that molecule, I need to time my approach." Again, the mental construct has grown in size. We could potentially add another shell to this Time Atom. Let's call this group TA5-1.

Our next group falls within the lines of TA5. They have the ability to detect wall, to taste/smell, to hear, and to see. However, they also have a sixth sense of some sort. These are the beings with sonar, like bats and dolphins. These beings would construct reality based off of sight like the TA5-1 group but they also have an added layer of sensory information. Let's call this group TA5-2. Again, we see a large jump in the number of universes that may be captured. Humans and dolphins are examples of TA5 beings.

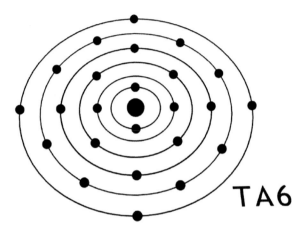

Figure 95: This image represents a type 6 Time Atom. This being would have the ability to naturally travel through time.

The next group of beings comes from our theoretical aliens in "Your Influence in Space." This being has the ability to see and travel through time just as easy as we see the stars at night. This being would have a similar gap in evolutionary advancement to us as we do to earthworms. With the ability to see and walk-through wormholes, you could say this being has a greater sense of awareness. It would have one more shell in its mental construct. "I exist. That looks like it was good at one point. Let's go back in time for that molecule." This being would have a TA6.

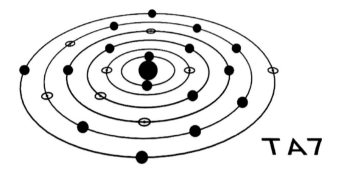

Figure 96: This image represents a type 7 Time Atom. This being would have the ability to walk-through dimensions.

What you see is that for every sense or dimensional construct we have added a shell for universes to orbit in. All of the beings we just mentioned would be accepting of the same universe particles. Our next being is the first type that has the ability to accept a different universe type. This theoretical being would be one that could travel not only through time, but dimensions as well. "I exist. That looks like it was good at one point. Let's see what it looks like in another dimension." It would have more universe shells than the previous type. For our model, we will call this a TA7. (It is important to note that there may also be beings of lower TA number that also accept multiple universe types. These would be considered special exceptions from our humanly understanding. Perhaps we could add a suffix based on universe types accepted. For example, TA1 (ab) and TA3 (ac).)

Conscious or Time Atom Packing

All objects want to go towards equilibrium. An easy way to put it is, "Earth goes to Earth, water goes to water, air goes to air, and space need not bother." However, in the smaller sense, when it comes to crystals and atoms, they tend to pack as tightly together as possible in an effort to preserve energy. There are basic shapes that come from this packing of spheres.

The five major shape types that exist are the tetrahedron, the cube, the octahedron, the icosahedron, and the dodecahedron. Obviously, there may be more shapes but these are the main shapes that crystal formations naturally tend to favor.

Let's now theorize on how these Time Atoms may pack based on the number of universes they may contain. Considering universes orbit the center of Time similar to electrons, it may be reasonable to follow the current crystalline structures that exist in our periodic table of elements. Here are a few examples of what the packing of Time Atoms may look like in a crystalline formation.

TA1 Crystal

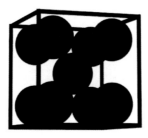

Figure 97: This image is a theoretical packing of TA1 beings.

It is unknown at this time what the true packing nature of a TA1 being may be, however for a being with one shell it may pack similar to hydrogen.

TA2 Crystal

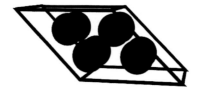

Figure 98: This image is a theoretical representation of what TA2 beings may look like in a crystal.

Again, the true state of the Time Crystal packing is unknown. We use Beryllium in this example to illustrate the packing of Time Atoms with two shells.

TA3 Crystal

Figure 99: Represents the theoretical packing of a TA3 crystal.

The TA3 crystal would be one that has three shells of universes orbiting it. What you see is that the structures created by Time Atoms may vary greatly. This structure resembles the packing of silicone.

TA5 Crystal

(Human?)

Figure 100: Represents the theoretical packing of a TA5 crystal.

There are many different crystals that exist in nature. Taking a note from our ancestors, perhaps this is the crystalline structure associated with human consciousness.

There are two other main characteristics worth covering when it comes to crystal formations. One, would be the concept of minerals. The other, would be the concept of having universal bonds between atoms, similar to ionic, covalent, and metallic. What could those imply in our consciousness universe model?

Bonds Between Atoms

In nature, there are a few bonds that allow for the sharing of electrons. In our model, this would imply the sharing of universes between Time Atoms. This translates into the ability to consciously interact with one another. The common types are ionic, covalent, and metallic.

Ionic Bonds

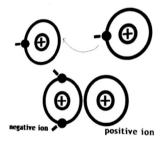

Figure 101: This image depicts a typical ionic bond.

The graphic is an example of an ionic bond. One atom loses its electron and gives it to the other. This creates both a negative and a positive ion. The negative ion now has both electrons and the positive ion has lost one. At first glance, this doesn't seem like a model we would be interested looking further into. However, we will return to it.

Covalent Bonds

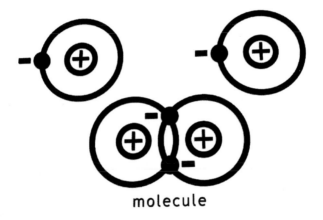

molecule

Figure 102: This is a representation of a covalent bond.

Covalent bonds form when the outer shell of the atom is sharing an electron with one or more atoms. For the sake of conscious generation by passing universes, this model may be the key. It also may lead us into answering some of the tougher yet unanswered questions of modern physics. Such as, what is quantum entanglement?

Metallic Bonds

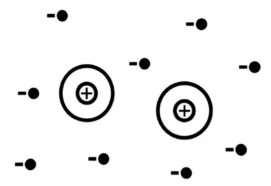

Figure 103: This image depicts a metallic bond.

Metallic bonds exist when the charge of the outer most shell of an atom is satisfied by a cloud of free-floating electrons. This model may or may not have practical uses when looking at the Time Atom. For now, let's let it be.

Minerals of Time Atoms

A mineral, in the most generic sense, is a crystalline structure composed of two or more elements. The crystals in the above section represented pure crystals with no impurities. However, a quart crystal is composed of silicone and oxygen. The combination of these individual elements or atoms makes a new structure with characteristics that are unique to the two original atoms. That is interesting on its own, but let's stay focused on solely that elements may imbed themselves into the crystalline structure of another element. Pyrite is a good example of a mineral. It is composed of one Iron atom and two Sulfur atoms. It has characteristics of both ionic and covalent bonds.

When translating this into our consciousness models, we see that the number of shared universes is an indicator of which types of beings may coexist on a conscious level. Let's take a look at a pyrite mineral and compare this to the potential experience of a starfish and protozoa.

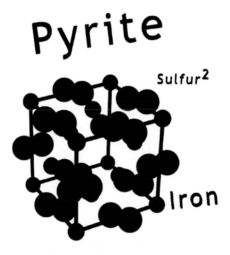

Figure 104: This image represents the crystalline structure of Pyrite.

In the periodic table of elements, Iron is shown to have four shells for electrons to fall into. Sulfur is shown to have three. For this example, let's pretend Iron is a TA4 being and Sulfur is like a TA3 being. An example of a TA4 being would be a starfish, and an example of a TA3 being might be a protozoon or other single-celled being.

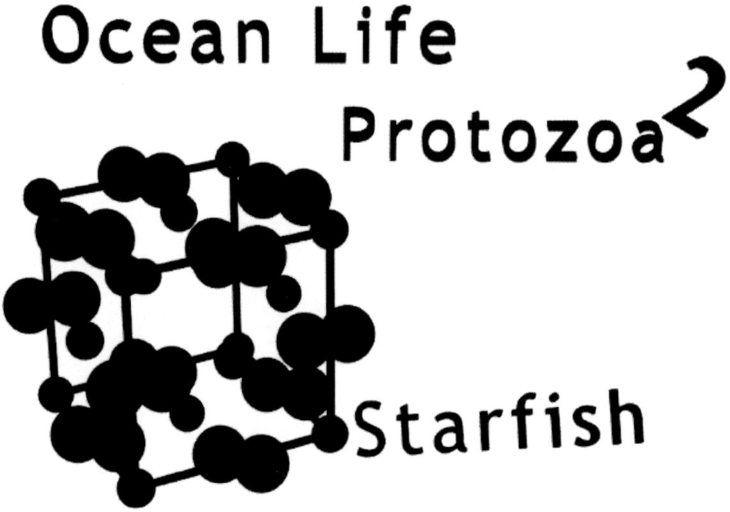

Ocean Life

Protozoa

Starfish

Figure 105: This image represents a mineral composed of starfish and protozoan consciousnesses.

Here you can see that a starfish and protozoa may pack together to form a coconscious reality They share information via sharing universes via ionic and covalent bonds. This is a very simple example showing a crystal of cocreation. The universes that are being shared are of similar type and create a stabile charge. The cluster shares a center.

Cluster Origins

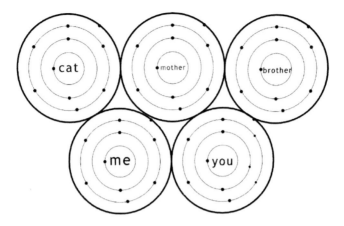

Figure 106: Is a simple example of how contact between atoms may relate directly to the level of quantum entanglement.

Not all conscious crystals in Time are in direct contact with each other. This creates clusters of conscious cocreation. A simple example may be a family. Imagine a father, a mother, a son, a daughter, and maybe a cat or dog. They may have their own coconscious reality that is then exchanged via a metallic bonding of sorts with other conscious crystals. This would translate directly into the types of "cliques" or gangs that exist in the human population. We are all humans that live on Earth, and so you would assume we have the same goals and general constructs of reality. However, in practice they are much different. They are almost of their own cocreated consciousnesses or grains of Time.

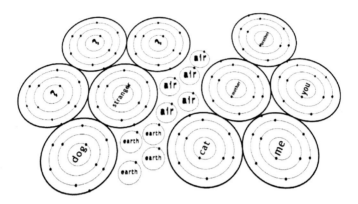

Figure 107: This image represents two grains or clusters of Time separated by a fissure or crack.

You can see with this simple representation how the two individual grains may experience different viewpoints on cultural issues. There has not been enough exchange of universes for them to be properly tuned to each other. The more time between sharing universes, the more different the cultures of coconscious creations become. However, once direct covalent bonds have been made it is likely the individual experiences, viewpoints, or rather expectations will merge.

An Altered State of Consciousness

What does an altered state of consciousness do to a Time Atom? Brain harmonics relate directly to frequency. It is not too farfetched to reason that a change in your brain harmonics will cause a change in which universe particles you will be capturing or interpreting into your consciousness.

There are many types of altered states of consciousness which may be induced in several ways. Hypnosis is a commonly used method to create a sort of super focus within the person being hypnotized. Past events may be replayed and seen in different perspectives. True healing may come from this. This type of altered consciousness does not seem to allow for new universes to enter. It does, however, seem to allow the user to float more freely through the Fluid of Time.

Another altered state of consciousness that we all experience at night would be sleep. Here we see the increase of the hormone melatonin into the blood stream. Sleep is extremely interesting when considering interdimensional travel. Remember, universe type accepted is related to brain or conscious harmonics. When you are sleeping your brain goes through a variety of changes. Each one of these changes gives the sleeper a new conscious experience. One brain wave pattern that may be of interest is the delta wave pattern. The long wave format appears to be several times that of the alpha wave. Theoretically, based on wave addition and subtraction, the delta pattern may be collecting information from another universe particle.

The use of hallucinogens is also commonly known to alter someone's state of consciousness. Some common types are MDMA, LSD and DMT. All of these hallucinogens cause one's brain chemistry and harmonics to change dramatically.

It is said that DMT may be a direct key to unlock the conscious path to a higher dimension. It is the molecule produced in the pineal gland and released at the moment of death. People that have experienced near death experiences (NDE) account similar stories. There are many accounts of people communicating with lost or still living family members, witnessing events unfolding, and of course, the tunnel of white light. There are also accounts of speaking with angels or potentially extraterrestrials from another dimension. Are these beings real? Where, how, and what could be happening?

A Shift in Standing Energy

Standing brain wave frequency is a direct result of wave function. In a normal waking environment, you are conscious of our normal waking world. Our brain waves are in a beta state which is a vibratory frequency of 13-30hz. Based off the model, you would be experiencing normal waking universes.

Just before sleep, humans are in an alpha state which is 8-13hz. When you fall into the delta wave function, your wavelengths become almost seven times longer. Relating this solely to frequency, you could say that the universes captured would need to be seven times in wavelength or size as well. Let's call that the Deltaverse. It is the conscious creation of brain harmony tuned to delta waves. This could be related to the molecule melatonin.

While experiencing DMT, there is increase in slow and fast-gamma waves. Slow-Gamma waves range from 30hz to 50hz and fast-gamma waves range from 50hz to 100hz. Here again, you see space for another universe type to be perceived.

Let's now think logically about wave tuning. You could see that for every common factor or multiple of human consciousness a different universe type may exist. We may say that alpha is 10hz. Then, it is only logical that experiences would be captured at multiples of that vibration. Let's just see how this works and then see what we may infer from that.

Very quickly a hertz (hz) is how many times the wave occurs in a second. So, alpha is 10hz. 10hz divided by 2 is 5hz. 5hz puts us into theta waves which are associated with sleep. Divide that by 2 and you are at 2.5hz. That puts us in the Deltaverse, similar to a deep sleep. Now let's go the other way. 10hz times 2 is 20hz. The 20hz frequency relates directly to the beta waves or Betaverse. This is our normal waking state. You could say we all mostly live in the Betaverse. Again, let's multiply by 2 and that gets us to 40hz. We are now in the Slow-Gammaverse. Multiply that by two and we are at 80hz. This wave function is associated with extremely heightened perception. We are now in the Fast-Gammaverse similar to a DMT experience. This is the state of mind when out of body experiences occur. That would be the end of normal human brainwave function. However, what universe would we be in if we doubled our conscious harmonic one more time?

80hz times 2 goes to 160hz. Is there a universe to be experienced at every harmonic resonance? I would argue that at each interval an experience may be had and that we may use tools in order to perceive these higher dimensions of consciousness. This would include 160hz, 320hz, 640hz, 1280hz, 2560hz and so on.

Understanding this, we may now fill our Table of Universes more accurately. However, before we do that, let's compare the delta wavelength to the longest wave perceivable as determined in "The Liquid-Light State Universe."

An Interesting Piece of Evidence

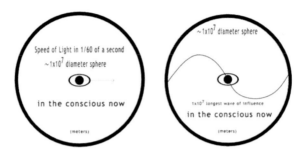

In "The Liquid-Light State Universe," we calculated the size of the conscious snapshot by saying that we take a picture with our brain sixty times a second. We then multiplied this by the speed of light to see a theoretical diameter for our consciousness. It ended up being 3x10^8 m/s x 1/60 s and we got 5,000,000 meters as our radius. We then multiplied that by two to get the diameter of a sphere. From this, we theorized on the longest wavelength we could manipulate with conscious preparations. This number ended up being 1x10^7m. This would relate directly to the longest wavelength human consciousness could perceive or manipulate based off light-state theory alone.

From "The Crystal of Time," we see that our habitable zones are places where our acceleration is equal to the speed of light. However, let's turn that around. Another way to perceive a universe is if it is circling us at a rate that would cause it to accelerate towards center at light speed. Let us now calculate the diameter associated with acceleration at light speed of the delta wave.

The longest delta wave occurs roughly at 1.2 hz. We know that our frequency of rotation is 1.2hz. We know that acceleration towards center must be equal to the speed of light. From this, we are able to calculate a theoretical radius where our delta waves may manifest or universes orbit.

$(2 \times 3.14 \times r)/v = 1/1.2$ goes to $7.536r = v$

then we use $a = (v^2)/r$ goes to $a(r) = 56.79r^2$

$a = c$ $c/56.79 = r$ $r = 5.3 \times 10^6$ m

this would make the diameter 1.05×10^7 m

deltaverse may exist in a cloud that orbits our center of time at a radius of

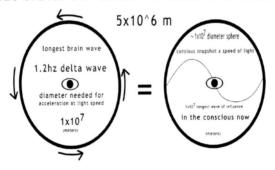

5x10^6 m

In an astronomical sense, this is extremely significant. Take a moment to understand this. All of our consciousness associated with the delta wave type may be in a cloud surrounding our golden spot at a radius of 5x10^6 meters.

Let's add this average cloud diameter to the Table of Universes as well.

Table of Universes

Universe	Brain Wave	hz Frequency	hz Harmonic Frequency	m Cloud Diameter
Deltaverse	delta	1-3	2.5	2.4×10^6
Thetaverse	theta	4-8	5	6×10^5
Aplhaverse	aplha	9-13	10	1.5×10^5
Betaverse	beta	14-30	20	40,000
Slow Gammaverse	slow-gamma	30-49	40	10,000
Fast Gammaverse	fast-gamma	50-100	80	2,500
Aleverse	omega	101-220	160	625
Dimiverse	zeta	221-400	320	156.25

Figure 108: Here we introduce the Table of Universes. Our normal conscious experience is an overlapping of the Deltaverse through the Fast-Gammaverse universe types.

Inducing Higher Frequencies

There may be ways in which we may theoretically induce higher brain wave function. Several tools currently exist on the market that help people focus their minds. Transcranial Magnetic Stimulation or TMS is one of the most commonly used devices at the moment. Professional video gamers and drone pilots use them to get an advantage. However, they are all being used to work in the Betaverse.

It may be possible to use a similar device and induce smooth brain harmonics in the 160hz range. It would require someone who is well versed in mental focus and meditation. It would be very interesting to see what would happen at each of these harmonic intervals, 160hz, 320hz, 640hz, 1280hz, and 2560hz.

A More Defined Time Atom Model

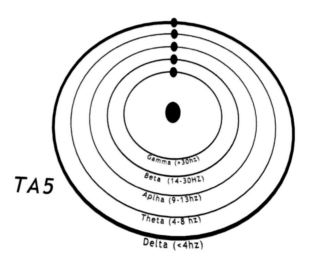

Figure 109: This figure represents a more defined Time Atom model. Here you can see we have added frequencies to the orbits.

Based on what we have seen in brain wave function we may now make a guess on the frequency involved with each of the orbital states.

We could say that the slowest orbital may be related to delta waves and the highest naturally may be related to gamma waves. Therefore, the orbital frequency of the exterior shell would be near 2.5hz. The orbital frequency of the second would be 5hz and so on. Earlier, we depicted the size of the shell based on the number of senses. That was a good start. However, it may be more appropriate to consider brain or conscious harmonics which is now more properly shown.

Here you can see theoretical frequencies associated with each shell type. Let's add two more shells of brain capability to get to our TA7 being.

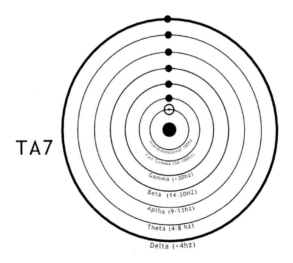

Figure 110: This image represents the conscious harmonics of a TA7 being.

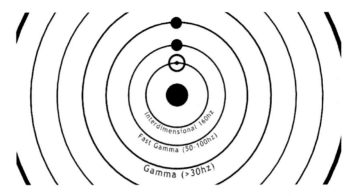

Figure 111: This is a closeup of the center of the TA7 being that would be inhabiting our conscious timeline.

Back to the Magic Sphere

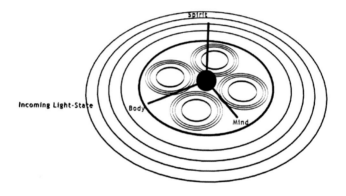

Figure 112: This image represents a magic sphere.

In "The Liquid-Light State Universe," we introduce the concept of the magic sphere. Let us now relate this to brain function and higher order consciousness.

Consider this a mind and spirit antenna. The magic sphere with no interior rings would make a single center peak. This center peak represents the standing wave harmonic of any system in the light-state. Here, we are talking about the human brain.

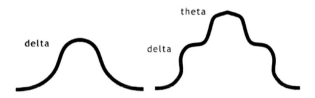

Figure 113: This is a side or profile view relating to harmonic amplitude generation.

You can see that the one hump relates to the delta wave. By adding the second set of rings in perfect harmony we are able to have two peaks. This pattern may continue to repeat as long as the vibrations remain in harmony. Here you can see the vibrations have added twice more.

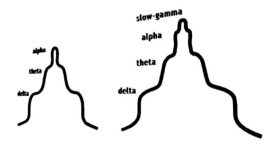

Figure 114: The harmonic resonance within the magic sphere allows for synchronous wave building.

We are now into the slow-gamma ability. By continuing to maintain perfect harmony within the brain, it is possible to increase this antenna to reach even higher and higher states of consciousness. Our next example shows a being with the ability to perform brain waves at 160hz and 320hz.

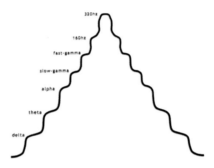

Figure 115: The potential for wave building within the magic sphere is infinite.

You can see the potential in the calming of a mind while stimulating through TMS to create these wave patterns. It would be very interesting to see what conscious reality a being would perceive with these wave functions occurring in mind. Another important consideration is, that with properly timed waves, it does not take that much energy to build upon itself. A trained practitioner of meditation may easily be able to increase their brain function to the "DMT" state and beyond.

Use of molecules or drugs during training will only allow for so much advancement. In order to reach sustained higher levels of consciousness, it must be done without additives.

Clouds of Universes

From this model you can see that your entire construct of consciousness is being formed by orbiting clouds of universes that accelerate towards your conscious center. The harmonic state of your brain determines which universes you are tuned too and what you will ultimately experience.

Cloud Technologies

Based on the concept of various universe clouds orbiting our center of consciousness, there may be a way to manipulate the incoming light-state to have them fall naturally within our perception. In a way, this seems more logical than using technology to increase our brain wave function. It is probably healthier as well. You wouldn't have to maintain the 80hz or 160hz wave harmonic. Instead, you could experience the higher dimension in your normal waking state.

Light-state technology gives us clues on how to manipulate the natural nodes of manifestation within our physical Universe. Using these techniques, we could essentially warp the local sphere to have the higher dimensions fall within our natural radius or Betaverse.

The easiest universe to attempt to shift first would be the Fast-Gammaverse. This is the wave associated with near death experiences and DMT journeys. Let's logically think about this for a minute.

In the light-state model, the Fast-Gammaverse is a cloud of universes that orbits at an average distance of 2,500 meters from your conscious center. Our Betaverse orbits at approximately 40,000 meters away from our conscious center. This is a factor of 16 times. We would want to expand the cloud of Fast-Gammaverse particles from 2,500 meters to encompass the 40,000 meter sphere. While doing this, the process would naturally push away any interfering Betaverse particles. They would essentially be shifted out of waking consciousness and be somewhere in the dreamland.

Gravity, magnets, lenses, and dense structures all have an influence on incoming light-state. In this case, we would want to create an expanded light-state. This would be one that slows incoming EM from all directions, or rather puffs out space. You would need a sort of negative gravity field that could create a time dilation equal to 16 times normal motion. At the same time, you would need to make sure that the particles are still accelerating towards you at the speed of light. When you expand the light-state it does not slow down the rates of rotation. At this point you would have a sphere of Fast-Gammaverse particles with an orbital frequency of 80hz. You would also need to slow down the speed to match that of the Betaverse which would be 20 Hz. The rotation rate would need to be slowed by 4 times.

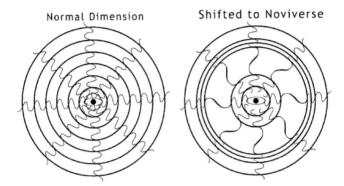

Normal Dimension   Shifted to Noviverse

Figure 116: The field lines represent the "smoothness" of normal space. The image on the right has been transported into another dimension.

In short, in order for the Fast-Gammaverse to be experienced in normal waking reality, you would need to expand the light-state by 16 times and create a counter rotation of 4 times. It may be possible that it is first easier to expand the state then rotate it or possibly to do them both at the same time. Just an important side note, you would want to make sure the physical space you encompass is not being warped, just the spherical volume starting at the distance of where it would naturally be. To explain a little more, you'd want the counter-torsion field generator to start at about 2,400 meters away and extend to about 40,000 meters away. That would most likely create an environment in which you could experience the Fast-Gammaverse in your normal Betaverse state of mind. This would allow you to physically walk around and experience this alternate dimension.

Relativity is Relativity

Everything is relative. Currently, we use an average of 2.5hz as our cycle of time for the delta wave. This is completely related to the number of cycles per second. The concept of a second is a very human thing.

For us, the relative ratios of mind go from 2.5hz in our delta wave state to 80hz in our fast-gamma state. You could imagine that our 2.5hz could be similar to the 80hz of another species within Time. Meaning, instead of their range going from 2.5hz to 80hz, it may go from 80hz to the number of harmonics away from that. Let me show you. Here, we will multiply our sets by 2 and see how they relate.

2.5hz, 5hz, 10hz, 20hz, 40hz, and 80hz for humans would correlate to 80hz, 160hz, 320hz, 640hz, 1280hz, and 2560hz for a being that is in a completely shifted dimension. Similarly, to how we call our current frequency range of universes the Universe, we could call this secondary frequency ranges the Noviverse.

Table of Universes

Universe	Brain Wave	hz Frequency	hz Harmonic Frequency	m Cloud Diameter
Deltaverse	delta	1-3	2.5	2.4×10^6
Thetaverse	theta	4-8	5	6×10^5
Aplhaverse	aplha	9-13	10	1.5×10^5
Betaverse	beta	14-30	20	40,000
Slow Gammaverse	slow-gamma	30-49	40	10,000
Fast Gammaverse	fast-gamma	50-100	80	2,500
Aleverse	omega	101-220	160	625
Dimiverse	zeta	221-400	320	156.25
Stellaverse	epsilon	401-800	640	39
Petraverse	omicron	801-1600	1280	9.75
Mikaverse	iota	1601-3400	2560	2.4

Figure 117: Our Table of Universes has grown to include the Noviverse. This pattern will continue indefinitely into lower and higher harmonics.

In other words, the DMT high-gamma state for humans could be the "delta state" of a being that has access to different dimensions or universe particles. The time dilation associated would be directly related to the Lorentz contraction.

The diameter of a 2.5hz wave is 2.4x10^6 meters. The diameter of an 80hz wave is 2,500 meters. Here you can see the amount of Lorentz contraction this equates to and then infer a time dilation between the two dimensions of waking life. Basically, the ratio is (2.4x10^6 meters)/(2,500 m) which goes about 1000. That is our multiplying factor. Theoretically, you could say, as far as waking perception, that for every 1 second that passes here in the Betaverse, 1000 seconds passes in the Betaverse equivalent of Noviverse. 640hz or Stellaverse, would be their "beta state." So, a diameter of 40,000m /39.06m goes to roughly 1,000.

The 4 rotations a second would also add to the time dilation. It may be a safer assumption to say the total time dilation would be 4,000 to 1. This goes to 1 second being equivalent to 1 hour and 1 minute.

The same could be true for a harmonic of lower frequency. There could be a set of harmonics that exist there as well. Our 2.5hz of the delta state would be the equivalent to their 2.5hz "fast-gamma."

This being said, it is almost like our highest levels of brain function matches the lowest of the next ring. Theoretically, someone on DMT may be able to connect consciously with an ET or angel that is sleeping.

The Layering of Conscious Types within Time

Here you can now see the potential for the layering of conscious types or universes within the Crystal of Time. The physical manifestations could all be existing simultaneously but in longer wave form and time dilated. The 1 second of time experienced by a Betaverse mind would be related to 1 hour of time in the normal waking world of the Noviverse. Likewise, 1 hour of time in our dimension would be equivalent to 1 second of time in the dimension shifted to longer waves.

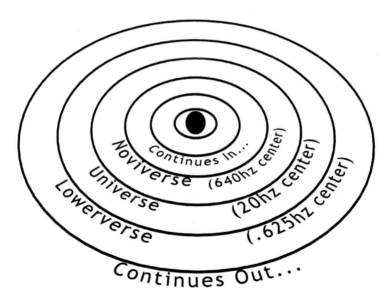

Figure 118: Represents the fractal nature of dimensions.

Have we just uncovered wheels within wheels? What is it that determines existence? If a 1 second experience in our Universe translates into 1 hour in the Noviverse, then the difference between the Lowerverse and Noviverse would be even greater. The ratio would be (4000 to 1) times (4000 to 1) which is 4000^2. This would make a time dilation between two habitable phases equal to 16 million. Meaning, for every second that passes in the Lowerverse roughly 16 million seconds would happen in the Noviverse. 16 million seconds is equal to 2,666,666 minutes which is equal to 44,444.44 hours. 44,444 hours is equal to 185.185185 days. It is interesting just to compare that to cycles here on Earth which is most closely related to 1/2 a year. The next cycle after that would be related to (4000^3)(note: the actual number to use is 3,840 not 4,000, astronomers like to simplify.). 4000^3 equals 64 billion seconds which translates into 2029 years.

# of shifts	Dilation Factor per Second
0	1 second
1	1 hour
2	185 days
3	2029 years
4	8.1 million years
5	32 billion years
6	130 trillion years

Figure 119: If our Universe is 18 billion years old, then the Noviverse would be 69,120 billion years old. This would make the Lowerverse only 4.6 million years old.

You can see by the nature of the Crystal of Time that this cycle will continue onward indefinitely.

Interdimensional Telescope

By understanding the light-state, brain harmonics, and the conscious connection, we may theoretically design an interdimensional telescope that may look into these hidden dimensions. The telescope would function on the premises of the cloud technologies mentioned earlier. However, for this interdimensional telescope concept you would only be creating a window in which you could look into these alternate dimensions. Potentially, you may also be able to physically walk into it, but we would have to build one to see.

Again, we would be using light-state theory to create the desired shifting and stretching of nodes to create this effect. You would be at point 0 (in meters) and need to create a field that extends from about 2,400 meters to 40,000 meters away. This would be 1.5 miles to 24.85 miles. In other words, the field generated would need to be 25 miles long.

Within this tunnel, you would want to uniformly expand and stretch the light so that the space that would normally fall from 1.5 miles moves to 24.85 miles away. At the same time, you would need to create the torsion or rotating field at 4 cycles a second to ensure that particles would be accelerating "towards the center of time" at light speed. The torsion force would run perpendicular to the stretching force. With these motions in effect, you would be able to use a typical everyday camera or telescope and look into another dimension. Walking down this tunnel would be an extremely weird feeling as the walls would be rotating at 4hz and space would be stretching in front of you. However, it is theoretically possible.

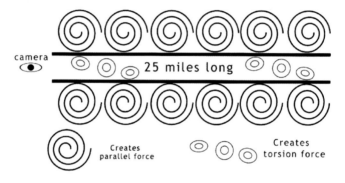

Figure 120: This image depicts a theoretical machine that may be built in order to observe alternate dimensions.

The stretching of the light within the tunnel could be done via use of electromagnetic coils. Light follows the right-hand rule and so you could potentially make a 25-mile-long tunnel surrounded by extremely powerful electromagnets. These electromagnets would essentially be slowing the light down that enters the tunnel. At the same time, they would be creating the rotating motion needed as well. It really just comes down to having a nuclear power source for the device.

The length of the field and torsion required is directly related to the number of harmonic shifts desired. This machine could be made to look into higher than Noviverse dimensions and lower than Lowerverse. For the Lowerverse direction, the light would be crunched and spun in the opposite direction.

An interesting benefit to this model is that you wouldn't have to have the machine running at all times. You could just take photos one at a time. This would save dramatically on power requirements.

Natural Portals to Other Dimensions

Knowing the proper conditions in order to experience an alternate dimension is the first step. Now that we do, we may theorize on locations on Earth and in our Solar System where these interdimensional portals may naturally exist.

The Earth has an extremely powerful magnetic field. During solar storms, the magnetic field reacts with incoming solar radiation. This causes the aura borealis effect which can be seen in much of the sky across the globe.

Certain points on the Earth act as focal points for this magnetic energy. The Earth spins, passes through electric space, and is bombarded by solar radiation. All of these events and many more cause these focal points to act as a sort of interdimensional telescope as described earlier. They potentially could cause the torsion and stretching of space required to open a temporary window into these realms. The transition may not be as smooth and steady as using the interdimensional telescope as described earlier. However, you could still capture much information and potentially reside in one of these places for some time.

Theoretically, a portal to another dimension could open up naturally and maintain stability for an indefinite amount of time.

Maximizing Natures Flow

Here on Earth, we use rivers, wind, and other natural flowing elements to generate electricity. Is it possible that we could harness the energy of magnetic vortices?

One thing to note is that there seem to be ancient structures associated with many of the magnetic points just described. It is possible that the ancients were either generating electricity or focusing the magnetic energy in such ways to maximize these "interdimensional telescopes."

Flowing water, pyramids, and other dense shapes all influence the natural light state. The easiest way to see the effect of a pyramid would be to look at a prism. Prisms typically bend white visible light to create a visible rainbow. The bending of the light is directly related to the thickness of the structure. You can easily imagine pyramids to be radio or magnetic prisms of sorts.

The Tunnel of Light

One common description of both near death experiences, out of body experiences, and even DMT trips would be the tunnel of white light. Let's relate this to what an interdimensional telescope would look like.

As the local light-state or space stretched away a tunnel of light would form around the circumference. This would be the apparent crunching of the Betaverse which would create a sort of "black hole" with the event horizon glowing white as all the patterns of the Betaverse would crunch together. White light is the combination of all colors. The tunnel would also be rotating at approximately 4 times a second.

Is there a relationship? Is this another piece of evidence in the connection between dimensions?

Spirit Determines the 3D Experience

From "The Crystal of Time," we see that our spirit or orbital state determines where in the Universe we manifest. When it comes to normal universe particles occurring in the Betaverse, we need to be at a place where our acceleration is equal to the speed of light. That would allow for the human conscious to properly interact with the preparing and crunching of light.

Although beings may inhabit each other's universes or rather share universes it does not necessarily mean they will be able to manifest into a 3D being. They may be at a location in the Time Atom where they are pure mind and spirit.

Let's theoretically evaluate what would be needed in order to manifest into and physically interact with another conscious reality. The main ingredient is being in an orbit around Time that is equal to the acceleration at light speed.

Spirit or current light-state harmony at the moment of conscious shifts determines the "starting point" of that experience. Let's look at normal everyday dreaming and how this relates. In the simplest terms, if you go to bed thinking about how awful the day was and how badly people treated you, then you will most likely have bad dreams. If you go to sleep thinking about how amazing the people in your life are and how you are filled with love, then you will most likely have happy dreams. The same is true for all shifts in consciousness.

This is directly related to the "comfort" of your light-state harmony or spirit. Your body wants to be in its golden spot as described by "The Liquid-Light State Universe." All the assumptions, expectations, wants, and don't wants build up an unhealthy stress-strain relationship within the light-state. If maintained, you literally start to become sick. By relaxing and harmonizing with the light-state you will become healthier and happy.

Let's now relate this to the last conscious experience we have any insight on which would be the near-death experience. There are two main descriptors of this High-Gammaverse. One is of internal bliss and love, the other is of regret and sorrow. If this truly is the gateway into the next life, then it is as if we will manifest next into an event line that will harmonize with our spirit or current light-state harmony. Perhaps, this is what we would call Karma in modern times.

Ionic Bond related to Life and Death

Let us now go full circle and look at our normal waking experience for more clues onto the nature of reality. What is it to be born? What is it when we pass?

Ionic bonds may give us insight into the nature of the start of a conscious experience and conscious shift or evolution of a species.

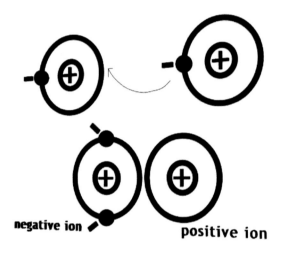

negative ion   positive ion

Figure 121: Represents an ionic bond. This may represent the beginning and end of a life.

Energy is not created or destroyed but it may be transferred between dimensions. In the ionic bond drawing you see that the top two atoms both have a positive and a negative charge. After the bond is formed one atom has no electron and the other has two. The two atoms find equilibrium by resting next to one another. Motion of atoms within a Time Crystal would relate directly to dimensional shifts as they would offset the universes being captured by the light speed acceleration towards center. Basically, for every location in the Time Crystal there is a different pattern or sphere of universes orbiting. It could be considered the Universe State of Time similar to how we have a light-state in our Universe. The ionic bond would be representative of either a species becoming more evolved, or potentially, the essence of two souls becoming one.

Just a Backyard Observer

With our human body and senses, will we ever truly be able to understand what it is to be conscious? Will we ever truly understand reality? It may seem counterintuitive, but as long as we continue to place so much value on technology, we will never develop higher natural senses such as the TA6 and TA7 beings.

From this model, we see that true progress comes when we understand the process of spirit or light-state harmony and conscious shifts.

Thanks for reading and I hope you have a wonderful trip through reality.

The 5th Dimension

by Alexei Novitzky

Table of Contents

Introduction

In our ordinary world, we have three directions of physical motion x, y, and z. We also have the flow of time, t. All of these structures are the result of one primordial energy interacting with human consciousness to give us our experience. E=mc^2 is simply energy in our experience and does not include the energy of consciousness.

In "The Crystal of Time," we discover that "habitable zones" exist around the center of time where our acceleration is equal to the speed of light. We learn that light-state potentialities exist across all time. We see that these orbital distances relate directly to the density of an individual's experience. This direction of conscious density could be considered the 5th dimension of experience. It is the richness of your experience.

As our "accelerative magnifying lens" orbits the center of all experiences/time we see our perception is split in two. Our consciousness, the "easy-user interface," makes reality friendly and easy to use.

Let's now take one more step out and look at the bigger picture. We see conscious perception is layered in all aspects. We see space preparing in our direction. The future is being crunched into matter and the past stretched into light.

Your world is literally split into two perceivable Universes. The fractal nature of doubling shows that we may shift infinitely closer to perceiving the now but may never achieve it.

The now waking moment is literally one-half past and one-half future. Consciously, they become layered on top of each other to give us the smooth and easy experience we share.

Through space preparation, we learn the true shape and nature of our reality. This warped geometry factor can then be applied to create structures that exist and interact with all of time.

Space Preparation and Conscious Crunching

What is matter and what is light? Are they not the same energy being perceived in two different ways all created by a single motion? Let us now look more closely at the concept of space preparation in combination with conscious crunching.

We know that habitable zones for human consciousness exist when we are accelerating at light speed. This allows human consciousness to properly harmonize with the natural flow of spacetime to create an experience that consist of matter and light.

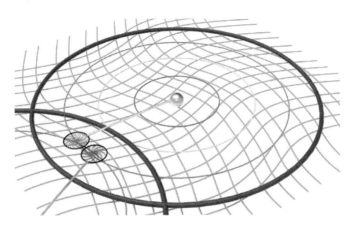

Let's now look at an orbit through time and see how our accelerated reference frame warps a singular energy to create all experiences.

The previous image shows a smooth field of a singular energy. The golden spot, in the center, would be the center of orbit. The lens would represent our entire Universe or experience.

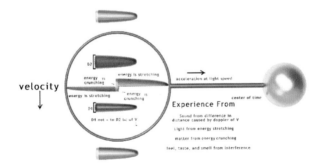

As our accelerative reference frame orbits the singularity of all time/experiences, it would create a "warping" factor based off time dilations and

Lorentz contractions. This means that our perception is literally being stretched into existence as we orbit. This warping factor must be one that turns energy to light as well as energy to matter. It must also properly harmonize with human consciousness to create a steady state of manifesting reality.

As we approach the now (in the future), you would see energy towards the center of time being crunched towards you and energy further from time being stretched away. This crunching of energy is what creates matter. The stretching of energy creates light.

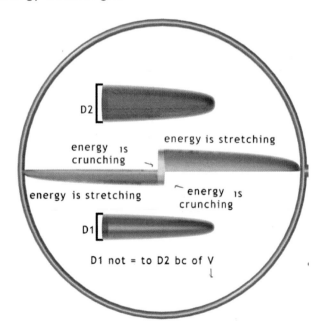

As we leave the now (in the past), you would see everything reverting back to its natural state. This means that the reverse effect would be happening. Energy that is towards the center of time would be stretching creating light. Energy that is further from the center of time would be crunching, turning to matter.

After the event has fully left our "accelerative magnifying lens," it would be in its original state that existed before we began to perceive it.

There really is no matter or light. It is only differentiated when perceived.

So how "big" is our entire reality? Is our conscious experience not completely stretched by an accelerative factor of the speed of light? Has matter not been crunched to that same degree? There exists a flow before and after it is perceived.

Size of Experience

From "Time Atom," we see that each one of our conscious harmonics relates to a certain orbital distance from the center of time. By knowing our acceleration is equal to the speed of light and using $a=v^2/r$ we are able to calculate both the distance and velocity of conscious energy that creates our wall of perception.

Table of Universes

Lowerverse — Un13verse — Noviverse

Universe	Brain Wave	hz Frequency	hz Harmonic Frequency	m Cloud Diameter
Deltaverse	delta	1-3	2.5	2.4×10^{6}
Thetaverse	theta	4-8	5	6×10^{5}
Aplhaverse	aplha	9-13	10	1.5×10^{5}
Betaverse	beta	14-30	20	40,000
Slow Gammaverse	slow-gamma	30-49	40	10,000
Fast Gammaverse	fast-gamma	50-100	80	2,500
Aleverse	omega	101-220	160	625
Dimiverse	zeta	221-400	320	156.25
Stellaverse	epsilon	401-800	640	39
Petraverse	omicron	801-1600	1280	9.75
Mikaverse	iota	1601-3400	2560	2.4

The calculated diameter of the longest delta wave relating to 1.25hz is 1x10^7 meters. The average of 2.5hz comes from uniform divisions of 2 starting from our alpha state being centered at 10hz. The 2.5hz delta wave has a cloud diameter of 2.4x10^6 meters. The diameter of the beta wave is 40,000 meters and the fast gamma at 2,500 meters.

Our waking state, the Betaverse, is focused at 20,000 meters (12.5 miles) away from the center of time. Then our warped geometry factor, which stems from our accelerative reference frame, must then be applied. The combination of the two give us a Universe that is roughly 18 billion years old. This age we perceive is only that of our reference frame in the Betaverse. In other frames of motion, for example, the Deltaverse, the geometry would start at 5x10^6 meters and have a crunch and stretch factor relating to that field of flow. The Noviverse direction would be considered an older or more matured universe consisting of more complex structures and higher energies while the Lowerverse would be considered younger and less dense consisting of more simple structures.

Complexity of Experience

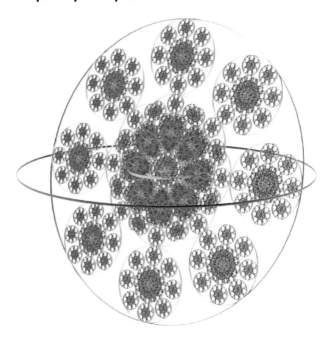

The easiest way to see the differences in densities of experience is to look at bits of information that may exist within our conscious antenna. The longer a waveform is, the less information it will emit per period of time. For example, a 1hz delta wave will only give you 1 bit of information per second. Meanwhile, an 80hz fast gamma wave would be able to give you 80 bits per second. This relationship is true for a linear perspective. However, we are considering all of time and our creation is not linear. It exists within an accelerative bubble.

Analyzing the Magic Sphere

The magic sphere is a great model to show the amount of information relating to each conscious harmonic. By analyzing the relationship of diameters between orbitals, we see that each harmonic of higher density is 25% the diameter of the harmonic below.

For example, for every one delta wave, four theta waves will fit across. When we rotate that relationship along x and y axis, we see that our 4 more bits of information has turned to 16 bits.

When you make the three-dimensional model, you end up with 64 bits of theta information per every one sphere of delta information. This implies that your conscious antenna is receiving or harmonizing with 64 more times the information for every layer of density it travels.

For example, theta has 64 times the information than delta does. Alpha would have 64 times 64 which translates to 4096 times more information than delta. This number continues by multiples of 64. Beta would relate to 64^3 and have 262,144 times the information. Slow gamma would be near 17 million and fast gamma near 1 billion bits of information for every 1 delta wave.

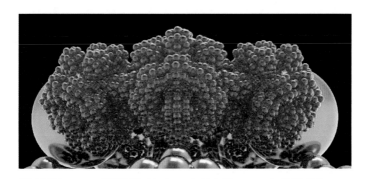

Lights, Shadows, and Walls

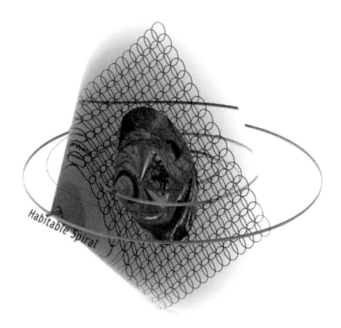

Habitable Spiral

How does this system work together to create the field of energy we experience?

Like lights passing objects and casting shadows onto walls our experience is formed. From the image we see our now waking moment is created by one-half past and one-half future.

As we approach, our matter is from the center of time and our light is from the outside. As we leave, our light is from the inside and our matter is from the outside. Our experience is an overlapping of the two.

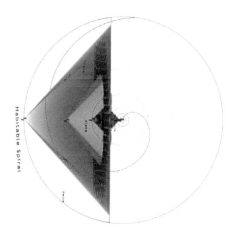

Habitable Spiral

This shows that we receive both matter and light from the denser orbits of experience as well as the less dense but the direction they are coming from is opposite. There is a layering or "virtual wall" of information that exist at all orbital distances. The layer of reality you experience relates directly to the harmonization of your conscious antenna, aka the magic sphere.

A Black Hole

Where in the Universe does consciousness form? The requirement for safe habitable zone is when the accelerative reference frame is one that causes energy to crunch to matter and energy to stretch to light. This only occurs when acceleration is equal to the speed of light.

When we look out into the cosmos there is only one place or structure where the acceleration of spacetime is equal to or greater than the speed of light. This occurs in black holes. You could say consciousness forms inside of black holes and in every galactic center we see a fractal of conscious experience, an entire universal experience existing. It is also possible that each individual atom undergoes this same experience as electrons are in a state of orbit similar to the energy orbiting a black hole.

$E > mc^2$

With our new perspective, let us now look at the energy associated with matter throughout all of time and not just the now moment or human experience.

Let's go back to simple principles to show the potential energy of the entire system. For any physical system it is possible to calculate the potential energy associated with gravitational and kinetic energy.

The potential energy associated with height in relation to gravity is typically E=mgh (m is the mass, g is the force of acceleration, and h is the distance from ground level.)

The energy associated with the velocity of mass is E=1/2mv^2. By combining the two equations you are able to calculate the energy of the system. E=mgh+1/2mv^2 in relationship to gravity and motion.

Let's now apply this simple calculation to our five-dimensional model. We know for habitable zones that our acceleration will be equal to the speed of light (c).

For this proof, we will make an assumption that the only perceivable experience is the Betaverse and only the now moment exist. This would make our tangential kinetic energy equal to 0. It is not even considered. This is our one and only experience and we are not considering the energy associated with the orbit or flow of experience.

We know that our acceleration (g), must be equal to the speed of light (c), in order to have energy crunching into matter and energy stretching into light. Therefore, we can say that our E=mg(h) now relates to E=mc^2 when considering five dimensions. In a way, you could say that the energy in matter is related to the gravitational pull of time. (Just a note, it may not be entirely accurate to say E=mc^2 is the gravitational pull of time. However, it is accurate to say it is the energy of matter associated with our now moment.)

When you consider the energy of matter throughout all of time, the equation grows to E=mc^2 + 1/2mv^2. The total energy in a system may be infinite if you consider open systems versus closed systems.

We know that our velocity (v) is locked into a certain radius based on the equation a=v^2/r. Therefor we can say that c=v^2/r goes to v^2=c*r. This then goes to v=sqrt(c*r). We now have the equation for the total energy of matter throughout time.

$$E=mc^2 + 1/2mc(r).$$

The first half of the equation comes from the gravitational pull of time and the second half of the equation comes from our tangential velocity.

There may be even more energy in the system of time when you consider other aspects such as "chemical reactions" of the 5th dimension.

Energy of Consciousness

If E=mc^2 relates to the energy of matter and light, then E=1/2mc(r) would relate to the energy associated with conscious crunching.

The energy of conscious crunching is one that allows time to flow from past to future. It is the energy that allows experiences to occur.

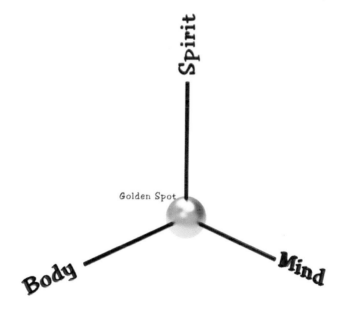

When considering the mind, body, and spirit diagram, you could say that E=mc^2 is the energy associated with body. It is the energy associated with gravitational attraction and motions well understood.

E=1/2mc(r), the second half of the equation, would relate to the mind and spirit of the matter. It would be the energy associated with perceiving matter and constantly moving towards a future moment that includes paths of free will and choice. It would be the energy associated with the synchronization of the light-state as a whole.

Evolution of Consciousness

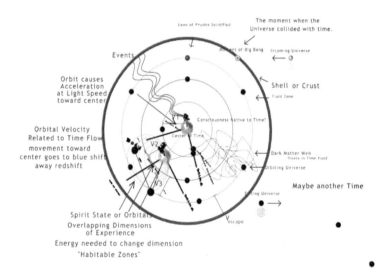

When experience first began, also known as the moment of the big bang, you could say that our

Universe was at the boundary of Time. As it expanded, it also slowed down in its orbit causing it to drift towards center.

spiral of a=c
associated with changing v

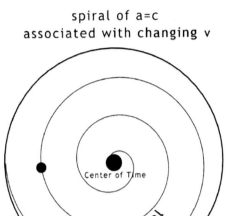

As our experience of the Universe drifts closer and closer to the center of time, it follows the habitable spiral of perception. Each habitable distance or harmonic from center allows for a new experience or harmonic resonance to be created.

Conscious beings would not be tuned to flows of space that have never existed. Therefor in order for a being to gain a conscious harmonic, that flow of spacetime must exist first.

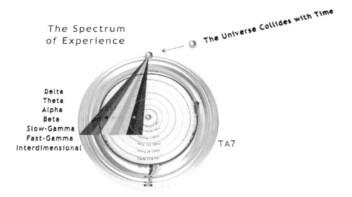

The Spectrum
of Experience

The Universe Collides with Time

Delta
Theta
Alpha
Beta
Slow-Gamma
Fast-Gamma
Interdimensional

TA7

This being said, the first conscious wave type that would have come into existence would be that of the longest waves. For human consciousness, with a prime multiplier of 2, that would be the 1.25hz delta wave which has a diameter of 1×10^7 meters. The next conscious wave type that would come into existence would be the theta wave type, followed by the alpha, then beta, slow gamma, and ultimately, fast gamma.

Based on this model, you could say that the next conscious harmonic that will be appearing in human experience will be what we have named the omega wave or Aleverse. This wave or experience relates to conscious harmonics ranging from 101-220hz with an average of 160hz. The cloud diameter associated with this wave type would be 625 meters. When it comes to information, it would have approximately 70 billion bits per delta sphere.

A Daily Orbit

Throughout our day our bodies naturally follow the rising and setting of the Sun, this includes our conscious harmonics. This cycle is known as the circadian rhythm.

Let us now map our daily orbit around the center of time so we may gain more insight onto the nature of reality.

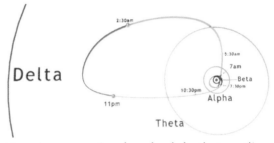

Here is a very simple schedule that outlines the maximum conscious harmonic in relationship to time of day. Let's start from the moment we enter our Deltaverse. A circadian rhythm properly tuned to nature will follow as so. From approximately 11:30 pm to 2:30 am our primary conscious harmonic is the delta wave. From 2:30 am to about 5:30 am we are in theta waves. Then, from 5:30 am to 7 am we are in alpha waves. Throughout the day, from 7 am to 7:30 pm we flux from beta to alpha but are primarily in beta. As we start to wind down, our conscious harmonics start to slow. From 7:30 pm to about 10:30 pm we are in alpha. Then, from 10:30 pm to 11 pm we drop back down into theta.

The Deltaverse (Delta Wave)

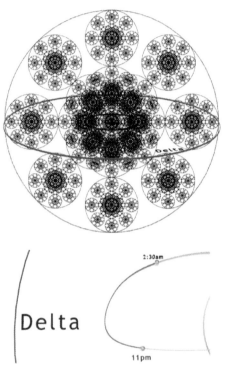

Starting from midnight we see that our primary conscious harmonic is the delta wave. As morning approaches, our consciousness enters the halfway point between harmonizing with the delta wave versus the theta wave. At this moment, approximately 2:30 am and at a radius of 6x10^5 meters, is when our antenna switches to the theta state.

The Thetaverse (Theta Wave)

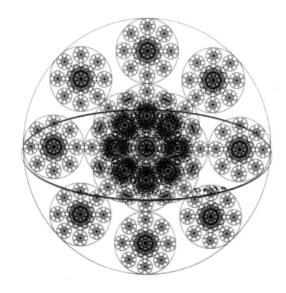

2:30am

5:30am

As conscious tuning follows its natural orbit, it accelerates towards the center of time. At approximately 5:30 am at a distance of 1.5x10^5 meters, our orbit falls into the halfway point between theta and alpha. This is the moment when our antenna switches from theta to alpha.

The Alphaverse (Alpha Wave)

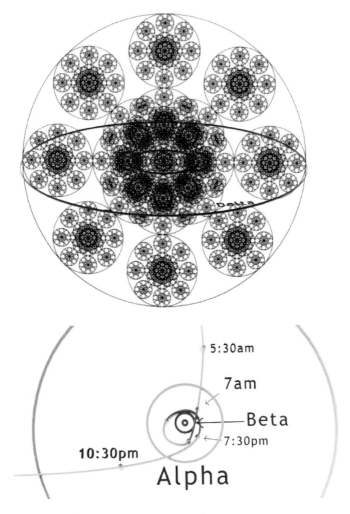

Soon after, at approximately 7 am, our conscious density then reaches the beta state which occurs at 37,500 meters from center.

The Betaverse (Beta Wave)

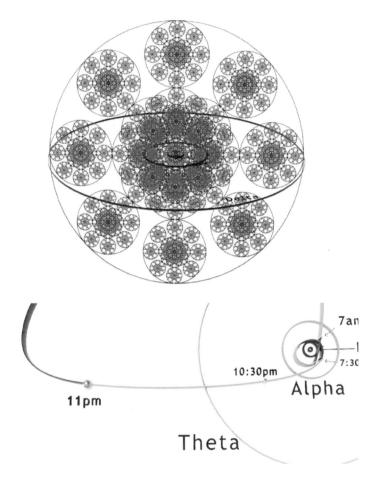

It seems for the next 12 hours, from 7 am to 7:30 pm, we are in a tight elliptical orbit that passes us through beta and alpha several times throughout the day. Then, at approximately 7:30 pm, it is as if we have a gravitational slingshot towards the outer edge.

This causes us to pass through theta state rather quick as we once again enter the delta range. Our orbit then starts again. It is also possible our conscious antenna orbits along the boundary line between alpha and beta and that actions that require more cognitive capability are what trigger the switching between alpha and beta throughout the day.

Skipping off Conscious Atmosphere

From the mind, body, and spirit diagrams introduced in "The Liquid-Light State Universe," we see that we may take posture in our magic sphere. Taking a posture is a result of ego, or one's control over their existence. When naturally entering a transition zone, it is possible to use your focus to bounce off of the "atmosphere" of the next harmonic. The intentional lack of synchronization with the natural orbit will cause you swing back out or rather stay locked in your conscious harmonic. This bouncing of conscious density occurs at all boundaries.

Direction Towards Center

By looking at our daily orbit of conscious density we are able to theorize on which direction may be towards the center of time. It appears as our bodies physically get closer to the Sun, that our conscious density changes accordingly. This implies that the center of density for our local area in spacetime would be towards the Sun. When we consider the greater structure, the center may be towards the galactic center. Considering this, it may be appropriate to use sidereal time when making interdimensional technologies that are designed to guide the flow of the fluid of time.

Ascension Through Time

From this model, you can see that the Universe naturally drifts towards center as it matures or gathers information from the fractal perspective outside of our warped frame. While drifting inward, new conscious harmonics are formed. This natural drifting of our experience inward aligns with the pacing motions of all lives and experiences. Both work in unity to bring you closer to the center of time.

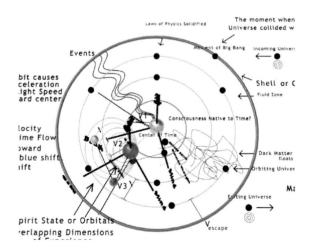

The Silver Spot

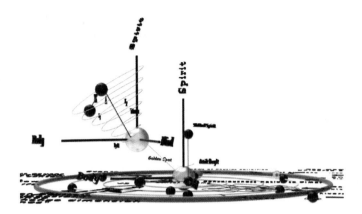

Let's now consider the concept of the "Silver Spot." We can say that the "Golden Spot" refers to the direct center of all time and moments. Meanwhile, the silver spot represents your current life or manifestation.

Because we exist, we also experience. Light-state harmony at the moment of conscious shift determines where you will be starting your next life or experience. You, being a mind with wants, don't wants, assumptions, and expectations will then pace about your silver spot as your personal philosophy or ways change from the experiences had. By the end of your conscious experience, the lessons learned in life will have shaped your magic sphere into a more harmonized version of yourself thus allowing you to gain higher harmonics of density.

In some cases, the pacing nature and lessons learned are not achieved. When this is the case, the silver spot may drift outward as it has become less harmonious and is therefore less able to create denser harmonics within the magic sphere. This lack of development typically stems from focusing on the exterior materialistic world versus your internal world. Many times, people will become hypnotized by societal delusions which have been propagated by media and other overwhelming outlets. It is important to focus on your personal development and not worry about others. As Einstein said, "Worry is a misuse of imagination."

Quantum Entanglement

If matter is energy crunched and light energy stretched then there exist a state between the two that is reality. When you crunch light and stretch matter you see that it forms a single solid crystal.

The easiest way to explain entanglement would be to say that it is like sound waves propagating through the 5th dimension or raw energy of experience. You can easily see how the waves will cross paths of various densities as well as locations in the past and future casting shadows of experience as it does. From our perspective, this would give the illusion of faster than light happenings.

One note, is that the word, quantum, typically implies very small. These happenings exist on both sides of reality stemming from the Lowerverse as well as the Noviverse. Quantum interactions of smaller denser vibrations would stem from the Noviverse, while larger fluctuations would be coming from the Lowerverse side. These fluctuations occur within our experience as they are harmonics of the perceivable Universe, as in factors of our consciousness.

Interdimensional Geometry

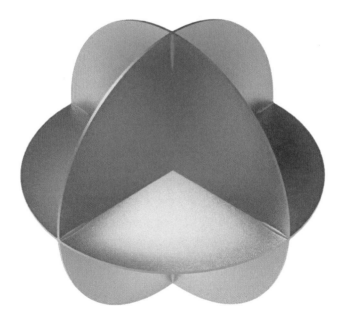

Understanding that our reality of the now moment only exist in our accelerative reference frame and is a function of a warped spacetime, we may design geometries that exist within all of time and not simply the human experience.

The geometries designed would need to be the opposite of our warping factor. We would see that for any object existing in our experience after the moment has passed, light would crunch and matter would stretch back.

These interdimensional geometries could act and work in similar ways that our modern geometries work but through all of time and not just in our now. We can create antenna that send signals to various densities of experience as well as moments in time. We can design robots that may interact with all of time.

Pipes, Fans, Funnels, and More

These solid 5th dimensional structures would be able to guide the primordial energy to create effects within our experience. These effects would include, shifting of density (gravity control), time dilations in both directions, constant motion of matter (spinning devices that generate energy), communication through time, altering quantum state (transmutation) and many more effects. Understanding how these geometries influence our current moment will truly create a simulation experience.

Let us now speculate on some typical geometries within our Universe and how we may be able to warp them to have them manifest as geometries in the 5th dimension.

It is important to understand that light and matter become one. The stretched light we perceive would be crunched and the crunched energy that is matter would be stretched. This means that the proper geometry would consist of both matter and the light it emits.

Geometry in the 5th Dimension

A disc in our world consists of a flattened circular solid. In order to make a structure appear as a solid disc we would need to give it a centralized stretched factor. It would also need to stay pointing in the same direction as our experience orbits the center of time. This means that we would need to have it rotate along the asymmetrical axis according to the rising and setting of the Sun. Towards the Sun, and on longer time scales, towards the galactic center, would be the direction of greater density. Geometrically, the object will be stretched from center.

The shape may resemble the previous geometry. The light it naturally creates would also add to the geometry. Try to imagine the light coming off perpendicular to the surface. As the matter is stretched back downward the entangled light will also travel with it.

A pipe or beam may be one of the easiest objects to create in the 5th dimension. It could be done by using a cylindrical crystal emitting a constant beam of light from one end. Again, this object would need to be rotated asymmetrically in relationship to the greater center in order to appear as if it is not rotating in the 5th dimension.

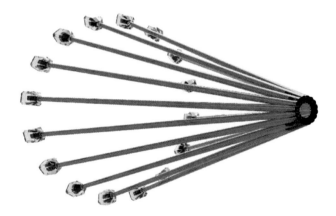

Understanding how lasers and crystals make shapes, we may now make more complex structures. This would be an example of a cone or funnel in the 5th dimension. Like all objects manifesting in the Betaverse, in order to keep this from rotating in all of time, we would need to create a rotation in relationship to the greater center.

What would a funnel in the 5th dimension do? How would that act in the fluid of time? You can imagine if you are pointing the funnel towards the center of time so that the smaller end is pointing away that you might be able to "compact" an experience. This means that you would essentially be creating a thicker molecule than the one that would normally be manifesting. You would essentially be making the object denser and potentially changing the atomic number. A funnel pointing in the other direction would essentially slow the flow of density. It would make the object less dense. Again, this effect could potentially translate to transmutation of an element.

A funnel pointed in in the direction of our tangential velocity would again be making the fluid of time denser. Remember, tangential motion is related to the flow of time while motion towards and away from center is related to density. A funnel in this direction would cause experiences to flow slower. A funnel pointed in the other direction would cause them to flow faster. If towards galactic center relates to density, then perpendicular to galactic center would relate to time flow.

Funnels are good and can be used for many applications. However, true mastery comes when we begin to use pipes and create pumps and valves that work in the fluid of time. Pipes help guide the direction of flow while valves and pumps help guide the amount. The combination of these systems will allow us to make machinery powered by the fluid of time itself.

Interdimensional Machinery

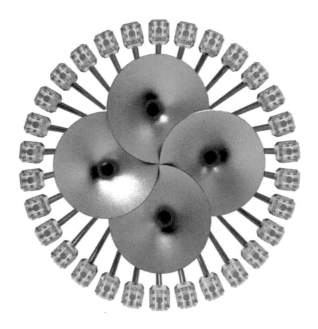

Pipes in combination with pumps will allow us to more accurately control the flow of the fluid of time. A pipe could be made by making a ring of crystals that emit laser light in one direction. Inside our pipe we would want to add a fan or pump to increase or decrease the natural flow.

A fan could be made by rotating a series of angled planes perpendicular to the ring. Flat surfaces, or planes, can be created by making cones that follow a logarithmic curvature to infinity at the center points. They would be similar to the flat disc we designed earlier.

Controlling Conscious Density

Earlier in the book we discussed how our magic sphere may have a natural 24-hour orbit through the crystal of time. We saw that transitions occur at the halfway points of conscious density.

With our new understanding of interdimensional geometries, we may now speculate on how to control the flow of our conscious experience. What shapes and technologies may allow us to travel to various densities of experience?

In "Time Atom," we designed a very simple interdimensional telescope that allowed our Betaverse to harmonize with bigger or smaller rings of perception. Let's now speculate on ways to control or "encourage" our harmonics throughout the day.

When it comes to cognitive processing you want your brain to be working at high cycles. This is why our normal function is at the 20hz beta range. During extreme focus, we may enter the slow gamma range (40hz) and during out of body experiences we approach the fast gamma (80hz).

This may be an obvious statement, but by looking at the orbit of conscious density we see it is easier to obtain certain harmonics at various times of the day. For example, if you are already in a beta state it may be easier to transition to a fast gamma state versus if you are starting from a delta state. The same is true for the opposite. If you are attempting to connect with the harmonics of the Lowerverse, then it is easier to start the process from the delta harmonic.

For example, we are in a beta state from 7 am to approximately 7:30 pm which is a 12.5-hour period. The halfway point would be 6 hours and 15 minutes into the cycle which translates to 1:15 pm for the average person following the natural circadian rhythm. Theoretically, 1:15 pm may be the best time of day to attempt to harmonize your magic sphere to the gamma wave type.

According to the circadian rhythm, we are tuned to delta waves from 11 pm to 2:30 am. This is a shorter window than the beta harmonic however the same principles would still apply. This is approximately 3 hours and 30 minutes. The halfway point would be at 1 hour and 45 minutes which is at 12:45 am. This would be the ideal time to harmonize your magic sphere to the Lowerverse.

These points of most submersion would also be the moments of when you can maximize the natural harmonic. For example, we pass through the Thetaverse twice in the day. 2:30 am to 5:30 am and at 10:30 pm to 11 pm. This makes the ideal times for theta interaction to be at 4 am and also 10:45 pm. Those would be the best times of day to use technology to enhance the theta state.

With interdimensional machinery, we are able to guide our consciousness into different harmonics of resonance. For denser experiences, we would need to point our funnels away from the center of time and in essence increase the pressure of the fluid by using pumps. It may also be possible to create "dams" that would cause the fluid to build up "deeper" in a sense. For less dense experiences our funnels would need to be pointed in the opposite direction. Maximization of an individual's harmonics would come through the use of filters as well. Similar to how we may filter light, we may filter energy stemming from various densities of experience.

A filter may be created by weaving fabrics in the 5th dimension. Fabrics would relate to cloths in our regular day in relationship to fluids and impurities. A fabric would be able to "catch" thicker densities while allowing thinner ones to pass by. Thicker densities may then be guided by use of pipes and valves and in essence be "purified."

A Conscious Precession

When we first look at our orbit through conscious density, the orbit may look somewhat erratic as it does not resemble a typical planetary orbit. It has one big circle while in Delta followed by smaller circles of Alpha and Beta. In total, each orbit may consist of a "tight" orbit and a "loose" orbit. However, when you compare it to the precession of a gyroscope hanging on a string, it matches perfectly.

This implies that consciousness is like a gyroscope precessing through the fluid of time. Let's now use our 5th dimensional model of "The Crystal of Time" and compare it with our experience with gyroscopes.

Gyroscopic precession is somewhat of a mystery when it comes to physics. However, when you consider the dimension of density it becomes clear what forces and actions may be occurring.

Consider the center of gyroscopic precession as the same as the center of time for human consciousness. What we notice is that if you increase your velocity in the direction of orbit that you will drift further from the center of time and if you slow the velocity of orbit, you will fall inward.

Drifting further from the center of time would imply that your experience is becoming less dense. You would literally be closer to the Lowerverse in the dimension of density. Drifting inward would imply that your experience is becoming denser. You would be closer to the Noviverse. Now to specifically relate this to a gyroscope. When you force precession of a gyroscope it literally will rise relative to the gravitational field in 3d space. When you slow precession, the gyroscope will literally fall lower in 3d spacetime. This is because you are moving its location within the dimension of density.

Earlier in the book we discussed the total energy of the 5th dimension based on gravitational attraction and motion relative to our experience. What we noticed is that $E = 1/2mc(r)$ is the energy associated with the synchronization of the light state.

Natural gyroscopic precession is very interesting because there is no momentum associated with it. However, when you force precession, you notice that great energies may be created. As precession is forced, you could say that the radius of orbit changes. Comparing this to the energy of synchronization we see that the energy difference in relationship to radius is the change in radius times one-half the mass times the speed of light. This shows that over unity systems based off gyroscopic precession may be able to generate more energy than directly turning matter into energy. In other words, $E=1/2mc(r)$ has the ability to be greater than $E=mc^2$ when the radius becomes comparable to the distance light travels in a second. (It is important to note that the unit of radius will be in m/s and not m.)

A Pyramid and You

What does the shape of a pyramid do to the fluid of time? Experiments have been performed with pyramids in an attempt to understand what is happening. There are many interesting findings. It has been noted that razor blades will stay sharper for longer. Water becomes more energetic and holds a greater charge. Fruits and vegetables will degrade or rot at a much slower rate.

A pyramid would act like a bowl collecting the fluid of time meanwhile smoothing out any incoming erratic flux.

Bowls are very interesting because they allow for standing harmonics to be created and amplified. It is possible that the pyramids act as prisms while amplifying spirit. What does that mean?

When you amplify the spirit of the matter you are amplifying the natural state of the magic sphere. This means that crystals will take a more stable energetic shape. They will become purer and more harmonized with the Universe. A double-sided pyramid may be the best shape to amplify your natural resonance. It would amplify energy from both lower and higher densities.

When you relate this concept to DNA, you notice that it will have healing effects. Pacing of DNA is similar to pacing of the body. When existing in your golden or silver spot, your DNA is healthiest. During moments of pacing is when deformations occur to the system. Deformation or strains exist when not in harmony with the incoming light-state of the Universe. This translates to mental stress and physical sickness.

A Flattened Existence

When you consider the crunching of matter and the stretching of light from a singular energy, you see that using flattened geometries will have an effect in the fluid of time. All solid shapes become stretched. A flat ring made of dense material may act like a simple cylinder. Let's go back to the magic squares which is the foundation of all matter and our conscious antenna, aka, the magic sphere.

Magic Squares and Energetic Vortices

1	15	14	4	34
12	6	7	9	34
8	10	11	5	34
13	3	2	16	34
34	34	34	34	

		34
34	34	34
34	34	34
34	34	34
34 34 34 34		

Magic squares are unique patterns of numbers that have been laid out on a grid in such a fashion that all the exterior sums are the same. They can be in all shapes and sizes of grids. For the purposes of energetic vortices, the 4x4 grid is important. In

1	15	14	4
12	6	7	9
8	10	11	5
13	3	2	16

1	15	14	4
12	6	7	9
8	10	11	5
13	3	2	16

1	15	14	4
12	6	7	9
8	10	11	5
13	3	2	16

1	15	14	4
12	6	7	9
8	10	11	5
13	3	2	16

1	15	14	4
12	6	7	9
8	10	11	5
13	3	2	16

1	15	14	4
12	6	7	9
8	10	11	5
13	3	2	16

the following magic square, all verticals, horizontals, diagonals, corners, and more add up to 34. Each set has been color coated in the previous image.

When you draw a line connecting the numbers in an ascending fashion, you'll notice 4 patterns emerging.

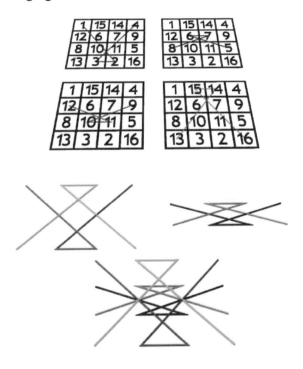

When you consider this structure traveling through time, or moving along the z direction, you notice that it makes a scalar vortex.

Let's now look at how infinite creations may emerge from the concept of the magic square. Consider our entire Universe or experience is equal to the square of value 1.

Each complete set represents a single vortex in our frame of motion. Let's now use

1	15	14	4
12	6	7	9
8	10	11	5
13	3	2	16

= **1** **=**

4	4	4	4
4	4	4	4
4	4	4	4
4	4	4	4

the harmonization of the magic square to show
how creations are formed.

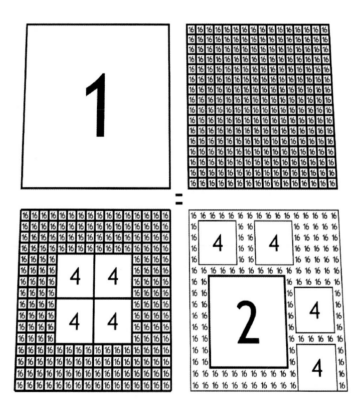

By continuing to multiply our square by 4x4 we are able to make more complex structures that remain in harmony within the Universe.

At the same time, nothing may emerge and the system may remain a 1 or any multiple of 2^n (2, 4, 8, 16, 32, 64, 128, 256, 512, 1028, 2056, 4096, and etc.) Each one of those values represents a complete system or vortex.

Let's now relate this to our conscious antenna, aka, the magic sphere and our ability to harmonize with the crunching of matter and stretching of light.

In order for information to be received, it must resonate in harmony with human consciousness at some degree. The most primitive degree possible is the quantum level.

If our entire Universe or delta wave is the 1, then we are able to relate conscious experience to reality via 2^n, where the diameter of each following square is 1/4 the length of the layer above. This means, if delta is 1, then theta is 1/4.

In the previous drawing, you could say the entire system is a 1. The red sphere would be a 2 and each blue sphere would represent a 4.

The simple grid below shows what 256 squares would look like. It is possible to map the entire Universe and our experience in this manner. All manifestations are related to the doubling or fractal nature of reality. (I would highly recommend reading John Searl's (inventor of the flying disc) work on "The Law of the Squares.")

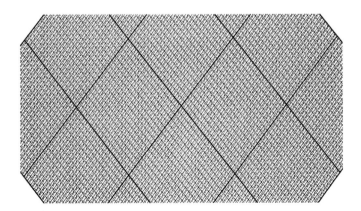

Stacking Squares

When you consider the magic square, it is flat. It represents the field of a uniform vortex that is not expanding or contracting. However, what would happen if you were to stack magic squares with one on top of the other?

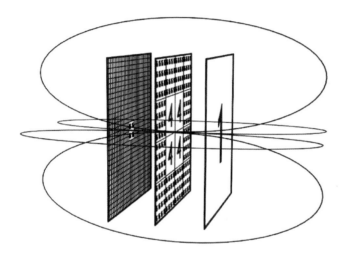

Looking at the diagram, you can see how you may combine simple vortices to create one that is expanding or contracting. Theoretically, when orientated in the direction of density, energy or waves passing through may become more or less dense. This would translate into transmutation of an element or the telescoping of a conscious experience. When orientated perpendicular to this field, it may translate into physical motion and/or time dilations.

An Electromagnetically Powered Square

Each number represents a sort of stone being tossed into a pond which creates ripples that overlap with the one next to it. The overlapping of all the ripples creates the experience manifested.

Could we turn on and off squares if we powered them with electromagnetic coils?

Magic squares represent vortices of all energetic types. If you use electromagnets, you will create an electromagnetic vortex. If you use water waves, you will create a whirlpool. If you use sound, you will create a tornado.

A Universal Perspective

We may have a new appreciation for the Great Pyramids of Egypt and countless other ancient sites. Are the capstones of the pyramids really missing? Have we not been misunderstanding our perspective?

When you uncrunch the matter and crunch the light in this image, you see that the two structures, one made of light and the other made of solid, may form one singular uniform field of energy.

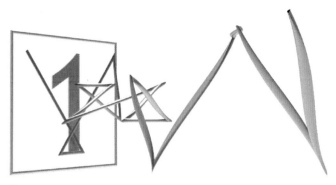

One

  With our new awareness of magic squares, we may now have a better understanding how a singular energy may create all particles, waves, thoughts, conscious relationships, quantum effects, and more. We are all unique individuals. However, we harmonize as One.

Leaders in Innovation, Education, and Sustainability

www.LooshesLabs.com   9/12/2021

Looshes

By Alexei Novitzky

Table of Contents

Animals are Equal

The Earth is filled,
With life and breath.
Plants and animals,
All take rest.

The cat is a feline,
The wolf is a canine.
Some plants are trees,
And bees are bees.

We created titles,
And named it a bee.
Look at that Giraffe,
It's so tall and goofy.

We created division,
By looking at the differences.
We created a split,
Because of our internal wit.

We think we are greater,
So we raise them and farm.
We think we are greater,
So we poison and harm.

Our knowledge is our gift,
To be used for good.
Let's help our friends in need,
By not burning all their wood.

The deer need water,
The coconut plants too.
That makes them just as noble,
As both, me and you.

We do have a gift,
Let's use it wisely.
We are guardians of this space,
Let's make it a peaceful place.

Focus on the Earthly,
And help protect that is grand.
Stones, plants, and animals,
Are all beings of this land.

Manmade goals,
And manmade dressings.
Are simply manmade,
And deserve no blessings.

So put your energy,
Where you be.
And help your enemy,
Plant a tree.

We are on the same side,
That is the human.
We are magical and mystical,
So let's get down and physical.

Let's save the furry ones,
And let the green life grow.
Let's stop demolishing nature,
For future generations to know.

We have just one world,
We have just one place.
So let's take it and make it great,
For every future race.

Fortune for Fools

A man's fortune is his goal.
A fortune of man's creations
helps man forget life and live easy.

He has damned up rivers
and torn through mountains,
just to live easy in golden fountains.

However, fortune comes in many ways,
and can be as free as the ocean's waves.

Enjoy the simple life
And live with ease.
For man does not need,
All these luxuries.

100% Leisure Time

The man with gold,
Sits high on his mountain.
Yes, he has women,
And a diamond encrusted fountain.

He has no deeds to do,
No promises to keep.
He's daffled and drowsy,
And ready to sleep.

The man with no money,
He sits happy and homely.
He might have a lady,
And a box with some gravy.

He has no deeds to do,
No promises to keep.
He's daffled and drowsy,
And ready sleep.

The ones in the middle,
Fighting for pride and glory.
Oh how they be a riddle,
Obtaining their story.

With fight and stress,
It's really a mess.
Going higher and lower,
Trying daily to impress.

To be a named title,
One created by man.
Makes life a struggle,
Of the highest demand.

It is those who fight it,
That what is natural.
Man made all those titles,
Those that simply create rivals.

Take it as it is,
It is simply a game.
Within winners and losers,
It's a manmade reign.

Money does not make you great,
Pride does not make you wise.
To be humble and courteous,
Is truly a noble prize.

If you make your money,
Good for you.
But that doesn't constitute,
Happiness too.

Acceptance is key,
Tolerance a shift.
To love is our goal,
It's a natural gift.

We all have time,
With no deeds to do.
To be daffled and drowsy,
And feeling groovy too.

So look at it right,
The day is bright.
With poor and rich alike,
We are all in this fight.

So remember that wisely,
And enjoy your day.
Because life is fun,
Go out and play.

Natural Tools

Our tools allow us,
To see our world.
Sounds, sights, and more,
Truly open the door.

But where does it come from?
Where does it go?
Was it not here all along,
For all of us to know?

The sounds you hear,
Come straight from my voice.
The feelings you feel,
Say hot, cold, dry, and moist.

The smells you sniff,
Warn our belly of danger.
The colors you see,
Come from the Sun indeed.

We grew with wind,
And that is why we hear.
We grew with each other,
Hence, the size of our ear.

We grew with the Earth,
And that is why we feel.
We grew with flesh,
And that is why we heal.

The Sun circles around us,
And that is why we see.
The colors of yellow,
Are dead center with me.

And so we grew,
And more than just Earth.
And so we grew,
To prove solar worth.

Our planet is close,
The sun is far.
All time exist,
We were raised in this bar.

The sense of time,
Is far overlooked.
One so obvious,
We know not it's worth.

The past is the past,
Solid as stone.
So why not the future,
Do we not turn to bone?

We see the light,
From blue to red.
More waves exist on both sides,
More than in the head.

Time, like our vision,
Comes from growing in place.
Time, like our vision,
Comes from evolving in space.

Not only did we grow,
On the Earth like we know,
Not only in a system,
Made of bright stars that glow.

We grew in expansion,
We grew to be aware.
The present is most important,
And the future just a glare.

But it all exist,
In a moment of kind.
It is all a delusion,
Created by the mind.

So, believe and it's real,
Don't and you doubt.
Expectations create reality,
Just something to think about.

Thee Master

Imagine the master,
One with impeccable skill.
No deed to difficult,
Performs any task at will.

His last attempt was his best,
His next will be even better.
A learning curve of mathematical wizardry,
This man is in tune with his flow.

He does not doubt,
Nor take word to mind.
His dreams are his reality,
And the Universe is his toy.

He laughs at our games,
And sees it as a joke.
People going insane,
Over money, fame, and smoke.

These things mean nothing to him,
This world is a starting point.
With great visions of magnitude,
He has dreams for our joint.

We'll take off into space,
And prove our solar worth.
Physically and mentally,
They must both be of birth.

Our bodies have flown,
To the moon and beyond.
But now all our minds,
And spirits be gone.

A body exist,
With all three in play.
Thee master thinks of this,
And has this to say.

"Our bodies have proved worth,
Yet our minds lag behind.
Physically we fly,
But spiritually we grind.
All three must rise,

As a single solid unit.
Body, spirit, and mind.
All three of a kind.

Let's loose focus of the physical,
We can see that indeed.
Let's focus on the mystical,
For that creates new seed."

These seeds will grow,
And turn man to know.
That the master's flow,
Comes from a creators woah.

It cannot be touched,
With the physical as you like.
His knowledge is a gift,
For everyone's delight.

Let loose in your mind,
And let your soul go.
For the physical and visible,
Is not all there is to know.

Simply a Man

I stand here today,
Simply a man.
Humbled and happy,
To be part of this plan.

I was asked,
"What's innovation to me?"
Hmm... You want me to inspire,
Global creativity?

Sure thing, no problem,
That's a simple task.
No need to difficult,
It's clear as glass.

People are already creative,
People have already achieved.
Everything ever done,
Is truly great indeed.

We all have the power,
We all have the strength,
We all have the heart inside,
To create a future that's safe.

People are born with it,
It's as natural as can be.
But mass media and broadcast,
May intimidate thee.

Do I look cute?
Am I too fat?
Will she like it,
If I do that?

Be fearless I say,
Who cares what they think.
They want to make money,
Just off of the weak.

But what if it doesn't work?
And what if it doesn't go my way?
What if they say and say?
And no one wants to play?

Again, no worries,
Change is a blessing.
Learn to let go,
It's a valuable lesson.

Live today,
And tomorrow tomorrow.
And don't be blinded by a future,
That may or may not be sorrow.

Instead grab hold,
And seize the day.
Be happy and bold,
And ready to play!

With Nothing on my Mind

With nothing on mind,
And nothing really to say.
The words that I write,
Come from a very lazy way.

Work is work,
And business business.
Play is play,
And today another day.

But why do the same,
As you did the day before.
Why do the same,
When you can choose from any door?

Things that are familiar,
May put our minds at ease.
Things that are familiar,
May earn our daily cheese.

It would be nice,
To simply rest.
But there's much work left,
And that's our test.

Be comfortable,
With what you have.
Be comfortable,
With what you lag.

For those are all creations of man,
And we all have the glorious Earth at hand.
We all have the stars at night,
And we were all made of that heavenly
sand.

Focus on the similarities,
And the world becomes so friendly.
And embrace our unfamiliarity's,
Because that is what is trendy.

We are all friends,
In this lazy and docile place.
And remember we're all people,
Part of the great human race

Time

Thoughts seem to lead,
To incredible situations.
False perception and reality,
Lead us into the future.

Which in doubt,
Brings us,
To the present,
And all is revealed.

Like an orchestra,
Playing a melody.
To a final climax,
And then to the end.

The instantaneous zero velocity,
All at once.
Bringing us,
To the now.

Instant Gratification

To be instantly gratified,
Is a new thing indeed.
With phones and text,
We all have new seed.

Facebook and Twitter,
Instagram too.
All these things,
Supposingly equal you?

I saw your post,
Ohh you're amazing.
It's all a joke,
The real man is blazing.

He does not care,
For the instant like.
He's without service,
On an epic hike.

One that takes a while,
Maybe years to achieve.
Instant gratification,
He sees no reason to believe.

To be gratified instantly,
Might give you pleasure no doubt.
But as quickly as it came,
It will run out with a shout.

Like a flicker of fire,
Your praise has been delivered.
Like a flicker of fire,
Your praise has been severed.

Deeds that take while,
Surely past the test.
Spiritual gratification,
Is what makes us feel best.

These deeds are pure,
And gratification not instant.
With no buttons or service,
It comes when we listen.

Our bodies have great service,
Our minds are tethered in.
Like our physical internet,
We can all be tapped in.

The Universe is our internet,
Our hearts are our like buttons.
So show like to another,
As if they were your brother.

True gratification,
And mental and spiritual ease.
It is all at our fingertips,
And even cheaper than cheese.

Simply walk your line,
And make your days way.
For instant is not natural,
To man's early day.

Baby

Energy is gathered,
From an unknown place.
It rolls and folds,
As it enters our race.

The body is grown,
Made by the spirit of two.
And out comes a baby,
And everything is new.

With no knowledge of life,
It knows what we teach it.
With no knowledge of life,
We best keep it treated.

Why teach baby of evil and good?
Why preach of right and wrong?
Only show right and right,
And wrong does not have a fight.

Baby learns what we show,
So why even negative we go?
Teach the good and only good,
And that is all baby will ever know.

We create wrong,
And baby follows our day.
Let baby write their own song,
And show only good along the way.

Baby is pure,
Keep baby that way.
For evil has no chance,
With baby today.

Death

Life is but a journey,
And we all turn to dust.
But fear not the end,
And that is a must.

I say this so,
For reasons you know.
That change can be scary,
When times are hairy.

Passing is not fearful,
It is glorious indeed.
For you will start a new journey,
With no tales to proceed.

Every place you go in life,
Has tales from the man before.
This gives you insight,
Before you go through the door.

Have people ever truly gone,
And come back to see the light?
Are their tales and their stories,
Of the true afterlife?

We cannot tell,
With manmade bails.
We cannot tell,
Without death sails.

That is a blessing,
Like a journey far away.
Imagine traveling forward,
With no maps or prior say.

It might seem scary,
Without modern mans tools.
To be naked without a body,
And flying with the ghouls.

But fear it not,
For it is divine.
To have crossed over,
This beautiful line.

It is an adventure,
With new bodies and gifts.
It is an experience,
One day, we all get to lift.

Doubt

The man who doubts,
Has nowhere to go.
He sits and pouts,
And denies his show.

It will never work,
That could never happen.
His motto is defeated,
And is vision depleted.

The cloud of doubt does blind,
Even with the most brilliant of mind.
You will tumble and toil,
Which could make your blood boil.

The angry fearful man,
All filled with doubt.
He looks to the past,
And regrets his last route.

Nothing is accomplished,
Even when the deeds are done.
He dreams and wishes,
It was sung by another one.

This man is pathetic,
And helps no one be grand.
However, this man is a man,
And part of the master plan.

So, let's be nice,
And help our friend.
Because we all have heart,
And that's the trend.

Faith

A man with faith,
Will always win.
With hope and glory,
He's proud of his story.

Anything is possible,
It will work if we try.
His motto is that's great,
And his vision so high.

Faith will awaken,
And allow you to see.
You will triumph and fly,
And truly be happy.

A faithful man,
All filled with cheer.
He looks to the future,
And makes ways to be safe.

Every action a victory,
Even if he did not succeed.
He's glad that he tried,
And learns something indeed.

This man is amazing,
And helps others be grand.
However, this man is a man,
And part of the master plan.

So be careful to glorify,
For he is simply a man.
We were all created equal,
By the same glorious hand.

Space Preparation

Everything is everywhere,
And everything is known.
Light moves at the speed of light,
No matter how fast you've grown.

Light going with you,
Is solid as stone.
Light coming off you,
Has free reign to roam.

We already exist,
At the edge of space.
We people are proud,
We are the human race.

A trick played by light,
Has blinded our best.
Einstein fell too,
To this electromagnetic slew.

Matter can travel fast,
Much faster than light.
But it will not look like it,
Because light is what fills our night.

The sources of magnetism,
Our information exchange.
Nothing will ever look like,
It's faster than light.

It's the Universe's greatest trick,
That makes us sit like a brick,
Our eyes do deceive us,
And here is my wick.

Space is prepared,
Before matter shines.
And proof lies within,
Differential lines.

To the man that is going,
Near simply light speed.
Our light has been stretched,
Maybe two times indeed.
It has traveled far,

A superior distance.
So how does that compare,
To this stellar instance?

For the man traveling,
At infinite speed.
Our wave is extended,
To infinity indeed.

As you see,
Our light exists.
It is everywhere at once,
But not always dense.

We have effect,
At the edge of space.
But our energy is strongest,
Where we stand in place.

Space gets prepared,
From long waves to short.
As you move forward through time,
You've already made rhyme.

What can we do,
With this secret of knowledge.
What can we make?
What can we create?

A machine so big,
It takes up our system.
With parts moving at speeds,
That would make awe and glisten.

This detector could see,
A transformation of waves.
This detector could see,
The future indeed.

It is all there,
In some light of a kind.
Remember space is first prepared,
By each and every mind.

You have the capacity,
And ability to perceive.
That your light exists everywhere,
At all moments indeed.

Recycling

It was once a treasure,
Now suits no good.
To the trash it goes,
To the dump we go.

This creates waste,
On our Earthly space.
This creates waste,
In our heavenly place.

To think before you make,
Is truly the key.
For resources are abundant,
And can come from a tree.

This does not pollute,
It's natural and good.
Plastics and smoke,
Are a big giant joke.

They cannot sustain,
They will only hold back.
Let's build a new lane,
And follow that track.

To create a product,
Is ok and dandy.
But wrappers galore,
Isn't always handy.

A wrapper from a leaf,
A box that's a bush.
Bamboo chute letters,
Let's all be go getters.

We can clean up our ways,
It's easy as pie.
It starts with the makers,
And that ain't no lie.

Time is but a Thought

Time is but a thought,
Built straight from your mind.
It cannot be sold or bought,
And thinks you fall behind.

Many stress,
As the hours go by.
With no place to rest,
Ask yourself "Why?"

Did man make the clock?
Yes, I believe we did.
So, is it solid like a rock,
No, it can be mended.

We create our days,
As we create our ways.
It is all a choice,
Although you may feel you have no voice.

Open your eyes,
And open your heart.
Notice the lies,
That's a great start.

Yes, time may equal money,
And can buy you endless honey.
But is your life yours?
Or is it controlled by your chores?

We live once for certain,
So do take advantage.
Dreams reveal the curtain,
With endless possibilities to manage.

Time is but a joke,
Created by man to listen.
There was then, now, and then,
All to make man, wealthy and glisten.

So do take note,
That time is just a tool.
It is fluid and you own it,
And that my friend, is truly cool.

Groovy Girl

An imperfectly,
Yet perfect lady.
The one that's got it,
To make you lazy.

Her eyes are warm,
Her heart filled with love.
She'll cure the weak,
Like a beautiful dove.

Her smile will lighten,
Her touch will heighten.
She is what is worth,
Saving this Earth.

A man is a man,
And does what he can.
But a woman's love,
Is of the highest demand.

Forgiving and caring,
Groovy girl is right.
There is no reason to struggle,
Or reason to fight.

She is wise and divine,
Her heart knows the truth.
She uses hugs and smiles,
To spread infinite youth.

No need for tools,
Or guns a blazing.
Her warmth is her shield,
That gets hairs a raising.

We all want to be,
So perfectly groovy.
And she lets us see,
It's so very easy.

Just sit and relax,
We're creating our tension.
Everything is fine,
No need to mention.

Forgetful in forgiveness,
A warm heart is key.
A groovy girl is needed,
Explanations need not be.

The past is made of stories,
And the future pure fantasy.
She says live as it's today,
And troubles will go away.

With gusto and hope,
Groovy girl spreads her love.
A smile is contagious,
And who knows where it goes.

A smile from a villain,
May go completely unnoticed.
A smile from groovy girl,
Will spread like nobody's business.

The energy will go,
From one to another.
The energy so familiar,
It feels like your mother.

It warms and cares,
Let's you know you're fine.
There's nothing to worry about,
It's all in your mind.

This heart is one,
That we all possess.
Let's smile bright,
And take a rest.

Rock Star

The rock star is king,
He takes nothing from anyone.
He lives by his flow,
And that's all he'll know.

People say don't,
People say you can't.
To the rock star, well,
That's a challenging rant.

He will not back down,
He will speak his voice.
He will let you be yourself,
And make your rock star choice.

He doesn't say you can't,
He doesn't say you won't.
He says be yourself,
Get your rock star off that shelf.

We are all rock stars,
Burning bright in our own way.
Focus on yourself,
Others will come and play.

To mimic another,
Is the compliment of the highest.
But you will never rock,
By striving for a perfect mock.

The rock star is unique,
He follows his way.
He does not think twice,
About what others say.

Some will take offense,
Their insecurities heighten.
Some will take defense,
They will surely run and frighten.

To be yourself,
In a world like today.
Takes boundless courage,
Because so many say.

The radio, the news,
The internet too.
Will all complicate,
What is truly you.

Forget that noise,
Forget that racket.
Be that rock star,
The one that cracked it.

Crack that mold,
Break free of its grasp.
Crack that hold,
Release the clasp.

You are a rock star,
We all shine bright.
Find yourself,
That is what is right.

Let yourself glow,
And let yourself know.
We are all rock stars,
In this magnificent and Earthly show.

Gravity

It pulls us down,
And keeps us on the ground.
It pulls us down,
And makes the Earth be round.

The flow of our rivers,
The height of our hills.
Are all influenced,
By it's magical spells.

The strength of our bones,
How high we can jump.
It controls it all,
As things flow and fall.

Earth goes to Earth,
And water goes to water.
Air goes to air,
And space need not bother.

Create space and you will go high,
Create Earth and you will go low.
But what if low is high?
And what if high is low?

What if the Earth pushes,
Instead of a continuous pull?
What if it's a shield,
Allowing us to grow?

Imagine all the stars,
That fill our heavenly space.
Imagine that their light,
Creates the gravity race.

It could explain the expansion,
From far far away.
It would explain the compression,
That we see in our daily day.

Gravity is from above,
And the Earth is a shield.
It keeps us in place,
As we travel and wield.

Who says it pulls?
And who says it pushes?
Does it matter at all?
It's up to your wishes.

But if it pushes,
Instead of pulls.
We need flip the sign,
And rework our hulls.

Maybe we can ride,
This stellar wind.
By simply switching,
Our electron spin.

It is so abundant,
And yet abused.
Gravity is sad,
And not amused.

Let's think again,
Before we equate.
Maybe it's from above,
That's up for debate.

Recycled Past

People from the past,
Were they as smart as stone?
People from the past,
How could they roam?

With no trace of tools,
They must have been fools.
With no trace of tools,
They had no magical jewels.

The pyramids are grand,
The stone statues too.
But how can they make this,
Without me or you?

Think of the cycle,
Of how technology grows.
Think of this trend,
It's like the wind blows.

Our direction is clean,
If you know what I mean.
Advanced technology,
Is hard to see.

It is made of stone,
At the nano level.
It is made from sand,
Without hand or bevel.

The further we go,
We leave less trace you know.
So maybe they were smart,
And focused on art.

Flying was mastered,
Knowledge of the stars too.
But green and clean,
They left us no clue.

Except for the stones,
That left modern man speechless.
Except for the bones,
That make them look seedless.

With no trace of pollution,
They give us a solution.
That advancements in mind,
Live with no trace behind.

Let's take visions of our past,
And make real things that last.
And show our future generation,
Just a wee bit of inspiration.

Let's turn our world green,
And get rid of the grey.
Let's transform our scene,
And save the day.

Leaders in Innovation, Education, and Sustainability
www.LooshesLabs.com   (2014)

Philosophical Implications

The next few readings take a scientific approach to the greater implications that rise. These ideas do have scientific evidence to support them, however there is no physical way to prove these claims accurate or inaccurate. They are purely philosophical in that sense.

Thinking with the Universe: We explore our connection with our mind to the Universe.

A Shift in Natural Selection: This section discusses how the focus of mate selection, which was once instinctual, is now dominated by manmade infrastructures.

Dreaming at Light Speed: Here we combine the theory of relativity, and the concept of space preparation to show how dreams may last much longer in the mind than in physical reality.

A Universal Conscious: In this section, we consider the Universe to be a living organism. What is the goal of this being and where do we as humans fit in?

Thinking With the Universe

When people learn new ideas, they tend to try to associate them with something that relates. People tend to make categories and put any item up for discussion immediately into one. Categories could include concepts from different scientific fields to physical objects, like a car versus a boat. Both are vehicles put they may be categorized further by where the vehicle is used. Essentially, the main point, is that any item may be put into a category. This happens on a day-to-day basis because of typical learning methods. Most modern people today go through an education system that is well established. Techniques have been developed and ideas put into subjects. Because of this, our minds essentially categorize information into a sort of tree of knowledge where one idea may be attached to another.

Categorizing Creates Predisposed Relations

Categorizing any concept in your mind automatically limits your ability to fully understand what is happening. You have already created predisposed relations and so it is less likely you will be able to use the knowledge learned to its maximum potential. Concepts become attached and inseparable to one another. For example, when most people visualize a car wheel, they automatically see both tire and wheel. They might even see concrete, the side of a car, and some bushes. This is because these items are commonly seen together that it is unusual to have one without the other. This is just a simple case to get you thinking.

Tree Branches of Knowledge

Tree branches of knowledge are a result of a modern educational system. It is probably true that almost every system uses the concept of different subjects. For example, the phrase alone, "We are now studying Math," as opposed tot studying History or English already puts the brain into a new mode, Math mode. When bits of knowledge are given names to them, they become categorized. Categorizations create limitations in one's ability to maximize the data.

For example, when studying different fields, one may notice direct relationships are quite obvious but more profound links are not connected because the information is being blocked by parts of the tree that are not very close.

Experts in Their Fields

Consider learning the concept of acoustic waves. One might study air temperature and pressure. One could become the leading expert in sound waves traveling through solids. If someone wants to know how fast a sound wave will travel, they know the answer because they are the best in acoustic waves. They have done test, performed experiments, and truly you understand sound waves.

On the other hand, you have a material expert. They are looking at crystal formations of different molecules. They are learning about the various types of cleavage rocks may have and their hardness levels. They notice how crystals deform and atoms move around. They notice how fast materials can break and become a materials master.

Now they are both sitting at dinner. You have one expert who is the expert at the speed of sound in all matter. You have the other who knows materials as if they are the back of his hand. They start talking. The sound expert talks and talks and eventually goes over his equations for the speed of sound. The materials expert then goes over his formulas. After a very lengthy discussion, he reveals his formula for crack propagations.

Do the two realize they are now talking about the almost the same exact identical concept and that there could be a giant connection between the speed of sound and how fast a crack can propagate through a material? It really depends on the number of tree branches in the way. In many cases, they would be completely separated because of the unrelated fields in which they learned.

Infinite Connections

The tree branch style of learning is good. It makes it easy to learn specific task. However, it is quite limiting to cognitive thinking and the innovative process. By removing tree branches of knowledge from the way you learn, you may see that you know much more than you think. Connections that once seemed unnoticeable will be staring at you in the face.

There are many ways to create this effect when learning. The easiest way is to not categorize anything ever. This may sound ridiculous, but ultimately everything is the same anyway because it's made of light. A great way to create this effect is to not preframe the person that is learning. The second you preframe the scenario the individual will attach the knowledge to branches. The goal is to have it be more of an absorbed knowledge. For the person learning, it is almost best to ignore the information. Sure, listen to it, maybe visualize, but the second the lesson is over, move on. You do not need to cognitively think about that information anymore. If it is a problem, do not categorize and simply let it go.

Learning with the Universe

Where does your conscious mind exist? The answer may be in your head. However, the mind and spirit are made of light and are part of the Universe. Every single atom or molecule is fundamentally made of the same material as your physical brain. When a thought occurs, there is basically a lightshow of electrical connections. Electrical synapses create electromagnetic fields and any electromagnetic field or energy may be considered light. Therefore, your thoughts are made of light.

Your thoughts then have the ability to interact with the electromagnetic waves of any other particle or wave that may be passing through your body. Going off the concept of space preparation, you could say that your mind's light encompasses the entire Universe. So why only think in your physical head?

Let your thoughts flow into the Universal mesh of knowledge and your will physically think less.

You will notice solutions to problems instantly and your sense of awareness will heighten.

Developing this Skill

Like the tree branch method of learning, any style of learning may be developed with practice. The tree branch method is good and creates desired results within a single field. However, the ultimate potential of full knowledge and ability to connect the dots may be much less. By full knowledge, I am referring to the amount of usable knowledge that may transfer into an intuitive notion.

An easy method to develop this skill is to cover a new topic every five to fifteen minutes. If the topic requires much more time, then discuss maybe for thirty minutes and then go use a completely different part of your brain for the next fifteen. This is almost like encouraging ADD but will teach you to let go of concepts cognitively and allow the Universe or subconscious mind to do all the thinking for you.

Universe versus the Head

In the head, you have to cognitively understand what is happening. Consider a savant that is amazing at Math. He or she has no idea what they are cognitively doing and cannot describe it, yet the numbers just appear in their brain. They can perform extremely advanced computation and more. It's truly incredible.

This type of thinking is almost impossible to cognitively wrap your head around and many of the calculations would take seconds to even mentally think about the steps involved. However, upon a simple glance, these savants know the answers. Where is their thinking happening? It is most likely not in the conscious mind and most likely in what some would call the subconscious or Universe.

Universal Mind

Your mental light and that of all beings extends to the edge of the Universe in at least one or more reference frames. Therefore, it is easy to see the mesh of knowledge that may exist within our experience. All knowledge of all time is accessible and once mastered, learning becomes more like remembering.

Remembering Knowledge

It is easy to remember knowledge that has not yet been told. Again, it comes down to perception. Do you think you are learning it for the first time, or are you simply experiencing it for the first time? Remember, through space preparation, that everything is somewhat everywhere and that the past and future may be just as solid as the present moment but your mind is only tuned to the now due to evolution within the expanding Universe. That means that it could already exist in your subconscious. The fact is, the experience exists somewhere in spacetime and therefor your mind has the ability to interact with it.

All knowledge of the Universe resides within the light it encompasses. Your thoughts exist at the edge of the Universe in any moment in spacetime. By removing cognitive thought and learning to think with the Universe, a greater knowledge and understanding of any topic will be the ultimate result.

A Shift in Natural Selection

Most people are familiar with the process of natural selection. It is the idea, that living things (plants, animals, bacteria, and etc.) that are best suited for the environment have the most chance of surviving long enough to produce fertile offspring. Therefore, although the individual creature may perish, the species continues to thrive. Slight changes in features over time could be considered evolution.

Using the theory of evolution, which has much scientific data to support it, we may say that humans have changed over millions of years to become the dominant species that we see today. Natural selection is apparent in all species and is rather peculiar when it comes to humans. The survival of all species depends on their ability to successfully interact with their environment. There has been a shift in the focus of mate selection due to modern technology and infrastructures.

Natural Focus

The earliest of humans did not have the luxuries of today's modern society. We may have scurried in bushes like animals looking for food on a daily basis (Remember, although we think we are different, we do inhabit animal bodies.) The idea of refrigeration and preservatives did not exist. Air-conditioned homes and proper plumbing did not exist. At this moment in history, humans could not read nor do math because mathematics and scripture had yet to be invented. Humans were at their most primitive state, completely unaware of the self.

At this time, survival was an instinct. It was common sense. It did not require thought because it was natural. Emotion or spiritual energy controlled their every action and the conscious mind was empty. Humans hunted and gathered their food. Farming did not yet exist. People traveled the Earth according to the changing seasons and food supply. This is a time when human survival depended on physical strength and intuitive notion. Humans were pure because their minds were unaware of their selves. Cognitive thought was not beneficial in most situations. Times were rough and to have a clear mind meant survival. The force empowering all human action was purely spiritual and instinctual. Natural selection and evolution were governed by human strength, the ability to find food, and the ability to care for children.

Primitive Speculations

Let's quickly speculate the societal demands of the early humans mentioned above. We may only speculate because it is a time long lost. A child would be born into the world. Whether a boy or girl, it most likely would have nursed from their mother. The child would then have learned from its elders and its surroundings on how things work. Encounters with biting insects and interactions with other humans would have shaped it into the being it became. (Speculation) For a woman, her purpose would have been to have babies and then ensure the success of their survival. For a man, his purpose would have been to make sure she has everything she needs in order to properly care for the children. This could imply supplying her with shelter and food. Neither male or female, had to go to school, be expected to get straight A's, win sporting competitions, be a super model, a rock star, a lawyer, or a doctor. They weren't concerned about making millions of dollars because money was of no significance. These duties had no importance in early human life because they did not exist. These positions of power, achieved successes, and wealth have all been created over the years by man. They have all come into being by trying to create structured environments in which to grow, almost like a human zoo.

Advanced Technology Blossoms

Over time a shift in natural selection has occurred. This shift has been gradually accelerating since the advent of technology. Primitive technologies such as spears and fire may be the precursors to all modern technology, from air conditioning to nuclear bombs. Early fire was used to keep people warm, ward off animals, and give us light at night. Our primitive fire has been replaced by air-conditioned dwellings that have electricity to give us light and walls to keep out animals (modern campfire.) Our spears and stones have been replaced by guns and grenades. Spears and stones require much more training and mastery to achieve desired results. Weapons like fully automatic machine guns take very little physical strength to gain power and cause serious harm.

This is where society is today, a place where a child with a fully automatic machine gun has more power over someone who has developed their intuitive notion over a lifetime. All the child must do is pull a trigger and our super developed human is gone. It takes years upon years of training to achieve levels of extreme athletic ability and intuitive notion. It takes an entire lifetime of dedication to effectively care for children and support others while on the hunt for food. Most people today have lost these ideals that fulfill our true nature and inner spirit. Again, this goes back to the advent of money and technology.

Creation of Leisure Time

What does technology do for us? It creates leisure time. Leisure time can be a blessing or a curse. What people choose to do with it can either be constructive or destructive. Constructive activities include, building relationships and long-lasting bonds, helping others and insuring the survival of not only the Earth, but the Universe as well. Destructive activities could be fighting, violence, and activities that might inadvertently have negative effects on the world. These activities aren't always intentionally meant to be negative, but are destructive because of the nature of the influence that initially caused it. Greed, jealousy, lust, anger, and other selfish human emotions may cause people to inadvertently have destructive behaviors.

A Man on the Mountain

The man with the most money and wealth is now the most fit to survive. He has no real obligation or duty and has 100% leisure time. He may buy armored vehicles and security guards to protect him at all cost. With the blink of an eye, he may have exotic foods delivered to the top of the highest mountains. He has the best doctors available and has many loves. He will live a long life. This man is the alpha male of the manmade race. A man with no money is seen as poor. He begs for money to buy food and the underpass is his home. He is regarded as dirty, lazy, and maybe even considered by some as the filth of the human society. He too, with no real obligation has 100% leisure time.

Money Equals Food

Humans have now evolved to rely on money more than food and survival techniques. It is obvious that money can buy food. If you are hungry, then you just go to the store and buy food. It no longer takes any physical ability or strength to buy sufficiently supply food for your family. Natural selection now favors the wealthy and not the wise. This trend has been around for at least the last 2000 years. If you say a new generation of humans is born every 20 years, then you could easily say that the last 100 generations of humans have been born with money being the driving factor for mate selection. If you assume that humans have been around for at least 100,000 years then you see that many more generations have been born with natural instincts and intuitive notion as the driving force for mate selection. It is obvious that a shift in human spirit is occurring.

A Shift in Spirit

This shift can most easily be seen in the case of human religions. Before this, we must understand the relationship between a monetary society and technology. Technology has given us free time to create manmade infrastructures which ultimately create wealth and disparities. For example, the monetary system, schools, government programs such as social security, transportation systems, media, communication systems, power grids, waste disposal, and etc. may all be considered manmade infrastructures. Every one of these systems has been designed to create more free time in one way or another. Money made trade easier. Schools made being educated easier and etc. However, the ultimate outcome over many generations may be destructive. Obligations and physical duties that are not natural to humans are now being forced upon all of society. If you do not follow these structures, you will be imprisoned and regarded as a quack or bum. So, it is obvious through the creation of leisure time that forced infrastructures now control our lives. Even before you are born, a general path of life has been laid out for you. You will most likely be born into a hospital and stay there for a couple days. You will grow up and go to school, get a job, get married, and have children. At night, you are supposed to watch TV and then sleep in air-conditioned homes. The focus of the human spirit has shifted. Most people now focus on living up to the standards previously mentioned. You must own a car, TV, internet, and all that fun stuff. Human focus is now controlled by science, technology, wealth, and other manmade infrastructures. Human focus has shifted from being purely instinctual to now being dominated by manmade infrastructure.

This has a dramatic effect on the human spirit, which has a direct negative effect on the way people treat each other. This may be related to one's spiritual beliefs whether it be in favor of science or traditional religion. Science may be considered mankind's attempts to quantify the known world. It is a way of categorizing phenomenon and using experimental evidence to create desired results. Faith, beliefs, and good intentions have no place in scientific exploration and in this modern scientifically dominated society.

The continuation of focusing on materialistic creations will not allow for the gaining of conscious density. It is similar to bouncing off conscious atmosphere when considering the orbit through conscious density in relationship to ascending though time.

Science versus Faith

The human spirit has been the dominating force for mate selection up until the advent of modern technology. This spirit is one that believed in faith, something greater than the self, and that there is much more to the world than the eye can see. From this primitive spirit came traditional religions such as Buddhism, Christianity, and etc. All of these religions basically have the same message. Love your fellow human and be a servant to the world. Be humble and love. None of them preach ambitious causes like war, presidential elections, alpha dog syndrome, and etc. Those are all modern focuses created by manmade infrastructure which are now the dominating spirit of mate selection. From this spirit came science and the theory of evolution. These concepts now rule the human spirit and are having an overall negative impact on the quality of human life. Strides towards earlier methods of natural selection. are of great importance. However, it is also important to carry the positive results from these last 100 generations

A New Spirit Will Emerge

It is impossible to instantly jump from one method of selection into another. It is not even feasible to consider jumping back to natural instincts being the deciding factor for human growth. We must not believe science has all the answers. Instead, we must learn to combine the two driving forces of mate selection. We must combine what we have learned from our modern scientific spirit with our prehistoric natural spirit. You cannot teach a worm politics and you definitely cannot fully explain the Universe with all of its mysteries (life and death) through quantifications.

Dreaming at Light Speed

Have you ever had a dream that seemed to last minutes, days, months, if not years, then to realize you have only been asleep for 60 seconds? How is this possible? How can so much mental time pass in such a short amount of physical time? To answer questions like this, we must first explore the nature of how and why humans perceive time, as well as the nature of time within our reality.

Human versus Universal Time

Seconds and minutes are all categorizations of manmade time. Humans defined the length of a minute and the length of a second. In social settings, it is used to organize events and meetings. It can be a helpful tool in organization. It is important to understand that it is manmade time and not Universal. Manmade time can pass at different rates in different reference frames and is a result of our 4-dimensional reality (x, y, z, and t.) Universal time is constant and solid throughout reality. It is the fluid Crystal of Time.

Reference Frames of Existence

Understanding the concept of a reference frame is crucial for understanding the concept of dreaming at light speed. A reference frame, in the simplest terms, is a place in space that may be considered stationary when compared to everything else in existence. Many people think of the Earth as being still when they walk. However, the Earth is spinning really fast and orbiting the Sun at a ridiculous speed. The reference frame is simply a definition that helps people compare two places in space with respect to each other. It is extremely important when considering doppler shifts and that our conscious experience is a result of the waves we interact with. Einstein's theory of relativity basically says when objects are moving near the speed of light relative to another object that they become time dilated, Lorentz contracted, and mass increases. This effect happens when any acceleration occurs and is directly related to the differences in velocities. This is not the case for the "Universal reference frame" of the 5th dimension which is based off Universal time (the Crystal of Time.)

The Greatest Magic Trick Recap

Einstein's theory of relativity might as well be the Universe's greatest magic trick. It is so great because, although flaw by human perception and understanding, it has value in modern technology. Einstein is correct when he says waves become time dilated and contracted. This is apparent in satellites. They must be corrected for time dilations as they orbit. Lorentz contractions and time dilations may all be solved through simple vector addition of accelerating reference frames and is relatively intuitive by nature. The magic trick created by the Universe is that light is the median in which we are able to detect any object. Objects can go faster than the speed of light but they will never look like it.

A Body of Light

The human perception of time in our physical Universe is a direct function of mental or spiritual shift in brain function. Times fly when you are having fun and seem to take forever when you are waiting for something. These are all perceptions of manmade time. Although two physical bodies may have experienced the same amount of time their spirits or souls may not have. The essence of life energy, chi, the spirit, the soul, or whatever you may call it, experiences much more time than the physical body. It may be hard to imagine because we are comparing manmade time to Universal time. In Universal time, everything is already everywhere in one frame or another. In manmade time, the core of modern human focus, due to evolution of the species within an expanding universe, time is defined and constant. The future has not yet happened.

The human body is solid and its spirit is made of light. The human consciousness or mind is the bridge that connects the two, creating our individual realities. This means that human focus, which is controlled by the mind, has the ability to jump from one reference frame to another. Our everyday life, morning routine, work, eating, and etc. is all in the solid frame which is a frame dominated by our bodies. In this solid frame, manmade infrastructures dominate and there is not much room for faith. In the spiritual frame, the one made of light, everything is somewhat everywhere. There is no questioning, because all is known. In this place, technology is of no use and Universal knowledge is certain. There is no time, solely existence.

Everything is Relative

Humans use patterns and rhythms to help them perceive manmade time, like heartbeats and shadow movements throughout the day. These are all tools that help us calculate time. So why then may dreams "last forever?" When you dream, the focus of your brain is not in the current moment. It is in a metaphysical world; one where manmade time has no power or control over the minds focus. This may confuse a being into thinking that many hours may have passed when only a few minutes have gone by on their physical clock. Your dreams are made of light and may be occurring at the edge of reality, in the Deltaverse.

A Universal Goal

Consider the Universe as conscious entity with the ability to grow and make decisions just as any other creature or living being. The Universe is alive and conscious of what is going on inside it. It can make decisions that lead to certain goals. The Universe may appear gigantic to humans, similar to how humans may appear large to a single animal cell. It takes thousands upon thousands of cells to make a human body. Similarly, it takes billions upon billions of galaxies to make our Universe.

Typical Life Cycle

The cells in a living being work together towards a single purpose or goal. This goal is to insure the life of the greater organism. Let's walk through the life cycle of any organism. First, comes birth. An organism is born into the world. Next, the organism grows. It becomes larger and more self-aware. At a certain point, it thrives to fulfill its purpose. For most organisms, you could say the sole purpose is to reproduce and to secure the prosperity of their kind. The last stage of any life is death.

First, there was Light

What is the goal of the Universe? Modern science tells us the Universe is expanding in all directions. It also tells us, at the beginning of time, all space and matter occupied a single point in our 4D space.

In the beginning, the Universe was a spore, similar to a human sex cell. It is not until an event occurs that the Universe begins to grow. This cause of the event is unknown to modern science and technology. In "The Crystal of Time," we say it is the moment when our Universe collided with time. How could that 5D realm relate to our 4D? In our human example, that is the moment when the sperm cell enters the woman's egg cell and cellular osmosis begins. The concept of replication and division of a single unit to attain a certain goal may be considered growth. The human sex cells begin to divide and grow into a functional organism that's ultimate goal is to reproduce and create fertile offspring.

The Universe also had a moment of initial growth. In the beginning of our experience, time didn't even exist because light didn't exist. Time is a measurement of the distance light travels. Humans have divided it further into 24 hours in a day with 60 minutes in an hour. This is manmade time and not the time being discussed here. The

Universe then began to expand. Once the Universe reached a certain size it then became possible for light to travel. This is the moment when our known Universe, with its laws of gravity, speed of light, and all other Universal laws came into existence. This is the moment when our Universe drifted into the "Habitable Zone" of conscious experiences. This is the moment when our Universe became self-aware and started working towards its ultimate goal.

Then Came the Elements

The first thing the Universe created were subatomic particles. These particles then coalesced to form electrons, protons, and other primal building blocks of matter. Electrons, protons, and neutrons then combined to make more complex structures. The first and only element was Hydrogen. Hydrogen started to combine and eventually formed burning stars. These stars become so massive that fusion reactions begin. Hydrogen atoms combine to form Helium. Helium then combined to form Lithium and so on. All of these early reactions are exothermic. It is only when you get to Iron that the reactions become endothermic. At this point, the star implodes and other heavier elements come into existence.

Planets did not yet exist. This process took millions of years in human time.

Molecules and Planets to Follow

It is only after the initial ancestral stars explode that the molecules come into existence. A molecule is a combination of elements that come together to make a new type of matter that has different properties than the parent elements that were used to create it. These molecules floated freely in space and eventually coalesced due to the force of gravity or synchronization of the light-state. These structures become so dense that stars begin to form once again. Material that does not become part of a star may be considered leftover materials and are what form the planets and other bodies that orbit the star system.

A Conscious was Awakened

A unique feature of life on Earth is that it is made of solid physical matter and are filled with spiritual energy or light. All Earthly organisms possess these two qualities, bacteria, plants, fish, birds, and etc. They are all made of matter filled with light. Yes, they do have a mind, however they are still mostly instinctual. Humans possess an incredibly powerful mind with the ability to think with the Universe. A stone is made of solid particles. A bacteria cell is made of solid particles filled with light. A human, the most advanced being we are aware of, is made of solid particles filled with light and controlled by an extremely powerful mind. The combination of the three mind, body, and spirit are what make humans unique to our realm.

We are Guardians

The Universe created particles. Particles created elements. The elements then combined to make molecules. The molecules then combined to make planets and stars. The interaction of planets and stars is what created life. So, what is the ultimate goal of the Universe? With this model is seems obvious that it is to create life. So how does life come into the ultimate goal of the Universe? What role do live beings have in this mysterious and Universal goal? Going back to our human example, the ultimate goal of the Universe may be to reproduce and have fertile offspring. Organisms, like people, are the white blood cells of the Universe. People have the ability to create or destroy any matter we choose fit. We were put here to insure the survival of our world and Universe.

A Blossoming Flower

With our new understanding of "The Infinite Pool of Experience and Awareness," we may see that our Universe is blossoming like a flower into the 6th dimension.

Water is Time

When we look at the flow of primordial energy from the perspective of the 6th dimension, we see it is part of a growing structure. Our Universal experience is a result of energy flowing into a black hole. In our experience, we see the spark of new conscious experiences as energy flows into the black hole of every galactic center.

We are one part of a structure that is growing into the 6th dimension. We are the harmonizers of that structure. Through love and synchronization, we flow like a river into the next layer of experience as it branches out like water in a lake heading out to sea or like a flower blossoming towards the Sun.

We are the water of the 1/6th dimension, the dimension inwards to where an electron is a universe. We flow like water. We are water and we are Time. We are all One.

Leaders in Innovation, Education, and Sustainability
www.LooshesLabs.com   2021

The Physics of Love

Synchronicity

by Alexei Novitzky

Table of Contents

Introduction

We are the harmonizers of the 5th dimension. "The Infinite Pool of Experience and Awareness" shows that our entire experience may be like a flower blossoming towards a "Greater Sun" into the 6th dimension. As individuals and as a collective, we see that through love and synchronization, we are the water and we are the fluid of time.

As consciousness gyroscopically precesses about the center, the quantum flow of the fluid determines the amount of intelligence which exist.

Laminar flows of the quantum state relate to much harmony and synchronization while turbulent flows relate to karmic cycles and lack of synchronization.

Through laminar flows we nurture the greater structure and perform our purpose. Our harmony is like water carrying nutrients to a source.

By use of the mind, body, and spirit diagrams, we see how our wants, don't wants, assumptions, and expectations influence the natural flow of the river.

The greatest intelligence may be found through perfect stillness or rather, egoless motions. Let us now sit quiet and truly explore experience.

Where Do We Begin?

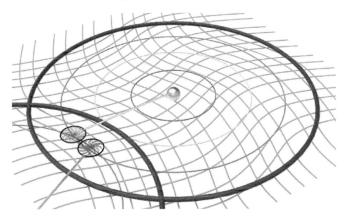

Quite honestly, where do you begin and where do you end? What is it that defines you and your space? From "The 5th Dimension," we see that our creation comes from the overlapping of all waves in the multiverse. They create a general light-state, a sort of pool of overlapping energy which remains in harmony as described by the magic square. I dare not call it EM because it is not EM and it is not matter. It is the state of matter being half stretched and light being half crunched. It is the state of the fluid of experience before it is perceived by a conscious entity. For our purposes, we will call this the "Loosh" state. It is the raw energy that is not in a state of perception.

Remember, reality is being stretched into existence as energy orbits and we precess. The perceived length and age of the Universe is directly related to the doppler shift associated with a light speed acceleration towards center. It is somewhat illusionary and depends entirely on your position within "The Crystal of Time."

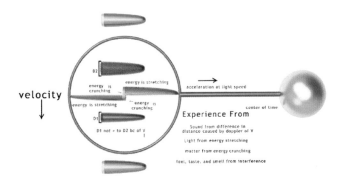

In the 5D sense, we are all literally created from the same field of overlapping energy. The same wave that makes you also makes me. We are all one. We all share the same ocean and 5D multiverse of potential experiences. Consciousness is not locked into an individual and it flows freely through the field of energy. It is only our egos and imaginations that separate us. All that exist is pure consciousness.

Relationship to Expanding and Contracting Universe

This gives us great insight as to why as the Universe appears to expand, matter also appears to become more and more dense. Considering the gravitational field of any body diminishes by a factor of r^2 we see that as we drift along the habitable spiral of perception, we would be drifting closer to the center of time. Our manifested experience is a direct relationship of the doppler shift associated to the degree of light speed acceleration towards center. Therefor you may see that as we drift closer to the center of time matter would appear to crunch more and light would appear to stretch more. This would give the appearance of the Universe increasing in size meanwhile matter would continue to become more and more dense creating the formation of black holes.

What might we expect if this is true? We may expect black holes to become even more dense into the future and as our experience of conscious experience drifts inwards towards greater density we may expect to see a "shedding" from black holes. It is possible, we may not be close enough to the center of time to have experienced any of these events or that they may be perceived as a big bang.

Laminar Flow

Laminar flow, in the simplest terms, is when a fluid has a nice continuous and uniformity about it. It is perfectly smooth and rounds corners easily. It would seem like a string or rope, perfectly in harmony with its motion. Laminar flows are the most efficient and transferring fluid from one source to another.

Turbulent Flow

A turbulent flow is one that is not uniform. You may find that there are gaps in the flow and often vortices or spirals of energy forming. In general, turbulent flows require more energy and take longer to reach their final destinations versus laminar flows.

A Series of Synchronizations

The flow of experience from past to present to future is somewhat illusionary as it is only perceivable from a specific spot in the 5D multiverse. However, each one has a sort of smoothness about it. For example, when a ball rolls down a hill, it will continue to do so with each progressive frame of time having the ball appear further and further down the hill. Now let's add some rocks to this hill. As the ball rolls, it may bounce off of a stone and take a different path. All the pebbles that now occupy the hill offer certain paths. However, between the collisions the rolling is somewhat uniform and laminar. It only changes directions when it collides with a stone. It is one event followed by another in a smooth fashion with turning points occurring at specific moments.

In this case, the turning points would be the locations of stones.

Let's now compare this to the natural flow of the light-state in relationship to laminar and turbulent flows.

A General Experience

The flow of the fluid your experience inhabits determines the degree of harmony within it. Experiences occurring in laminar flows would relate to much synchronizations and harmony. They are very easy going. A flow within a turbulent region would translate into much pacing about the golden spot. They lack synchronicity and would cause karmic cycling of events to repeat until synchronization with the laminar flow is achieved.

There is an Intelligence in Stillness

There is an intelligence in stillness. Rather, stillness promotes intelligence. As above is as below and as our experience of the expanding Universe drifts inwards towards center we see that we gain higher harmonics of consciousness.

You could say that the human base wave is the delta wave which it at 1hz. From there, we have gained denser and denser experiences. Our most heightened state is currently the Fast Gamma wave which is at 80hz. The next wave coming into human experience will be what we have named the Omega wave or Aleverse. It would be associated with brain harmony of approximately 160hz.

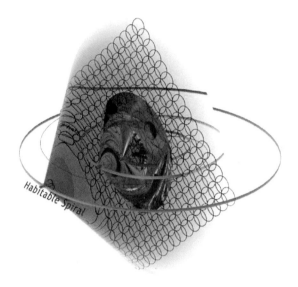

In general, as experiences drift towards center they gain higher harmonics of consciousness.

Quantum Experiences

From "Time Atom," we see there is a layering of conscious types that exist within our 5D multiverse. Each layer of reality is associated with a specific conscious harmonic.

The initial size of the conscious type depends directly on the flows of space that create it. From there, it drifts inward or potentially outward gaining more perceivable information.

Consciousness forms in black holes and so from our perspective you could say that every atom and every particle is essentially conscious. The evolution of the conscious type is directly related to the rate or quality of flow for the fluid. For example, if the flow is very turbulent then it is unlikely to drift inward. Individual atoms within the flow would be colliding creating friction. This friction does not allow for smooth transitions or long-lasting laminar flows. It would consist of short experiences that do not make it to the final destination.

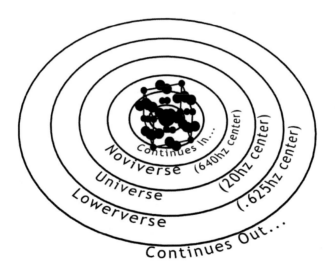

On the other hand, with laminar flows, consciousness can evolve rather quickly. "Time

Atom" shows that there exist time dilations between densities of experience.

(From Time Atom pg 44 - reminder)

Table of Universes

Universe	Brain Wave	hz Frequency	hz Harmonic Frequency	m Cloud Diameter
Deltaverse	delta	1-3	2.5	2.4×10^6
Thetaverse	theta	4-8	5	6×10^5
Aplhaverse	aplha	9-13	10	1.5×10^5
Betaverse	beta	14-30	20	40,000
Slow Gammaverse	slow-gamma	30-49	40	10,000
Fast Gammaverse	fast-gamma	50-100	80	2,500
Aleverse	omega	101-220	160	625
Dimiverse	zeta	221-400	320	156.25
Stellaverse	epsilon	401-800	640	39
Petraverse	omicron	801-1600	1280	9.75
Mikaverse	iota	1601-3400	2560	2.4

"The diameter of a 2.5hz wave is 2.4x10^6 meters. The diameter of an 80hz wave is 2,500 meters. Here you can see the amount of Lorentz contraction this equates to and then infer a time dilation between the two dimensions of waking life. Basically, the ratio is (2.4x10^6 meters)/(2,500 m) which goes about 1000. That is our multiplying factor. Theoretically, you could say, as far as waking perception, that for every 1 second that passes here in the Betaverse, 1000 seconds passes in the Betaverse equivalent of Noviverse. 640hz or Stellaverse, would be their "beta state." So, a diameter of 40,000m /39.06m goes to roughly 1,000.

The 4 rotations a second would also add to the time dilation. It may be a safer assumption to say the total time dilation would be 4,000 to 1. This goes to 1 second being equivalent to 1 hour and 1 minute."

# of shifts	Dilation Factor per Second
0	1 second
1	1 hour
2	185 days
3	2029 years
4	8.1 million years
5	32 billion years
6	130 trillion years

This shows that for 1 second of perfect laminar in our waking reality that 1 hour of time would have passed in the Stellaverse which is the Noviverse equivalent of our Betaverse.

To go another 5 steps of harmonic resonance, every second in our experience would be related to 185 days of evolution.

Betaverse is related to 2^4. The Stellaverse is related to 2^9. The next center would be related to 2^{14}. So, in general, the equation becomes $2^{(4+5D)}$ where D is the number of dimensional shifts towards the Noviverse. Relating this to our graph on the prior page, you can see that for one second of perfect stillness, 130 billion years may pass in the dimension of time relating to 2^{34}. This equates to a processing speed of roughly 17 billion hz.

Mind, Body, and Spirit Distortions

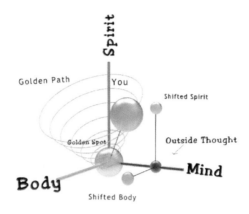

"The Liquid-Light State Universe" shows us how our wants, don't wants, assumptions, and expectations create all the pacing motions of our lives. Each one of those is related directly to an energetic vortex of sorts that has a length of time required to pace back to zero. It could be considered a karmic cycle of delusion. The pacing of our energy back to zero is represented the Fibonacci sequence spiraling inward along the major shifted axis.

Therefor, you can see how each of these offsets creates a general pacing. Remember, your creation consists of mind, body, and spirit. Pacing motions and spiraling actions exist in all three aspects. So, every thought creates a pacing within the 5D multiverse. Every action creates a pacing and so does every show of ego (light-state harmony).

Habitats within Time

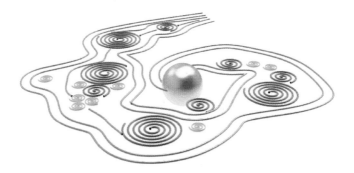

There are many habitats within the Loosh (the raw energy of experience.) Each of these flows of energy is related to a habitat of conscious density. Each of these exist as a conscious distortion of the being of a lower density. For example, the Sun is conscious and it creates the habitats for the planets. The planets are conscious and create the habitats for the beings that inhabit them. On Earth, humans are conscious and create the flows for denser harmonics of consciousness. All bodies increase in conscious density as they drift inward.

Turning Points in Relationship to Cycle Size

Smaller spirals within the Loosh are created by the mind, body, and spirit distortions projected by the consciousness inside. Each one is representative of a delusion or experience of sorts depending on your personal habits or ways.

Addictive actions will lead to the smallest spirals of creation while egoless motions and synchronicities lead to the greatest. For example, if you suffer a drug addiction, the furthest in time you will see is to your next "fix." You will be disconnected from the greater flow of reality.

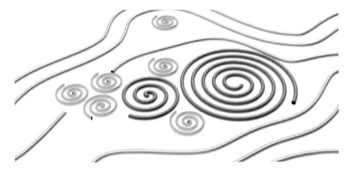

To synchronize with the planets, Sun, and stars is to synchronize with the greatest flow of our experience, although, greater synchronizations do exist. (We will speak on that later when we discuss interdimensional postures.) Consider the diameter of each spiral as your field of view or line of sight within time.

A Line of Sight

The quantum habitat one inhabits determines their level of conscious awareness or connectivity. This pacing motion is general related to one's level of overall confidence/faith versus that of insecurity/doubt. They are directly related because each represents the distance in time or into the future you may see. Beings connected to the greatest orbits of experience may see to the beginning and to the end of Time. Their conscious awareness inhabits all regions of the 5D multiverse and they may peer into the delusions inhabited by others. This allows for a greater understanding of the actions of others and allows for greater compassion. It becomes apparent why beings do what they do when you can see the delusion they inhabit.

Postures in Mind, Body, and Spirit

Many people are familiar with the concept of taking physical postures. It is a common exercise done in yoga, gymnastics, and many other sports. Some examples include standing on one foot, stretching upwards towards the sky, and of course touching your toes. These are all examples of physical posture.

You may also take a posture in mind. For example, you can walk around thinking that democrats are the best, or you can walk around thinking that republicans are the best. Another common example would be the lifelong assumptions of race and monetary separation. I highly recommend looking into the Stanford Prison-Guard Experiment.

In short, students were asked to play the roles of either prisoners or guards during what was supposed to be a multiweek long study. The study however, ended up being cut short only after seven days. This is because the participants started playing out their assumptions of those roles to such a degree that they were causing harm to themselves and to others. It was as if their assumptions and expectations created the results of the experiments. As is the state of the Earth. Very rarely are people removed of their delusions that have been instilled. From childhood, we are subconsciously taught how to treat each other and how to act. If your girlfriend leaves you, you're supposed to get upset. If someone steals from you too. Certain races do this and certain monetary classes do that. This really isn't true and is only the case because people are caught in their delusion.

It is a good practice during meditation to analyze the postures you have taken in mind. This could relate to past relationships and the thoughts your project towards people you believe have harmed you in the past. When you hold the posture of a "grudge" it does not allow for synchronization for anyone involved. All "grudges" must be let go of in order for everyone to reach their Golden Spots. In some cases, it is best to not be on the minds of others. This is certainly the case when inventing and creating artwork. All thoughtforms overlap and create the experience manifested.

It is also possible to take a posture in spirit or light-state harmony. This would relate more to your ego and how easily you go with the flow of our natural manifestation. It is important to understand that all experiences are manifested from a delusion of sorts. The removal of one will put you into a bigger one. This being said, it is important to find the greatest laminar flow before completely relaxing the ego.

Consider the ego as a sort of steering wheel through delusion. It is through the use of our mind, body, and spirit connections that we free ourselves from instilled smaller vortices within the 5D multiverse and connect ourselves to the greatest flow.

Healing through Posture Control

"The Liquid-Light State Universe" describes the concept of overlapping projections and how they influence one another. All waves overlap and their energy adds and subtracts. The energy you walk with directly influences all beings around you. Therefore, if you see someone that is caught in a destructive spiral of delusion you may use your knowledge of the mind, body, and spirit to guide or connect them to the greater flow.

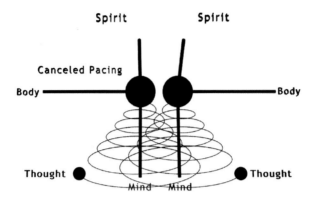

In some cases, they may require a timed dampener and in others a timed amplifier. It is not always necessary or proper to use the same offset force to correct the cause of the pacing.

For example, if one is caught in a delusion of abandonment, it is best to use the body to show care and compassion. A show of heart and physical presence will cleanse one of the feelings of abandonment or loss. A compassionate hug of everlasting care will be remembered.

Every pacing action has the most appropriate or quickest way to be calmed. This is individual based because each individual has a different mind, body, and spirit complex.

A Growing Flower

When a being is brought into this planet it is at its most pure state. It has not yet been taught the cultural ways of the society it has been born into. As individuals age, they are rewarded for certain actions and so depending on which society or culture you are born into is what you may strive for as success. Every single household will ultimately have its unique view of reality or level of conscious awareness. Each unique view may be considered a fractal or smaller vortex within the greater laminar flow.

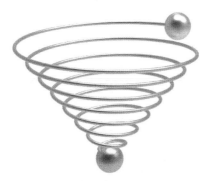

Consider this drawing as a being that has never experienced doubt. Doubt in this sense, would be considered any action in mind, body, or spirit that would have caused the being to shift from their Golden Spot or path. This would be a life of perfect health and quantum manifestations as it drifts inwards gaining higher harmonics of conscious experience.

The previous drawing would represent a being that had never accepted any of the vibratory responses of cultural guidance. They could be considered free of delusion. Let's now add cultural expectations to a being and see how this effects their natural growth or evolution.

Notice the spiraling energy that has "budded" from the growing flower. Each bud or spiral represents a sort of doubt or delusion of some sort. Each represents a conscious experience that has been created by the individual that must be "overcome" in order to return to the Golden Path.

It would require a supercomputer to track all the spiraling motions of every action but for our purposes this will suffice. In the previous drawing, you could say the start of life would be the "Silver Spot" on top. Then, as the being develops, it would naturally follow the Golden Path to center. However, we are constantly bombarded with societal delusions and therefor constantly shifted from our point of zero along the Golden Path. Each shift then requires a pacing back to the zero point before it may continue its journey of conscious evolution and spiritual development.

These spirals may represent various degrees of timescales. It may be possible to create one that relates to a day, another to the week, the month, the year, and a lifetime.

Here we see a spiral that has extended far away from the path to zero. This could be representative of someone dedicating their life to a fractal of institutional delusion such as a Religious, University, or Governmental Institution. These cycles tend to last many years as they are very overwhelming and may solidify postures in mind, body, and spirit.

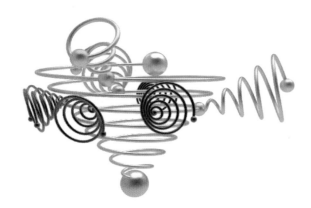

Returning to Zero

Returning to zero may be one of the healthiest actions any being may undergo. This is the act of being perfectly in balance in mind, body, and spirit. You would essentially be riding the laminar flow of the Golden Path. From here, you are balanced. You are stable.

Consider martial arts or any physical activity for that matter, it could even be opening a door. If your footing is not proper you may find that you lose balance or stumble as you pull or push on the door. Martial arts is a great example to use because individuals are performing punches and kicks. The rooting of the individual determines the ease of the maneuver or amount of force which may be transferred. After each move, the martial artist returns to a certain stance, one of power, or one of motion. Each stance is geared towards certain actions. Each returns the individual to a comforted and rooted position.

Now imagine if the martial artist was not properly rooted after each maneuver. For example, they kick and instead of returning to zero accidentally step on a small plastic toy and are now hopping on one foot. It will be very difficult to have any sort of power or strength behind a move stemming from that new position of "rest," hopping in pain.

Golden Connection

I highly stress the importance of creating from zero. Creations stemming from offset bodies in the mind, body, and spirit diagram will be continuously drifting further from zero. This action will not succeed or blossom into anything long-lasting. In order for a creation to be long lasting it must be in flow or in tune with the greatest laminar flows of reality.

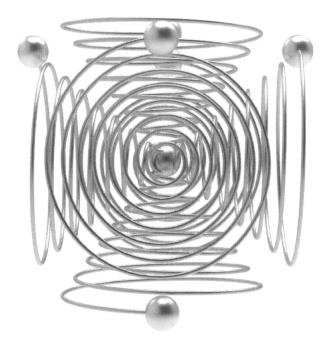

Notice how the image above looks much different than the previous "flower" that did not have experiences stemming from the Golden Spot. This would be considered a rare flower in modern day society and culture but is becoming more commonly seen as awareness of the Golden Spot increases.

Densities of Creation

Knowing our 4D manifestation is a result of motion through a 5D multiverse, we see that our physical experience stems from different densities within the Loosh.

The densest parts of our body, our bones, come from the denser parts of creation. Whereas, our lightest parts of the body, the air we breathe, stems from the less dense orbits of experience. Perhaps that's why we lose breath or stop breathing when we pass. Perhaps that's why our bones exist into the future within our physical plane.

Either way, your energy is being manifested from various densities of experience. Each distance is directly associated with a specific chakra. The highest frequencies would be near the center and lowest would be near the outer edges.

Interdimensional Alignment

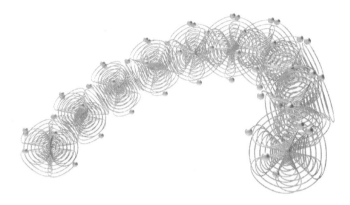

Interdimensional Alignment would be the concept of aligning the self to the greatest flows in reality. It would almost seem like chain formed by perfect flowers that have stemmed from the Golden Spot over several lifetimes. Let's call this a Golden Chain.

In a 6th dimensional view this could be considered a golden wire, similar to an electrical wire used to pass information or electricity in common household applications. In typical household wires, the more solid a wire is, the better it will perform.

You can see in the Golden Chain that the delusions overlap in such a way that energy or information may easily be transferred.

This would be an example of someone who has never achieved their golden spot. The reincarnations do still overlap and information may be passed from one to another. However, it is clearly not as efficient at doing so.

The quantum nature of reality shows us that all lives overlap within the Loosh. This means as you effectively remove delusion from your current life, past and future lives will also be affected.

Seed Crystals

Seed Crystals are commonly used in the fabrication of pure crystals. They are essentially a single grain that has a "perfect" three-dimensional structure which contains the desired structure for the material being "grown."

A very common application of this is in the fabrication of silicon wafers for computer chips. In short, in order to make perfect silicon wafers for computer chips you first start by melting a volume of silicone. Then, while the silicone (sand) is in a liquid state you slowly dip your seed crystal in from above. The seed crystal is not liquid. It is solid and has the shape of the desired formation.

The seed crystal is then slowly raised from the molten silicone and as it does the molten silicone sticks to it and rises with it. As the seed crystal continues to be lifted the molten material begins to solidify.

As the material solidifies it takes a crystal formation. Typical crystals solidifying in the "wild" are exposed to many different physical vibrations and so the crystal does not come out "perfect." However, with the use of a seed crystal and the method described, you may form perfect crystals of any size and of any material. We will return to this.

Cleansing Hitchhikers

Understanding that our mind, body, and spirit distortions create habitats within the Loosh we see that each delusion contains a degree of turbulence to it in relationship to the greater flow or river of time.

Let's now compare this drawing to a river.

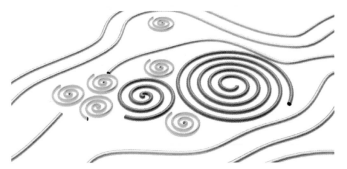

In a river, different animals and beings live in different parts. Some animals live where the water is deeper and some live where it is shallow. Some animals prefer faster moving water and some prefer slower moving water. It is the same within the river of Time. Different beings may inhabit different size vortices. Each of these beings is conscious and aware and wishes to continue to thrive like all animals. They want to reproduce, expand their habitats, and so on.

It may be challenging to see but there are beings that may only survive within doubtful flows of space. When it comes to conscious influencers within Time, they typically will guide you into a karmic loop of their liking. Very rarely is this beneficial for the "host."

The "host" will typically increase in pacing which causes all others connected to increase in pacing. This increases the size of the habitat that this being may inhabit. The 5th dimensional being may now grow even more.

It is important to be aware of what causes the pacing motions in your life. What actually triggered it? Was it a thought? Where did that thought come from? The human is naturally loving and caring. It is negative thoughts that then lead to destructive behaviors.

Remember, we may take posture in all three, mind, body, and spirit. It is possible to cleanse ourselves through posture control. The easiest way to cleanse the self is to connect to the greatest flows of reality. This would imply watching the Sun rise and watching the Sun set.

It is also possible that certain places on the Earth naturally contain habitats for beings of denser and less dense flows of space. These places would typically exist where there would be an expansion or compression of space and time. For example, the magnetic hotspots of Earth may naturally act like "pools" of habitable fields of energy.

Hurricanes in the Loosh

Let's now consider the concept of a hurricane and how it effects the ocean water as it passes. In short, the hurricane is basically an energetic vortex that moves along the Earth. The main driver of the hurricane is pressure differences.

This causes massive distortions on the surface of the ocean. It causes sea levels to rise and to flow onto the land causing destruction. The important point here is that the "height" of the water depends directly on the pressure differences created by the hurricane. The same effect is true for a tornado however the pressure is so high that the water will be sucked through the vortex in the center.

When you relate this to the mind, body, and spirit distortions created by pacing you see that each pacing also creates a certain amount of pressure within the fluid of experience. It would be a very similar bulge as to what a hurricane or tornado does as it passes over land or water. This shows that the "height" of the habitat depends directly on the intensity and duration of the cycle size.

It is somewhat reversed when it comes to perception. In a way, you can think of them as holes that are being created. This goes back to the concept of the "line of sight." If you are in a deep valley or hole, you cannot see very far. However, as you remove delusion and equalize your "tornado" with the natural flow of reality you may see you are now standing on top of a mountain, able to overlook and peer into the delusions of others. From this position, we may now offer a helping hand and pull others out of their holes or spirals of delusion.

Great Cycles in Relationship to Orbiting Universes

There are many orbits within the Loosh that may offer habitats to conscious beings. When we look at the relationship of our experience to the nearest habitable zones, we see that time dilations exist. Zones towards the Noviverse would be experiencing more time and zones towards the Lowerverse would be experiencing less time. Considering experiences are becoming denser we see that the Lowerverse side could be considered beings from the past, or of a purer nature.

The time dilation chart shown earlier depicted the alignments as we go inward. Every second we align with inner rings. When it comes to aligning with outer rings, this happens much less regular. For one second that passes in the next outer ring, 1 hour and 1 minute would pass in our experience. The next alignment would happen every 185 days. The alignment that we are currently undergoing is one that occurs roughly every 2029 years. The last great cycle could be related to the Age of the Pisces, or the coming of Jesus. Pure speculation, but the star of David may have been created by a temporary alignment of orbiting universes from the Lowerverse direction. We are now entering the Age of Aquarius.

To relate this to religion, God could be considered the greatest laminar flow of our entire experience or creation. Although we are all children or fractals of the flow, there are times when the most undisturbed and purest energy may fill our perspective. During these great alignments, reincarnating beings may return to reseed or fertilize the planet once more. These seeds then perform their purpose.

Cluster Origins (From "Time Atom" Pgs. 25 and 26)

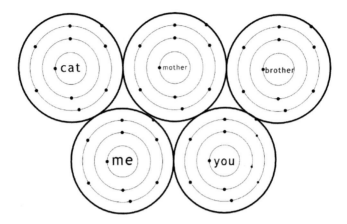

Figure 122: Is a simple example of how contact between atoms may relate directly to the level of quantum entanglement.

Not all conscious crystals in Time are in direct contact with each other. This creates clusters of conscious cocreation. A simple example may be a family. Imagine a father, a mother, a son, a daughter, and maybe a cat or dog. They may have their own coconscious reality that is then exchanged via a metallic bonding of sorts with other conscious crystals. This would translate directly into the types of "cliques" or gangs that exist in the human population. We are all humans that live on Earth, and so you would assume we have the same goals and general constructs of reality. However, in practice they are much different. They are almost of their own cocreated consciousnesses or grains of Time.

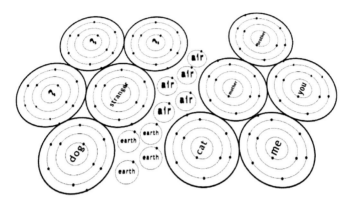

Figure 123: This image represents two grains or clusters of Time separated by a fissure or crack.

You can see with this simple representation how the two individual grains may experience different viewpoints on cultural issues. There has not been enough exchange of universes for them to be properly tuned to each other. The more time between sharing universes, the more different the cultures of coconscious creations become. However, once direct covalent bonds have been made it is likely the individual experiences, viewpoints, or rather expectations will merge.

Grains within Crystals

Let's now go back and consider the concept of seed crystals in relationship to making desired crystals of any type. In order for a crystal to properly take shape of the seed it must first be melted. For example, when relating to the silicone wafers, grains of silicone that are not fully melted will not be able to take the shape of the seed crystal as it rises from the batch of liquid sand. This would be considered an imperfection or unusable section of the wafer. Unusable material typically will be melted down again and used during the process of forming the next crystal.

Molten Distortions

Considering we are all composed of mind, body, and spirit, and understanding how postures of all three may solidify, we see that maintained experiences within fractals of delusion may cause our postures to solidify.

Understanding this and knowing we are somewhat born into fractals of delusion, we see that a liquifying of all selves is somewhat necessary in order to take a more "pure" vibration or crystal within the fluid of Time.

It is important that the crystal of consciousness reorganize itself periodically so that denser harmonics of conscious evolution may continue to exist. If the crystal becomes too granular then there is not enough stability or laminar flow within the fluid of experience in order for denser beings to evolve or exist.

The smaller the "grains of consciousness" are, the more turbulent the fluid of time becomes. Therefor there is a direct relationship with conscious grain size and conscious types that may exist. Grain size relates directly to tortuosity, so therefor the largest most stabile crystals will have the greatest laminar flows and most intelligent beings.

Grain Size in Relationship to Cooling Rates

There is also a direct relationship to grain size and the rate the material is cooled after becoming liquified. The quicker the material crystalizes the smaller the grains become. Molten material that cools over long periods of time form the largest grains of any material.

Fluid Perceptions

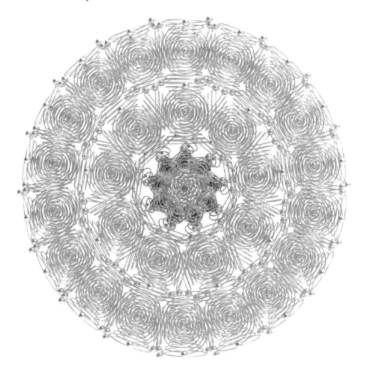

When you consider a molten mind, body, and spirit diagram versus one that has taken postures and solidified you see that much friction may exist. All beings rise in conscious density as our experience drifts inward and so a liquification is somewhat necessary in order for beings of higher density to continue to exist.

Current State of Society (Dec 21, 2021)

Over the last few years, potentially starting on Dec, 21, 2012, we have seen a liquifying of perceptions. It may have first started with an economic crisis. Soon after that, power struggles between political parties rose and with the use of media more and more separation has occurred.

The next "dissolver" of delusion may be considered the Covid 19 outbreak. This began towards the end of the year 2019. This forced every single person on the planet to completely change their lifestyles. Subconsciously, we have all been challenged to say the least.

People were told that they were "not essential" by media. They were told to follow the "social norm" of the leading manipulators (media) point of view. People went from feeling they had value to being called non-essential. People have also been locked into their homes and somewhat separated. Considering the advent of digital communications and switching of actions being done in person to actions being done online we see that physical connectivity has diminished. We have also seen rises in movements of equality.

When considering all of the above societal actions we see that a liquification of delusions has been occurring. The most recent release being that of the world governments admitting to the human population that UAP do exist.

A quick side, the fact that the world governments needed to tell people what to think to begin with shows the delusional state our Earthly population has existed within. Every day for years, people tell their neighbors of accounts of UAP and etc. Yet, the neighbors fail to believe because the mainstream thinking which has been prorogated through media and social shaming said they don't exist. It is important that people become in tune with the greatest flows of reality so that they may remove themselves from the delusions of others. The connection should be direct, you to the Universe, not you, government, then Universe.

Therefor, you may now understand how the collective mind, body, and spirit state of the human population has become "molten."

A New Manifestation Awaits

Let's now relate a seed crystal being dipped into a liquid batch of silicone to a Golden Chain being dipped into a batch of molten mind, body, and spirit distortions.

As the seed crystal within the silicone is pulled up, the rest of the liquid batch sticks and rises with it.

As the Golden Chain is lowered into the batch of molten distortions you see a crystallization of distortions takes place. This may be considered a converging moment within our 5D multiverse of potentiality. All potential timelines will converge.

Diverging and Converging Timelines in Relationship to 2012 - 2029. (Speculation)

There are many bodies, referring to universes, orbiting within the raw energy of experience. Each body has a push and pull on the ones next to it when looking from a 6th dimensional view. You could say it would be very similar as to how planets within our Solar System push and pull on each other as they pass one another.

For example, as Jupiter passes by the Earth in its closest orbit, it literally tugs on the planet and the Earth then drifts slightly away from the Sun. As Jupiter passes, the Earth then paces back to its original orbit as it finds it's new zero.

There is a dimensional alignment, somewhat of a syzygy of the 4 closest habitable zones every 2029 years. The next great cycle is related to 8.1 million years.

This shows that as the alignment approaches that our experience of the Universe will be pulled out of its typical laminar flow. It will literally orbit in a slightly less dense realm of experience. This tugging on our experience would translate into a turbulent flow as our experience paces back to its typical orbit within the fluid of time. It could almost be like a rock splashing water causing a divergent moment of timelines in relationship to the fluid of time. Then, the water that has splashed up in the bucket eventually settles and once again fills a certain space and makes a certain shape.

The resettling of the fluid of time would be symbolic of the converging of all splashed timelines. Our experience will once again orbit in its typical flow.

Relating this to our manifested experiences you could say that the moment of Dec 21, 2012 would be considered the moment our Universe was tugged outward. It has fallen back into the laminar flow as of March 21, 2021. On June 21, 2029 (also potentially 12/21/2029) our experience of the Universe will have drifted to maximum inwardness. Considering the concept of jumping shells within habitable zones of experience, this would be a day to remember.

Awakening Modern Science and Religion

The greatest shifts that may be seen will be in relationship to religious and scientific views. We will once again see how our science has been completely backwards.

Health of the body starts within your quantum manifestation of the mind, body and spirit complex. The use of pills to suppress symptoms will become obsolete as true healing begins to occur.

We will also see a much greater reality as our awareness of the 5D multiverse allows us to create technologies to travel through the various densities of experience. In the dimension of conscious density, we are literally inches from the star.

Religious Institutions

This new understanding of our reality in combination with the seed crystal that may be coming will not conflict with any religious views. In fact, it may actually solidify and cause a pacing within religious institutions as well. Remember, religious and customary methods have never intentionally meant to be destructive. It is over many generations that messages and true meanings become lost. Has there really ever been a difference between the great teachings stemming from religious figures such a Jesus and the Buddha? Don't they all basically say the same thing? Don't they all say unconditional love and forgiveness is key?

It is by the creation of infrastructures that we have lost our purpose in that regard. Remember, just like the governments needing to tell the human population that UAP are real is the same as needing a religious infrastructure to be connected with the greatest laminar flows of reality. The connection is direct. It is you to the 5D multiverse. It is not you, religious institute or accepted scientific view, then Universe.

You are the direct connection to the greatest flow.

The Age of Aquarius

You may now see how a single solid crystal of mind, body, and spirit may cause the rise in consciousness of a once entirely melted collective.

Mankind has had the technology to travel to the Moon and beyond for about a century. However, it is important that all three, mind, body, and spirit rise together.

This new spirit will be one that combines both the modern benefits of societal structures with our prehistoric method of mate selection. With our new ability of compassion and understanding for how we influence the denser experiences of creation, we may be better suited for exploring these once unforeseen realms.

"Our Harmony determines our Potentiality"

-Alexei Novitzky

We are all One.

www.LooshesLabs.com   12/22/21

Mind Body Spirit

Alexei Novitzky

"Mind, Body, & Spirit"

What is it that makes reality?

"Mind: The Shifter and Reorganizer of Nodes" discusses how the various conscious states influence the natural drifting of energy as it follows along the habitable spiral of perception. We see our consciousness is like a gyroscope hanging on a string at a 90-degree angle. We see perception orbits the center of time. (pgs. 3-47)

"Body: The Mind's Spaceship" shows us how matter, light, sound, and magnetism all emerge from the primal vortex of creation as we orbit the center of all moments. We see how our inertial reference frame creates perceivable layers of information all relative to your current position. Do we align consciousness to our bodies or do we align our bodies to consciousness? (pgs. 48-91)

"Spirit: The Vortex of Creation" shows how all motions are guided by the primary vortex of creation as they are all tidally locked fluids. Local spheres of influence guide the circadian rhythm of the human, the precessional cycle of the Earth, all the way down to the creation of atomic structures. (pgs. 92-128)

Mind

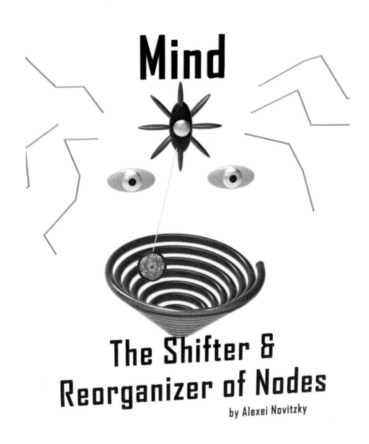

The Shifter &
Reorganizer of Nodes
by Alexei Novitzky

The Table of Contents

Introduction:

What is matter and what is light? Are they not the same energy being perceived in two different ways all created by a single motion?

"Mind: The Shifter and Reorganizer of Nodes" theoretically discusses how our mind's various states influence the natural drifting of energy as it follows along the Habitable Spiral of Perception.

There is only now and the now moment is created by one-half past and one-half future all existing within the Vortex of Time. Consciously, they become layered on top of each other to give us the smooth and easy experience we share.

Through Space Preparation we see the true shape and nature of our reality. Following the circadian rhythm along our daily orbit through conscious density and you see it is tuned to various harmonics depending on the time of day as it mimics a gyroscope hanging on a string at a 90-degree angle. However, it is all in the now.

Our wants, don't wants, assumptions, and expectations are in constant vibration working the fluid to best synchronize with our projections. It is the synchronization of all beings in the light-state that ultimately create our motion and manifested experience.

The Vortex of Time

All aspects of creation are in a state of motion and in a state of orbit. It is the nature of our existence. The human body orbits the center of the Earth. The Earth orbits the center of the Sun. The Sun orbits the center of a Galaxy. All those structures orbit the center of all Time with many steps between our universal system and the next. However, there is a greatest center of all moments.

Our physical experience is directly related to that greatest inertial reference frame. Considering we are human; information exchange is controlled by a factor of the speed of light outward and one time the speed of light inward. We cannot see past the smooth cosmic microwave background and we cannot see into black holes.

This is all somewhat illusionary because there is a perception interacting with a field of energy. Einstein's theory of Relativity shows us that time dilations and Lorentz contractions ultimately give us the stretching and crunching of a singular fluid to create all experiences.

It is all relative, which Universe you will experience and which energy may manifest. It is the relative crunching and stretching of a singular fluid that creates your current position and line of sight.

A Liquid-Light Sate Prediction

Speed of Light in 1/60 of a second

$\sim 1 \times 10^7$ diameter sphere

in the conscious now

(meters)

In "The Liquid-Light State Universe," we calculated a theoretical size for consciousness. There is always a starting point and so we start here.

How big is our consciousness in the now relative to our experience? Let's first examine our physical manifestation and the 5th dimensional vortex after.

Perception is based off frame rate and the human brain takes a picture of reality roughly 60 times in a second. The speed of light is approximately 3x10^8 m/s. This means that light from your physical body travels 5x10^6 meters per conscious snapshot. Let's call this the radius of the conscious now. When you multiply that by two you get 1x10^7 meters. This implies that the longest standing wave that may exist within our conscious snapshot is 1x10^7 meters.

"Time Atom" Prediction

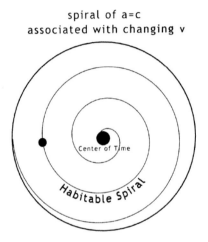

spiral of a=c
associated with changing v

"The Crystal of Time" shows us that matter and light are first differentiated when acceleration is equal to the speed of light. This is what creates the "Habitable Spiral of Perception." It is a harmonic relationship of energy orbiting a black hole determined by $a=v^2/r$. Acceleration (a) is equal to the speed of light and so the equation may read $c=v^2/r$. Our brains act like an antenna picking up information based on our maximum conscious harmonic.

Every point in our 3-dimensional space has a unique light-state. Meaning, each point has different incoming and outgoing energy and may be seen as the center of a black hole. Essentially, every point in space and time has a unique sphere of orbiting energy that creates it.

"Time Atom" puts you in the center of time and shows how your perceived experience or dimension is a direct relationship to the incoming energies that orbit you and the conscious harmonic of your mind.

You could say in a physical sense that our consciousness is created by waves consisting of delta to fast gamma. Each of those vibrations would then be tuned to a specific orbital rate and distance.

For example, at 1.2 Hz, the delta wave may be considered the longest wave in our experience. When you consider orbital motion of the 5th dimension consisting of light speed acceleration towards center, you see that each conscious harmonic manifest or interacts rather with a specific field of energy. This is what gives us the Table of Universes and implies our next conscious harmonic will be related to a frequency of 100-220 Hz centered around 160 Hz and 320 Hz to follow.

Astronomical Significance

deltaverse may exist in a cloud
that orbits our center of time at a radius of

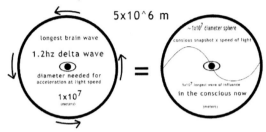

5x10^6 m

Take a moment to really look at what this may imply. We only perceive the now moment which is a creation of scaled waveforms as matter is being crunched in from the fluid and light stretched away. Our physical is illusionary in that nature.

The Still Pencil

In a physical sense, the pencil sitting still on the table is not moving. All we are seeing is the physical now. It is not the true past of the energy creating it or the true future of that flow. In a real sense, it is being manifested, blipping in and out of solidity at scales related to the plank second. It is a focusing, an emitting, and is a curling of fluid as it continues to drift inward. It is in a state of constant manifestation from scaled waveforms that pass through and continue onward.

The Table of Universes

Understanding that each harmonic is ultimately controlled by an orbit of the 5th dimension we may now create a table of perceivable Universes and theorize on other energies or flows which may offer us a conscious experience.

Table of Universes

Universe	Brain Wave	hz Frequency	hz Harmonic Frequency	m Cloud Diameter
Deltaverse	delta	1-3	2.5	2.4x10^6
Thetaverse	theta	4-8	5	6x10^5
Aplhaverse	aplha	9-13	10	1.5x10^5
Betaverse	beta	14-30	20	40,000
Slow Gammaverse	slow-gamma	30-49	40	10,000
Fast Gammaverse	fast-gamma	50-100	80	2,500
Aleverse	omega	101-220	160	625
Dimiverse	zeta	221-400	320	156.25

This also offers us insight into the total field of perceivable experiences for human conscious.

Remember, they are all related to 2^n for the Noviverse direction which would be considered denser and $1/2^n$ for the Lowerverse direction which is less dense. One thing to note, is that humans have a prime multiplier of 2 related to orbits within time. It may be possible that other complete conscious sets exist such as 3^n, 5^n and so on. These fields would require an extra bit of technology to properly harmonize. Either way, there exist more dense and less dense realms of creation in which we may harmonize.

Table of Universes

	Universe	Brain Wave	hz Frequency	hz Harmonic Frequency	m Cloud Diameter
	Deltaverse	delta	1-3	2.5	2.4×10^6
	Thetaverse	theta	4-8	5	6×10^5
	Aplhaverse	aplha	9-13	10	1.5×10^5
	Betaverse	beta	14-30	20	40,000
	Slow Gammaverse	slow-gamma	30-49	40	10,000
	Fast Gammaverse	fast-gamma	50-100	80	2,500
	Aleverse	omega	101-220	160	625
	Dimiverse	zeta	221-400	320	156.25
	Stellaverse	epsilon	401-800	640	39
	Petraverse	omicron	801-1600	1280	9.75
	Mikaverse	iota	1601-3400	2560	2.4

However, how does our conscious now effect the manifesting and manifested realms? How do our postures of mind, body, and spirit influence the past, present, and future?

Where do we Exist?

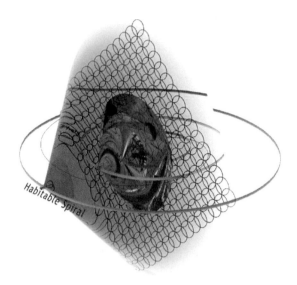

Habitable Spiral

From our perception, the physical body clearly exist within our dimension. However, when you consider your body throughout all of time, you see that your physical body is a manifestation of less dense and more dense realms overlapping to create a now moment. It is like the still pencil being manifested into the current position.

When looking at this from above, you could be a string of energy that starts from the most outer regions of the Lowerverse and spiraling inward into our waking Universe and then continuing onward towards the center of time.

Amplitude and Frequency of Thought Forms (From "The Liquid-Light State Universe")

There are many types of thought forms and for reasons here we will break it down to wants, don't wants, assumptions, and expectations. The "in the moment" short pacing, for example, getting a glass of water, a kind of "I'll just do this really quick," kind of thought would have a higher frequency when compared to a subconscious thought form relating to assumption and expectation about the general nature of reality.

This is easiest to see by looking at the theory or concept of Space Preparation. As the now manifest from the light-state, there is the crunching effect of the electromagnetic wave. It shows that the future of the light-state exists in extremely long wave form. The now exist in the state of matter. The light-state just before the now is composed of very short waves but not yet manifested.

The easy-user interface of the mind, body, and spirit is the shifter or reorganizer of nodes. The wants of the now work with the waves that are closer to being manifest. These would be of a very high frequency almost that of matter. The assumptions and expectations of a lifetime work in the longest of wavelengths. They start reorganizing the light-state from the greatest reaches of our consciousness.

A Daily Orbit (From "The 5ᵗʰ Dimension")

Throughout our day our bodies naturally follow the rising and setting of the Sun, this includes our conscious harmonics. This cycle is known as the circadian rhythm.

Let us now map our daily orbit around the center of time so we may gain more insight onto the nature of reality.

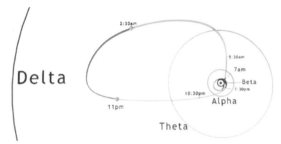

Here is a very simple schedule that outlines the maximum conscious harmonic in relationship to time of day. Let's start from the moment we enter our Deltaverse. A circadian rhythm properly tuned to nature will follow as so. From approximately 11:30 pm to 2:30 am our primary conscious harmonic is the delta wave. From 2:30 am to about 5:30 am we are in theta waves. Then, from 5:30 am to 7 am we are in alpha waves. Throughout the day, from 7 am to 7:30 pm we flux from beta to alpha but are primarily in beta. As we start to wind down, our conscious harmonics start to slow. From 7:30 pm to about 10:30 pm we are in alpha. Then, from 10:30 pm to 11 pm we drop back down into theta.

The Deltaverse (Delta Wave)

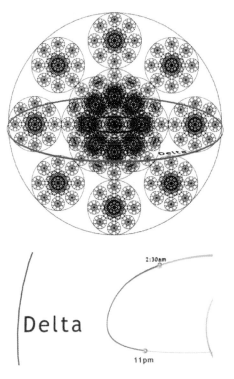

Starting from midnight we see that our primary conscious harmonic is the delta wave. As morning approaches, our consciousness enters the halfway point between harmonizing with the delta wave versus the theta wave. At this moment, approximately 2:30 am and at a radius of 6x10^5 meters, is when our antenna switches to the theta state.

The Thetaverse (Theta Wave)

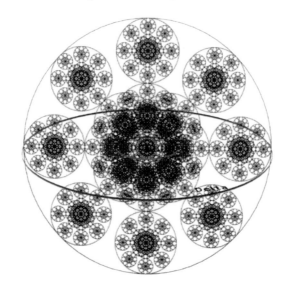

2:30am

5:30am

As conscious tuning follows its natural orbit, it accelerates towards the center of time. At approximately 5:30 am at a distance of 1.5x10^5 meters, our orbit falls into the halfway point between theta and alpha. This is the moment when our antenna switches from theta to alpha.

The Alphaverse (Alpha Wave)

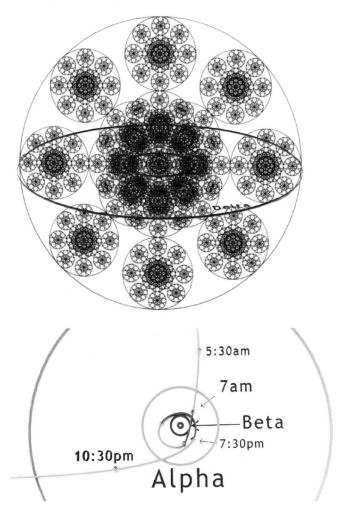

Soon after, at approximately 7 am, our conscious density then reaches the beta state which occurs at 37,500 meters from center.

The Betaverse (Beta Wave)

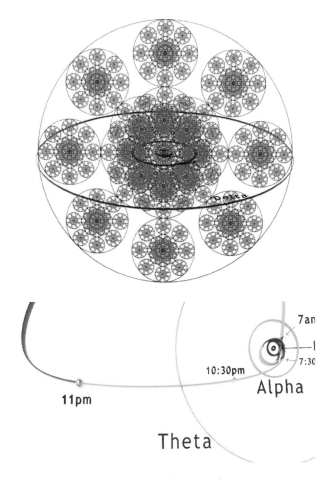

It seems for the next 12 hours, from 7 am to 7:30 pm, we are in a tight elliptical orbit that passes us through beta and alpha several times throughout the day. Then, at approximately 7:30 pm, it is as if we have a gravitational slingshot towards the outer edge.

This causes us to pass through theta state rather quick as we once again enter the delta range. Our orbit then starts again. It is also possible our conscious antenna orbits along the boundary line between alpha and beta and that actions that require more cognitive capability are what trigger the switching between alpha and beta throughout the day.

The Habitable Spiral of Perception

Considering our now moment in the wake state is a result of inward drifting energy in combination with our alpha and beta state you'd see that before energy interacts with our awake state it first interacts with all of the realms of the Lowerverse. The first conscious harmonic to interact with the fluid would be your delta wave. The second harmonic that may interact would be the theta.

Tidal Locking of Conscious Spheres

All energy that creates the body is synchronized in such a fashion to manifest. When you consider the natural manifestation of consciousness it seems to follow an orbit related to the precession of a gyroscope hanging on a string at a 90-degree angle. In essence, our perception is being dipped into a fluid and then undergoes precession as the fluid spirals through.

All orbits have influence on our experience. The pulls and pushes of the Noviverse realm are also apparent and we will speak on this in a later section. For now, let's stay focused on our typical conscious modes which are delta, theta, alpha, and beta.

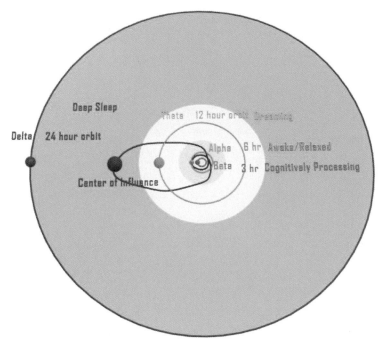

This shows that the 2.5 Hz rotation of the delta wave may be related to a 24-hour orbit within this fluid. The 5 Hz of the theta may be related to a 12-hour orbit. The 10 Hz of alpha would relate to a 6-hour orbit and beta would be related to a 3-hour orbit.

When you map the orbits of these 5th dimensional spheres you notice something peculiar. It seems as if our "center of influence" is related to the "center of mass" of these 5th dimensional spheres.

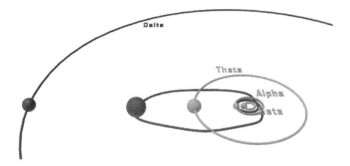

For example, starting at midnight you could say all the spheres are on the left side of this image. Then, throughout the day, the spheres all orbit at their tidally locked rates.

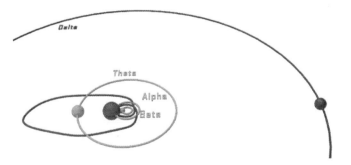

What you notice is that the only difference between midnight and noon is the sphere related to the delta wave.

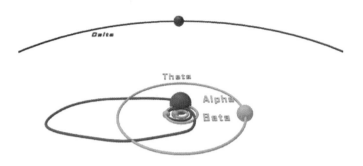

The only difference between 6 am and 6 pm is again the sphere related to the delta wave. This basically shows that our entire conscious experience is somewhat related to the orbiting of these 5th dimensional tidally locked spheres and that they cause our gyroscopic precession.

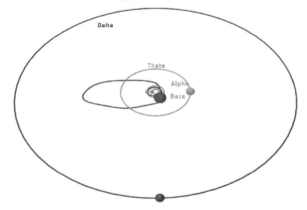

When you expand this outward and inward to include the dimensions of the Lowerverse and Noviverse, you see that more alignments exist within this tidally locked fluid. Great precessions related to dimensional alignments emerge.

Dimensional Alignments

What does this even mean? What is a dimensional alignment? Following the Circadian Rhythm, we see that conscious perception is somewhat guided by the orbiting of 6 spheres that are tidally locked within the 5th dimension. This is literally just our perception within Time. It is the tuning of energy to the human body which may be considered the mind's spaceship.

Our biggest orbit of experience is related to the delta wave which either has a 1 Hz processing speed or 1 day when relating to the vortex. Considering it's all harmonic ratios and human perception exist within delta to fast gamma we see that humans gather information from 6 harmonics of experience. Fast gamma may be our first step into the afterlife or denser realms.

When relating to our physical universe, we can say that delta and theta are dreamland or the past. alpha and beta is wake state, and that slow and fast gamma is towards the afterlife of future state of the greater now.

In order to be in a shifted dimension with slight overlap you'd either need to have your delta state shifted inward to the fast gamma towards the

Noviverse direction or fast gamma would need to be shifted outward to the Lowerverse.

For a dimension of the Noviverse being related to our Universe, we could say that a 2.5 Hz delta wave would relate to the 80 Hz wave of a being in a completely shifted dimension. The 5 Hz alpha wave would relate to a 160 Hz field. Each of these is related to a timescale of orbit. This is considering only brain wave activity. The alpha and beta state would then be 320 Hz and 640 Hz.

When you consider orbits of the fluid in the 5th dimension, delta relates to a 24-hour orbit. theta a 12-hour orbit, alpha a 6-hour, beta a 3-hour, slow gamma a 90-minute, fast gamma a 45 minute and so on. This shows that in the denser realms of the Noviverse that the 640 Hz conscious harmonic would then be related to a 337 second orbit. All of those inward experiences would align daily.

However, considering we are concerned with perceived experience it may make more sense to approximate dimensional relationships of time dilations and Lorentz contractions based off relative size and orbital rate.

For example, the delta wave of 2.5 hz has a diameter of 2.4 x 10^6 meters. The slow gamma wave of 40 Hz has a diameter of 10,000 meters. Here we see a difference in size of 240 times with a difference in rotation of 16 times. When you put the two together you get 3,840. However, it is a rough estimate and on the other side of the spectrum you get 4,096 times. A safe number to use for the time dilation factor between dimensions relating to 5 harmonic shifts would be 4,000 to 1.

You can now see how dimensional alignments emerge. This time dilation chart between dimensions would be related to 5 dimensional shifts, referring to dimensional shifts of perception. For example, one dimensional shift would relate to the time dilation between our 2.5 hz delta to the 40 hz slow gamma.

# of shifts	Dilation Factor per Second
0	1 second
1	1 hour
2	185 days
3	2029 years
4	8.1 million years
5	32 billion years
6	130 trillion years

The amount of time dilation between one harmonic would be 8 times and this is related to the diameter being 4 times as small while having the orbital frequency being twice as much.

Golden Alignment

Why even discuss fields of energy outside our perception? What does that have to do with our daily routine and the choices we make?

Synchronization of the light-state starts from the greatest reaches of our experience. We are a spiral of energy that is constantly drifting inward towards the center of Time.

"The Physics of Love: Synchronicity" shows that our natural manifestation is the end result of the synchronization of all the realms of the Lowerverse. Aligning with this flow is key for connecting to the universal mind and influencing denser realms of creation.

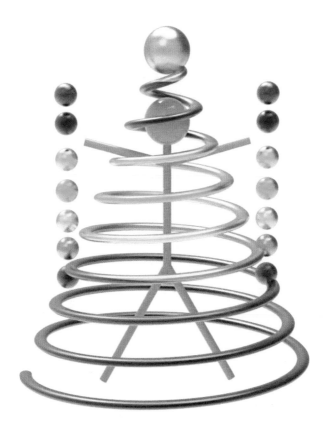

Creations stemming from offset bodies will not last in time. They will be continuously drifting further and further from the Golden Spot causing the laminar flow of your creation to become turbulent. It will increase the amount of pacing you ultimately undergo.

Consider water coming from a faucet in a smooth continuous flow. That could be considered the natural energy of creation. You could say you have the full strength of the laminar flow on your side when you work with it. Forcing a will or want that is not in your flow is like trying to fill a cup that is not underneath the faucet and attempting to fill it by splashing the water sideways with your hands.

What is one to do when the cup is not under the faucet and yet that is the one you want filled? You can either move the cup, or you can move the faucet. However, it is important to understand that this will not last as the projections of the Lowerverse will constantly be fighting you. Call this the intuition of the heart or our greatest sense, that of synchronicity.

Prayer

How might these concepts relate to modern day prayer and religions? Have we just theoretically discovered the foundations of prayer and how it may work?

Let's discuss what prayer might be considered and then discuss the greater picture involved. Prayer, in the simplest terms might be considered like asking God for something, maybe something physical or mental like guidance. It's a sort of way to connect consciously to God and to help others, help you forgive, and ultimately tends to create more love and harmony in your life.

Let's now consider the natural synchronization of the Lowerverse realms, the habitable spiral of perception, the circadian rhythm of the human, and the denser realms of the Noviverse.

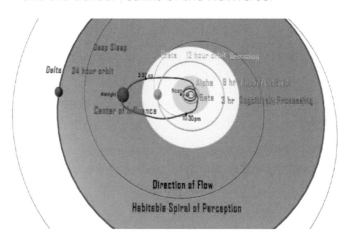

Let's start with our awake state and how that relates to our Universe. Our awake state is primarily focused within alpha and beta waves of conscious activity. While in awake state our conscious minds dominate our cognitive process while the subconscious or universal mind may be whispering.

The actions we make are in our physical realm. We may move objects and perform almost limitless actions within this space. However, we can really only go so far based on the spirit potentials that exist. Actions that pace too far from the laminar flow of your creation will cause you to spiral into delusions as they become disconnected from the laminar flow or faucet of creation.

Lowerverse Connections

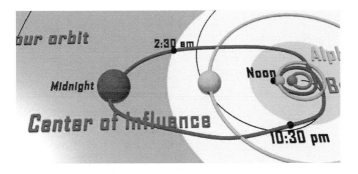

From the circadian rhythm, we see that we first encounter the theta wave type at 10:30 pm. We then enter the delta range at approximately 11 pm and then reenter the theta range at about 2:30 am. This shows that our point of most submersion into the Lowerverse is at about 12:45 am. Let's consider this a turning point in our conscious orbit. Is there a difference when moving into the Lowerverse versus moving out of it?

Orbiting Towards the Lowerverse

What we see from our gyroscopic precession is that after about 4 pm we are headed back towards the Lowerverse. This is the moment when we first start migrating back towards the purest realms of creation. It's important to understand that starting new activities at this time is not ideal and it may be better to be ending the daily routine at this point.

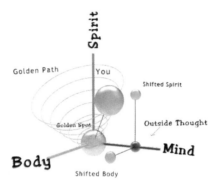

In an energetic sense, what are we doing? Energy is constantly spiraling inward towards denser creations so this time of day may be seen as swimming up river or against the wind. How does that translate into experience?

When riding a bicycle into the wind it is best to tuck to avoid drag. This drag may be related to the synchronization of our daily egos to the true you that exist without delusion. Considering our natural orbit is related to the focusing of experiences and we see that holding delusions will cause you to misalign with your incoming flow.

When relating to communication with beings of less dense realms, you see that this is when it's time to listen.

Orbiting Towards the Noviverse

After 12:45 am you could say that we transition from orbiting towards the Lowerverse to orbiting towards the Noviverse. At this point, you could say we are going with the wind.

Consider a gust of wind or wave in the ocean. Each gust or wave could be considered like a thought emerging from the Lowerverse. This is almost when it is best to ask for what you want.

Imagine surfing against the waves in an ocean. You really can't do it. While surfers paddle out, they almost do their best to avoid being caught. However, when going with the waves, the surfer can perform various maneuvers. They can cut up, cut down, do a hang ten, and any other move they choose all under one condition. They need to work with the wave that is coming and understand the limits of their experience as a surfer.

Only the most experience surfers catch the biggest waves on the planet. In the same sense, those waves have the ability to do much damage if you do not ride them all the way to the end.

In short, before bed it may actually be more beneficial to listen rather than to ask and project. When moving forward in the morning may be a better time to ask and guide the creation of your experience.

Sleep

When we sleep, our egos are somewhat removed. This may allow for the natural synchronization of energy to work more efficiently. Perhaps this is a key to the relationship between sleep and rejuvenation.

When we are awake, our postures of mind, body, and spirit may somewhat be controlled by the daily deeds of life. This implies going along with the delusions you have been born into along with the ones you may have picked up during your life's journey. Many of these actions are not natural to the Universe and are a result of societal expectations. They become compounded on top of each other and somewhat layered like the layers of an onion.

We are all fundamentally made of the same fluid of experience as every other bit of physical matter within our dimension. The true you in this sense may be the you that exist without delusions.

It is a perfect flow of laminar fluid that stems from the Lowerverse and drifts inward through wake state and continues all the way to the Noviverse.

The curling of this fluid is what creates your body. It is the curling of fluid as it drifts inwards. Holding postures creates turbulent flows around the center of your manifestation. When we sleep, our awake egos somewhat dissolve and the subconscious mind takes over. Lucid dreaming may be a partial exception of this.

The Subconscious Ego

The subconscious mind or universal mind is somewhat separated from the wake mind however they all work in harmony to create your experience. For purposes here, the subconscious mind may be more related to the assumptions and expectations that are not present in the cognitive process when it comes to perceiving experiences, associations, and actions we make.

Sometimes actions that required much training make their way to the subconscious. A good example is in martial arts. After a certain point, one does not focus so much on how they stand, how they kick, or how they defend. Those actions have become second nature through focused practice and intent.

The ability to speak may also be considered somewhat subconscious. Yes, we take several years to speak, but once you know the language and it becomes second hand nature, you no longer need to practice. The same is true for walking and riding a bicycle. Hence the saying "It's like riding a bike."

Almost all aspects of thought become categorized in a subconscious mind. Categorizations limit one's ability to make greater connections.

Tree Branches of Knowledge

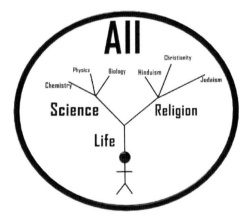

Information may attach itself to tree branches of knowledge and so concepts and ideologies become inseparable to the cognitive mind. At the same time, other concepts grow further and further from each other to the point where there is no overlap.

A quick example of items or flows becoming attached could be getting to work. Depending on your typical method of travel the idea alone of getting to work involves a car, traffic, buying gas, and etc. There are millions of ways to get to work. You could walk, jog, ride a bicycle, and even fly a helicopter. Once the process has become routine it becomes solidified.

Programmed Subconscious

Therefore, you may see how all of our minds become subconsciously programmed through our daily experiences. This is primarily the result of media, propaganda, and cultural expectations.

Be aware of marketing and media you watch. Modern society is geared towards control and making money and so most of everything you see being projected by another is simply an attempt to market and make money. They are not really true to the natural flow of creation. For example, people become attached to logos and brands because of this. They might even prefer an inferior product. Marketing may be one of the most dangerous inventions in modern society. It has the ability to make you feel as if you do not have value or on the other hand may make you feel as if you are more valuable than the person next to you. This ultimately leads to societies becoming completely out of tune with reality.

For example, it really doesn't make any sense for everyone to have perfect grass in their yards. In short, if we all had gardens that produced food the world would be a little different. Expand that thinking to all other aspects of society and you see that most societies are not sustainable. Yet, we are guided to believe this is success.

What does this have to do with dreaming and projected futures? Our dream state, somewhat guided by the subconscious, is constantly working the fluid of the less dense realms of the Lowerverse. Awareness of your subconscious assumptions and expectations is key for returning to zero and guiding the flow of your creation.

Assumptions and Expectations

Our assumptions and expectations start reorganizing the light-state from the greatest reaches of our influence. It is a synchronization of thoughts and wills that have been projected from a Lowerverse realm that then interact with ours. As we turn to dreamland, referring to the theta and delta brain waves, these need to pack properly with the incoming energy. This is the moment when we begin to dream.

It is almost as if our subconscious minds create the fabric of this dreamland and that the subconscious ways take charge. Meaning, like a trained martial artist that has learned to instinctually avoid kicks and punches, the actions you make in dreams are not consciously controlled. It is almost like an autopilot may have been turned on.

This is the time when you have most effect on the incoming flow of creation and therein lies the importance of proper subconscious trainings.

Training the Subconscious

Training the subconscious mind to let go of preconceived notions and reprogramming for desired results is possible. Like learning a new style of martial arts, you must first become aware of your footing. In this case, referring to the root of the thought process. Once the root of the thought is consciously perceived it is possible to retrain the mind to see possibilities in another way. If not lucid, the subconscious mind will guide your dreams.

"The Physics of Love: Synchronicity" shows how postures may solidify when maintained in a delusion. For example, if you are always "late" that will become solidified into the subconscious. Take a deep look at the self. Why am I always "late." What is the root of it? Once identified, take logical steps to change the thought process to a more "I'll be late if I do this." This also gives insight into fractals of potentiality based on the choices we make and increase your overall level of awareness.

Lucid Dreaming

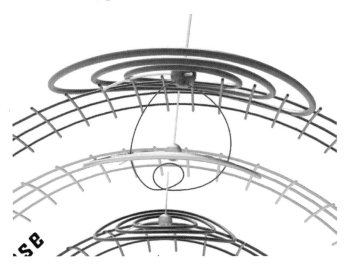

Lucid dreaming is the ability to be awake in your dream. It is the ability to control all aspects such as location, characters, and more. You can literally fly with no technology and visit places you've never been. There are many degrees to the lucidity of the dream. The most advanced practitioners may find solutions to problems and true learning may occur too.

There are many practices for lucid dreaming. A key aspect is having your energy properly harmonize into dreamland. The closer you are to your golden spot, the more lucid your dreams will become. The more lucid your dreams are, the more power you will have to influence the natural drifting of energy along the Habitable Spiral of Perception. In short, you want to be in the faucet of creation when heading into dreamland. If not, your awake mind will turn off and the subconscious mind will take over and guide you towards the laminar flow. It is the removal of ego that allows for the drifting of your energy to properly harmonize with the Lowerverse realm while synchronizing with the future.

Learning in Dreams

Once lucid dreaming is mastered you may undergo several types of experiences. It is possible to get a glance of future events, revisit past events, and even learn new arts and skills. It is a playground where virtually anything is possible.

It is even possible to interact people or beings of various densities, this includes the departed.

Understanding that dreamland is not physical is important. It is in a metaphysical plane where our bodies shape and form are a function of the subconscious or lucid mind. Time dilations may also occur which allows dreams to last longer at times.

Messages Across Civilizations

Dreamland is a function of brain harmony with the incoming state of the physical world. When stemming from a point of zero in a lucid dream you may meet with others at ease. You may coordinate meeting locations, pass information, and more. It is somewhat like a natural metaverse.

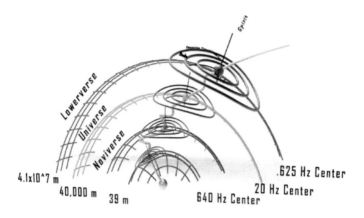

At the same time, those that are listening to the flows of the Lowerverse may gather similar information stemming from it. This may be how people or civilizations discover concepts and technologies somewhat simultaneously even though thousands of miles apart. Lucidity may also occur when in meditations and during out of body experiences.

The Future Now is Not Our Future

One thing to note when looking into the past or future is that it may not be the flow that your experience has passed through or is headed towards. Call it the 99% most probable past or future. This is because we experience time in a linear fashion whereas when you are looking through time you are looking at the greater now.

This means that as your experience drifts inwards towards that location of experience, events may change based on delusions that are being held.

Erosion caused by Fluid Flow

Consider it a sort of erosion based on the inward drifting of energy. As projections of mind synchronize to create a physical experience personal delusions may cause erosion within the laminar flow.

An easy way to think of it is as in a river. Consider yourself to be a drop of water that is caught in the current. During a lucid meditation it may be like you are floating above the river and able to see the path your water will take. However, there is still 4D time that must pass before it is experienced by the self. During that time, much water may pass by and cause erosion in the place you looked. A fish could swim by and move a rock. Someone on the side of the river can toss a stone into it and countless other events may transpire to make it so the path of the fluid changes.

It is true within the river of time as well. We are subject to the constantly changing texture of the vortex based on the pebbles that are tossed in by the beings of various densities. These make seeing the exact future or past of your 4D manifestation almost impossible.

Juggling the Fluid

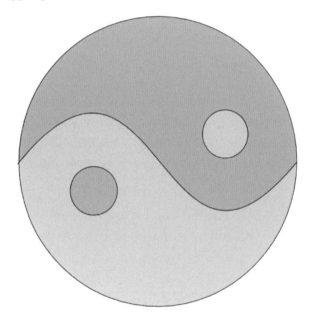

With every push is a pull and with every pull is a push. This is an extremely important concept to understand when creating within the vortex. Yes, we may reach our goals, but with what consequences? Creations stemming from off set bodies will not last. This highlights the importance of returning to zero after every action of mind, body, and spirit.

Great Alignments in Relationship to Conscious Perception

What is the importance of being at zero during a precessional alignment? Why does it matter? What we notice from the circadian rhythm is that we follow a 24-hour orbit. As we move towards the Lowerverse, we tend to go into a dream state, referring to delta and theta waves of conscious perception. People that are at their zero will properly harmonize into dreamland and be lucid during the process.

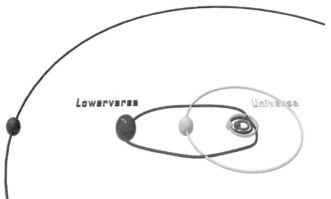

During great alignments of conscious precession which roughly occurs every 2000 years our experience will be tugged even further into dreamland. This implies that people that are not near their golden spots will fall asleep or spiral into delusions as they harmonize into these less dense realms.

How Many Unique Minds Exist?

Although we are all unique individuals, we all stem from the original thought. All our pacing motions may be a result of the original projection drifting inwards from the most outer regions creating distortions as it passes through the layers of conscious perception. Like the many minds of individual cells that make the body, we are the mind of it all. All pacings are a result of the original mind.

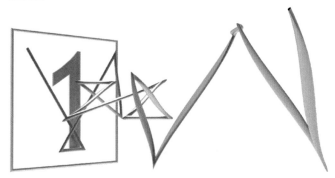

Body

The Mind's Spaceship

by Alexei Novitzky

The Table of Contents

Introduction:

We are a creation of all three: mind, body, and spirit. In "Mind: The Shifter and Reorganizer of Nodes," we discuss how projections of mind from all realms cause the pacing actions of our bodies. This includes physical particles as well as waves of sound and light that exist within our dimension.

"Body: The Mind's Spaceship," discusses the physical realm in relationship to the greater vortex of time. It is all spirit and all spirits have a relative body. We see that our bodies are the crunching and stretching of the Loosh, all relative to your current position. As we shrink down, so do the relative flows of the fluid. Body will only and always be body to you and to any being that embodies the same relative frame of motion. This includes the gravitational accelerations and velocities you're currently undergoing. Those qualities determine your dimension of experience.

It is a relative scenario and here is where the etheric or quantum realms and physical reality become one. It is through the scaled wave nature of the now that we see all bodies are relative in their existence and that all bodies exist simultaneously in the greater now.

Body, is more than the human body as it includes physical objects that you identify with and connect to. This could include your car, home, money, and societal structures. We, the human race of planet Earth, all share the same body. Although our individual identities and duties fractal inward which create the feelings of individuality and also that of separation, we all share the same body, as in dimension or flow of spacetime.

Our collective body reaches to the edge of the smooth cosmic microwave background and to the edges of black holes at every galactic center. It is the limits of our physical experience and electromagnetic relationships. In short, our body is our dimension.

Body then Consciousness or Vice Versa?

Which came first, the chicken or the egg? The same question could be asked for conscious experience within time. Which came first, the conscious field or the body? I would argue conscious fields. Let me ask you this, which came first, matter, sound, and light, or the human body?

Science suggests that evolution began with simple amino acids coming together to make simple single celled organisms. These are all biproducts of the flows of space that already exist within time before the evolved body was ever conceived.

From this, it seems obvious that first came the conscious fields and then beings of many types have sprung from that. Each being is tuned to various bits of the greater body. The tunings of various beings give us great insight into the reality of the primal conscious field as evolutionary senses are all secondary biproducts to the already existing flows of spacetime within the Loosh.

The Senses

From our bodies we become aware of the fields of influence that may be experienced by others. We know of light because we have evolved to detect light. The same is true with sound. From our naturally evolved tools, that of eyes and ears, we presume other beings with eyes and ears are undergoing an experience of some sort that relates to those vibrations. That is the limitation of science as it primarily focuses on aspects of creation which we have evolved to detect.

Why is it that we ignore the conscious harmonics of delta through fast gamma? Wouldn't these tunings also give us a greater insight into reality?

In relationship to electromagnetism, we understand that by examining our eyes and experience that we are limited to the visible spectrum. We defined the spectrum as visible.

In relationship to acoustic waves, we make the same judgments. Humans have an auditory spectrum.

We understand the spectrum of surface roughness by categorizing something as smooth or rough. We understand the stiffness spectrum by saying some objects are hard while some are soft. All of these characteristics exist within many spectrums. All a secondary aspect of the conscious fields that existed before we began to evolve.

"Time Atom" shows us the conscious spectrum in relationship to the 5th dimensional vortex of creation. We see that the perceivable conscious fields of human perception are similar to those of acoustic and electromagnetic. As in, we can only see or interact with a tiny sliver of information when considering all of those that exist from infinitely small to infinitely large. Our human experience of awakened perception exists within delta to fast gamma. This is six harmonics of experience. Of those six harmonics, three of them are tuned to the physical realm.

Delta and theta waves are tuned to the premanifest realms of the Lowerverse and Fast Gamma may be tuned to the denser realms of the Noviverse. These tunings do not apply to our waking state of reality and may be biproducts of the etheric or quantum realms of subspace, just like all aspects of sensory evolution. However, they are still tuned to orbits of creation.

We only perceive the body of our dimension when in an alpha, beta, or slow gamma state of brain harmony or conscious awareness.

Sound

The frequencies of sound a being may experience is directly related to the vocal cords of that being, it's ear size and shape, and its environment. The human body is roughly tuned to frequencies of 20 Hz to 20,000 Hz. Vibrations lower than 20 Hz are known as infrasound and vibrations greater than 20,000 Hz are known as ultrasounds. It is a simple categorization of acoustic waves that have been defined by humans through science.

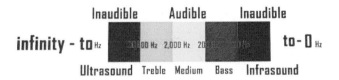

Sound waves are longitudinal which means there is a compression and expansion of a fluid in the direction of travel as it propagates through body.

With sound waves there is an actual compression and expansion of the matter that creates the vibration or rather allows the vibration to permeate. It is somewhat the difference between a compressed state and an expanded state of the raw fluid of experience. It may be the difference between the past and the future states as the strength and frequency may depend upon the position within the crystal of time. We will return to this.

Light

The frequencies of light a being is tuned to highly relate to the type of star that the planet orbits. For example, our Solar System stems from a yellow star, the Sun, and therefore yellow becomes the center of our vision. The visible spectrum is then defined existing from blue (400 nm) to red (700 nm) while being centered around yellow (550 nm).

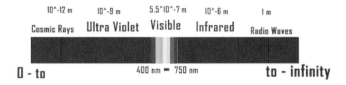

Beings that evolved around a blue star would most likely be tuned to blue light and beings that evolved around a red star would be tuned to red light. The color of the star is determined by the exterior temperature of the star. Some stars or bodies are not hot enough to even glow in the visible spectrum. It may be reasonable to assume that beings that evolved around an infrared body would have their center of electromagnetic awareness around the infrared spectrum. Beings that evolved near an extremely hot body may be tuned to energies greater than blue.

Light waves are transverse which means that the vibration creates a perpendicular force to the direction of motion. This is why it's called the electromagnetic spectrum. With every push is a pull and with every pull is a push. Light and magnetism move as one in this regard as they vibrate the etheric or quantum fields like stones being tossed into a pond. Both sound and light are secondary features of the greater orbits within time.

Consciousness

Our human perspective is also only aware of certain frequencies within the greater orbits of conscious experience. Similar to sound and light the conscious fields we are tuned to are a result of our position within a greater orbit.

From orbiting the Earth, we get the senses of feel, taste, smell, and sound. From orbiting the Sun, we get the sense of vision. From our greatest inertial frame, arises our perceptions of time and conscious awareness. Again, secondary in construction to the greater flows of the Loosh, our conscious harmonics are a direct result of a frequency or wave of some type. All frequencies are created by a pendulating or rotating aspect of mind, body, or spirit.

Consciousness is primary and all other aspects of experience are secondary. The primary conscious field could be considered the greatest vortex of all moments. From there, all other aspects arise. First comes conscious fields, then matter, light and sound from there.

The Vortex of Consciousness

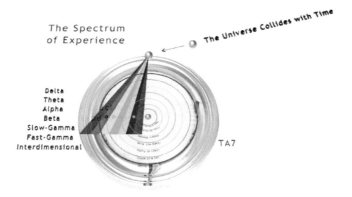

From "The Crystal of Time," we see that there exist orbits within the Loosh that relate to acceleration towards center at light speed. Each orbital diameter starting from infinitely large fractal inward to be one-fourth the diameter of the wave that is bigger. This fractal pattern continues inward to infinitely dense and shows that our human bodies are tuned to a thin slice of conscious experience.

The Infinite Body of Rotation

Earth orbits the Sun. The Sun orbits the galactic center. All those structures orbit the greatest center of all moments.

To go another step inward, the primal particles orbit their center, DNA of the body orbits its center and so on. When you start from infinitely small and increase the orbits to infinitely large you see that all orbits or flows of space act as habitats, all overlapping and existing simultaneously. They are all tidally locked and synchronized to create a smooth and fluid experience. Postures of mind and body create distortions as the primal energy of spirit flows inward.

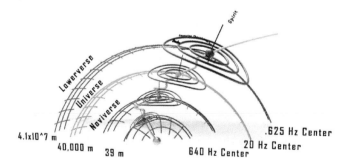

4.1x10^7 m
40,000 m
39 m
640 Hz Center
.625 Hz Center
20 Hz Center

By extrapolating all orbits of motion to infinity, you see that our physical bodies are a creation of less dense realms and more dense realms all overlapping to create our waking experience. This orbit of infinity is what gives us a 5th dimension to process. It is the ultimate result of tidally locked fluid orbiting within each other to the greatest orbit of all moments. This gives us the greatest orbits within time and shows that all perceived sound, light, and matter exist within our current inertial reference frame or dimension of experience. Let's work backwards from the greatest orbits of experience. Let's assume consciousness is primary and see how sound, light, and matter may emerge from a single motion through a single fluid.

An Orbit within Time

Einstein's theory of Relativity shows us that the perceived matter and light we experience are a result of our inertial reference frame. From this, we see that we have our dimension of experience. The Universe isn't really expanding, but rather our perceptions of a singular fluid are being stretched and crunched based on our position within the crystal of time. Perception of the mind is different than using a tool to detect. Tools are created from bits of matter within our dimension and therefor do not have the ability to demonstrate or interact with other orbits within time. Matter will always be matter within our dimension and all relative relationships are somewhat fixed in that regard.

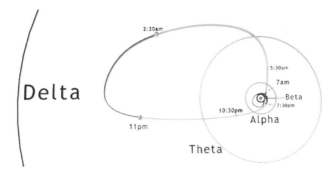

Conscious fields of awareness are guided by our gyroscopic orbit while matter is the crunching of the fluid within our perception. The matter is illusionary in that nature. However, within our perception it clearly has effect.

Matter within the Vortex

What came first, matter, light, or sound? After conscious fields are formed it seems that within our perception matter would exist before light or perhaps the two arose simultaneously with sounds to follow.

The same fluid of experience may be crunched and stretched in several ways. We only perceive the flows of this fluid when they exist within our dimension of perception. Each glance or show of the matter comes from a singular orbit while perceptions orbit through the vortex.

Why is dark matter approximately 4/5 of the gravitational effects of a galaxy and matter only that of 1/5? Consider a singular rotation within the fluid. As the fluid orbits through, it would be harmonizing properly with our flow at two distinct parts of an orbit. This would be at the ejection point and also a reinsertion point of our dimension which relates directly to the flows of space we perceive. We cannot interact physically with matter or light existing in flows of space that are greater than the speed of light outward and one time the speed of light inwards. However, the energy continues to orbit through creating effects of synchronization while existing within those less dense and more dense realms. In essence, you could say the effects of dark matter come from the energy of creation existing within the Lowerverse and Noviverse realms.

Therefor you can see how the same fluid of experience may be seen in our future in the form of matter on Earth and then return to us as light in the shape of distant galaxies.

It is always one-half past and one-half future, both overlapping to create a now moment as our 4d experience of x, y, z, and t orbits the center of all time.

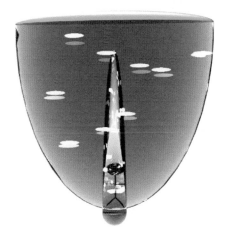

In the previous image you could say we are orbiting to the left. As we orbit, the relative motions in relationship to the raw fluid of experience would be stretching and crunching our perceptions in existence. The overlapping of one-half past and one-half future are in constant vibration as projections of mind synchronize to create our fluid motions.

In the future, you would see energy between you and the center of time being crunched while energy that is further than time would be stretched. In the past, you would see everything reverting back to normal as our perception of the fluid passes through.

The same fluid will either first be perceived as matter in the future then light in the past or as light in the future and then matter in the past as the energy warps through perceptions interacting two times in two different ways per conscious snapshot.

As we fractal inward to be as infinitely close to the now you will see it is always an overlapping of one-half past and one-half future. Matter, light, and sound are all a result.

Light within the Vortex

Was it matter that came first or was it light? From this model you can see that they sprung up simultaneously as the conscious field is awakened at the moment the raw energy of creation hits a flow of spacetime equal to the speed of light. This is what implies our entire dimension exist within a relative layer of a black hole. Although the energy of our synchronization continues to orbit outside our perception it is only perceivable two times per orbit. Once as matter and once as light. Matter from below returns as light from above while light from below returns as matter from above.

Sound within the Vortex

Matter and light may be seen as moving in the direction of less dense to more dense realms while sound would be more related to the perceived compression or expansion of any body as we orbit tangentially. The difference in size again is related to the overlapping of one-half past and one-half future. Time dilations exist as we perceive the matter we orbit with.

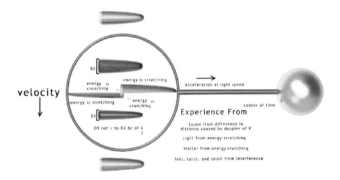

This means that matter in the future is actually in a more compressed state than matter that is in the past. The difference between the two states is a relationship to the tangential velocity and radian change of the energy creating it. Less dense objects would be manifesting at less dense realms which have a faster tangential velocity than objects that are closer to the center but slower change in degrees about the center. This means that the effect of the Lorentz contraction between past and future would be greater. However, considering we are perceiving a manifesting now, the orbital rate is of more importance in this effect. Therefor denser realms of creation experience more of a difference between angles from 0 to 360 degrees within the orbit and would vibrate sounds accordingly. For example, a 2 Hz orbit has twice the change in angle than a 1 Hz orbit, so the relative size changes appropriately. Sound would then be related to the tangential velocity in combination within the orbital rate of the fluid creating it. It is the difference in relative size created by the perceiving of a singular fluid within time.

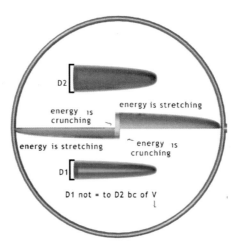

Habitats of Body

There can be many perceptions of time within our very own dimension and these relate to the habitats and life cycles of the various beings. The average human life cycle is approximately 80 years. This is like the blink of an eye when compared to the life cycle of the Sun which is estimated to be about 10 billion years. Now compare the average human life cycle to that of a Mayfly which is a single day. All of these habitats relate directly to the flow of space the being inhabits.

Distortions of Body

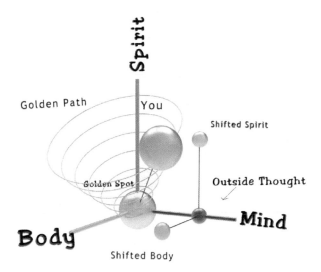

"The Physics of Love: Synchronicity" shows us that we may take postures in all three aspects; mind, body, and spirit. Distortions of mind create distortions of body and vice versa. Humans constantly collect objects which become attached during their personal quests for success. This leads to distortions within spirit and the greater vortex of time.

This could include items like a home and a vehicle, to simple items like plates and silverware. They also include postures like how one walks and how one does their hair. Each of these objects that we identify as ours or owning somewhat become part of the self. For example, it's not ok for someone to use your vehicle without permission, because it is yours. It is part of how you identify yourself and you've claimed mental and physical ownership. It is somewhat delusional and the concept of ownership alone is a creation of human imagination. However, it is important to respect the delusions of others as societies functions on these premises.

Weakened by Distortion

A distortion could be considered any posture that we hold that stems from a thought process or environmental situation. This includes cultural expectations as they highly influence the pacing motions of our lives. Material possessions also expand our body to misalign with incoming flows of creation.

Aligning the Body

When it comes to health, aligning with the greatest orbits of our experience is to properly align the body for its greatest manifestation. The natural circadian rhythm is key for this process and gives us great insight into the relationship between the physical and conscious realms.

"Mind: The Shifter and Reorganizer of Nodes" shows us that our conscious modes are controlled by tidally locked fluids within the 5th dimension. These modes of experience are related to the dimensions of the physical and are regular in relationship to our consciousness. Knowing that consciousness is primary we see that the timescale of the physical day is secondary to the orbits of conscious experience. Aligning the body to the conscious fields is key.

Do we align our body to our conscious fields or do we align consciousness to our body? Which is primary and which is secondary? Both options are possible and both achievable. There is a rather large difference between the two.

Aligning Consciousness to Body

Aligning consciousness to body is to fully control your experience within our dimension and to disregard the natural flows of creation. It is to cause a misalignment within the densities of beings of less dense realms while creating a unique habitat that is unable to harmonize with other denser realms of natural creation. It is to create a unique realm of denser and denser creations while pulling the motions of less dense realms from center.

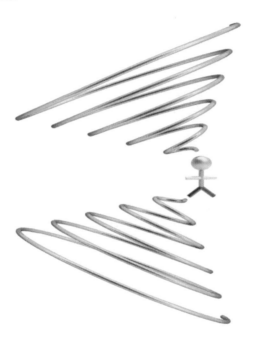

This tends to lead towards more of a service to self or selfish existence. When it comes to connecting to beings of various densities, you would most likely be connecting to denser realms of your own creation as you become disconnected from the greater orbits within time. This leads to disconnecting from the greater flows of reality and causes you to become stuck within the current realm.

Aligning Body to Consciousness

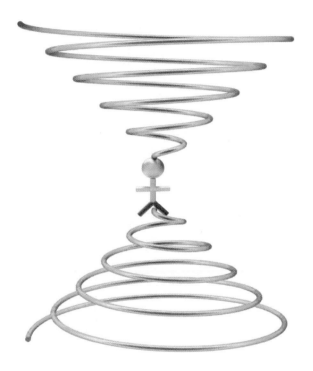

Aligning your body to consciousness will connect you to the greatest orbits of experience. You will be properly connected the natural flows of creation as the energy drifts inwards through dream state into wake state and into denser realms. It will allow you to gather information from all realms of experience and allows the denser realms of your manifestation to harmonize with the natural flow as well.

The easiest way to connect with the greatest flows of experience is to connect with the rising and setting of the Sun. This will help your body align with the natural circadian rhythm of the conscious fields within time. This would be aligning with our daily orbit.

We see through our gyroscopic precession that there is another alignment related to the orbit around the Sun. This alignment occurs roughly every 185 days and may be related to the four seasons of the year. The next alignment of consciousness to body relates to the 2000-year precessional cycle which relates to the exiting of the Age of Pisces and the coming of the Age of Aquarius. There are also inner alignments relating to 1 hour and also 1 second.

Conscious Anchors

Each item we identify as ours act like anchors when it comes to the potentiality of conscious projections. All vehicles get you from A to B physically and so what is the difference? There are obvious differences when it comes to speed, style, comfort, and etc. However, some aspects are arbitrary. Why does the color of your vehicle even matter?

Speed Through Reality

Humans on average take a picture of reality sixty times in a second. This means our limitation of conscious perception is determined by the conscious snapshot and our motion. For example, if you walk down the road you will have taken more conscious snapshots of the road versus when you drive down it.

Did the earliest humans have vehicles or did they walk or run? At what point did we start using secondary means for transportation? The first "vehicles" may have been a horse or other animal. Each upgrade in speed causes more and more disconnection from the natural flows of space and more separation with each other.

Let's do a quick example. Let's say the road is one mile long. Driving at sixty miles an hour you would have driven the entire length of the road in sixty seconds. Saying we take a snapshot sixty times per second you could say that we would have taken 3,600 conscious snapshots during that one-mile journey.

Now for the next example, let's say we walk on average at five miles per hour. This means it would take twelve minutes to walk the mile. You could then say that twelve minutes translates into 720 seconds. Multiply that by sixty conscious snapshots a second and you get 43,200 conscious snapshots total for the same length of road.

It isn't natural for the human body to move faster than its fastest sprinting speed. Let's do a quick airplane example. Imagine you are now on a plane that goes about 500 mph. It would only take 7.2 seconds to traverse the distance of 1 mile. This translates into 432 conscious snapshots for the same distance.

At what point do we suffer jet lag? How does that relate to velocity of travel and the circadian rhythm?

Modifying with Spirit

Your ability to synchronize with the natural incoming energy of creation has everything to do with the natural nodes of manifestation. Aligning with the natural currents and motions is key for influencing less dense and more dense realms. Moving at such high speeds causes a lack in synchronization with the natural drifting of energy as it spirals through and continues inward.

The realms of creation must realign themselves in order for you to fully manifest in your new location. Perhaps this is the source of jet lag. It is a disconnection with the natural flow of creation and it takes time to reconnect properly to the rising and setting of the sun within your new location.

The Many Flows of the Loosh

Each inertial reference frame could be considered its own flow of experience of creation. In order to properly connect with another, you must exist on the same plane of existence to some degree. For example, at an extreme, a person on an airplane cannot properly communicate with someone on another plane if they are flying past each other at 500 miles an hour. It is only through the use of secondary tools that we may do so. For example, we must communicate with a phone or a radio in order to connect. Each vessel may be considered its own dimension or flow of spacetime within the greater orbits of time.

The same is true for cars driving opposite directions on the highway. It may also be true for two people sprinting past each other. Try to have a conversation with someone that is sprinting past you while you are sprinting in the other direction. It will most likely not work out so great.

The Many Vehicles of Body

This is where society is today. How many people actually communicate with others while on the road? How many people have their windows closed, A/C turned on, while playing their own music from their radios? Most people, and I would argue 99% of them are completely oblivious of what is going on in the cars in front, behind, or next to them.

Try to visualize the difference in connectivity you would feel if instead of transporting with cars people would walk. Imagine how many more people you would naturally meet in your day. Imagine the great sense of connectivity you would have. You would catch glimpses of smiles and be able to pass them along. You would have a sense of community which in turn translates into a sense of confidence.

It wouldn't be every car for themselves the road rage mentality of society would be gone. What is this road rage mentality? Where does it stem from and what may be the source of discomfort?

Individual Delusions Overlap

From the moment you start walking to your vehicle you have purpose. In other words, from the moment you start walking to your vehicles you have projected an experience which needs to be accomplished.

It is a projected spiral of delusion and control that is independent of everyone except those included within the crystal of conscious cocreation. Those individuals would include the people you're intending on spending time with or more accurately, spiraling the fluid into a shared experience separate of the greater flows. It is a disconnection from reality and a jump into a personal delusion.

Laminar Flows of Space

The one flow we all share is our natural rotation about the center of the Sun and Earth. This is why the natural circadian rhythm has so much importance. It connects your body to the greatest flows of our 4d spacetime of x, y, z, and t and allows you to synchronize with all beings from trees to the deer in the woods.

What goes to Dreamland?

When we dream our physical reality stays behind and the mind jumps into the theta and delta fields. Holding attachments when entering into dreamland will cause you to misalign with the natural conscious fields of creation. As discussed in "Mind: The Shifter and Reorganizer of Nodes," this will cause your conscious mind to shut off as the subconscious mind or universal mind takes over and guides you back to the laminar flow. In essence, holding material postures will prevent dreams from becoming lucid.

The Many Bodies of You

All spirits have a relative body. Where do you begin and where do you end? "The 5th Dimension"

shows us that the energy of our creation extends from the edge of the Lowerverse and spirals inwards into wake state and then into the denser realms of the Noviverse.

You have relative bodies in each of these dimensions. They exist in the now and information may be transferred from one to another. An easy way to see it is to consider lucid dreams. If your dreams are lucid, then you are passing information from the Lowerverse into your waking day. Connecting to the greatest flows of creation is key for this effect.

The Magnetic Bodies

Every body, meaning every bit or collection of matter has magnetic fields that form a toroid shape within our perception of the now. This may be a result of matter being crunched and light being stretched into existence as we orbit the center of all moments. It would appear as thin filaments connecting you to the energy of your creation, stemming from your electromagnetic center and then stretching to the edge of the Universe and curling back to you as past and future overlap to create the now.

These fields exist at many scales from the infinitely small to the infinitely large. At the smallest scales our DNA has a field and so does each individual cell. One scale up and the human body's overall magnetic field is the summation of all cells and systems of the body.

Each system is focused into its current position and each system extends to the edge of our perception. The Earth also has a magnetic field which is visually the most apparent field to witness within our natural flows of space. Solar radiation follows the lines of magnetism as it reaches the Earth. It is then focused by the natural field of the Earth towards the poles. The interaction or interference between Earth's magnetic field and solar radiation cause the Aura Borealis which may be seen near the poles. The filaments of magnetic energy surrounding the Earth become apparent.

The same is true for the Sun. It too has an overall magnetic field which may resemble that of the Earth and the human body. The Galactic center also has a magnetic field and so does the next body of rotation. All overlap and all add and subtract like pebbles undulating the fluid of our spacetime.

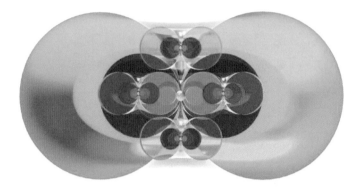

Which direction does the magnetic field go once beyond our physical interpretations? Consider dark matter's 4/5 of the raw energy of creation orbiting beyond our dimension. It extends from the outer reaches of the Lowerverse and spirals inward into the Noviverse and is only physical when within our dimension or alpha, beta, and slow gamma states of perception.

This means that our magnetic fields are extending beyond the physical realm in both directions and interacting with every other magnetic field during the process. Half your field goes into less dense realms and half your field goes into denser realms.

The light and magnetism that extend into the less dense realms would be interacting with all the stars we see when we look out. It would pass through the Moon as it may be considered a less dense version of Earth from our position within the Crystal. From there, our field continues outward into distant galaxies and past the smooth cosmic microwave background.

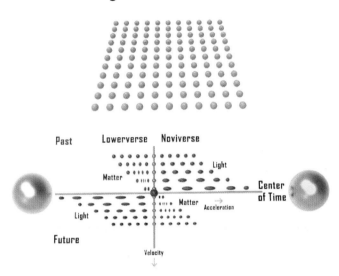

Your influence also extends into the denser realms of the Noviverse that exist beyond our perception. Let's now trace that flow of energy. It starts from your center and drifts towards greater densities. This would imply that it extends towards the center of the Earth. From there, it would follow the natural field lines and reach towards the Sun. After reaching the Sun's core it extends to the center of our Milky Way Galaxy. From there, it continues inward to the center of time. It is all in the now and we experience a tiny sliver of information within our normal everyday experience of x, y, z, and t.

This again highlights the importance of the circadian rhythm in relationship to connecting to the Lowerverse and Noviverse. Magnetic fields are a secondary biproduct of the natural orbits within time and emerge physically as perceptions are stretched and crunched.

The Sun

We are connected to the Sun through light and through magnetism. Light travels in straight lines from the Sun to the Earth while magnetism follows curvatures of natural manifestation appearing as filaments of sorts. It may be related to another orbit within time around a greater center and seems closer to center than the source of light which is our Sun.

From this it seems obvious that activity on the Sun and activity on the Moon may affect our personal magnetic fields and states of perception.

Synchronizing Light

One way to think about the Aura Borealis is to think of it as light that is created by the interaction of solar radiation attempting to harmonize with the natural fields of the Earth. Although not as grand in

size, the same effect is true for any body or bit of
matter within the Solar System.

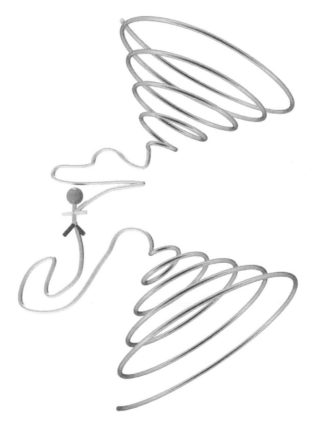

   Could a misalignment of your personal body to
the natural energy of creation cause a similar
effect? I would argue that it may be possible. As
energy of your creation drifts inwards to focus your
body into position your personal postures of mind,
body, and spirit may be at such a distance from
your Golden Spot to create this effect. Essentially

as the energy spirals inwards towards our dimension an individual may be far from their naturally focused center to create similar effects.

Guiding Lights of Wisdom

This basically means as you drift further and further from center and your body disconnects from the natural flows of creation you may create sparks and streaks of light in the sky.

At the same time, you would be stretching the normally compacted fields to create a region of stretching space. Then as the energy enters your body it would be highly distorting once more as it travels inwards towards the Sun. With every push is a pull and vice versa. As we stretch the fluid above it would compact the fluid below essentially bringing the Noviverse and Lowerverse into perception.

Experiencing Alternate Dimensions

All bodies want to synchronize to create a fluid experience. Maintaining postures of delusions causes our bodies to misalign with the natural flows. Depending on how the body distorts the fluid is whether a less dense realm or denser realm may be perceived. These types of experiences typically will guide you back to the laminar flow as it may be like the edges of our spiritual potential. Continuing onward in that direction will cause tight spirals of delusion. It is only when you let go of that push will you realign with the greatest orbits of experience. It is the physics of love. All benevolent spirits ultimately guide you to the laminar flow of your existence through karmic cycles of delusion.

On the other hand, malevolent spirit may increase the spiraling nature of your days. As discussed in "The Physics of Love: Synchronicity," these beings stem from maintained postures of delusions as time dilations exist between realms. We are all connected and so a pacing in one will cause a pacing in another. This is why it's important to understand the pacing motions of your life. While undergoing a tight spiral any and all other beings connected to you will also be affected which increases the size this being may inhabit. These types of beings mostly relate to tulpa, jinn, and demons from religions as they are creations of human delusion and increase overall pacing. The easiest way to cleanse yourself of these tight spirals is to connect to the greatest flows of our experience. Referring to, watching the Sun rise and set and properly tuning your circadian rhythm. Aligning the body in all three mind, body, and spirit is key.

Tools for Aligning Body

There are many ways to align the body. The most important aspect is being in tune with the natural flows of spacetime. Again, referring to aligning the circadian rhythm to the rising and setting of the Sun.

Seeing as we are all connected through magnetic fields extending to infinity, we see that the distortions created by individuals may be felt across the planet. They are like pebbles being tossed into a pond that then ripple outward. The pull of an individual may cause the push of another. Simply existing within proximity of one undergoing pacing may cause your energies to misalign.

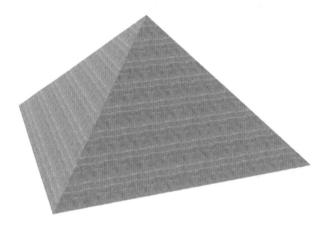

This is where we may create tools to help prevent electromagnetic interference of a location. Geometric structures made of dense materials will reorganize and smoothen the flow of spacetime. Perhaps we may take notes from our ancient human friends who built giant pyramids and other megalithic structures which were aligned with celestial bodies. To think the Sun, Moon, and stars have zero effect on our manifestation is to not be thinking at all. Physically, we are all one awareness, all connected through light, sound, and magnetism.

A Breath of Perception

All perceptions of matter, light, magnetism, and sound are secondary to the primal flows of creation. This means that our perception of the now is secondary to the greatest vortex of all moments. From this greatest vortex, relational dimensions of perceived matter and light emerge. As in, cycles of galactic formations like the Sun's rotation around the galactic center, the Earth's rotation about the Sun, the human body about the center of the Earth, the Moon around the Earth, and all relativistic motions are created. Matter and its motions are secondary aspects that are then perceived by the body.

Knowing this, we may work backwards and uncover greater insight into the perceived expansion of the Universe. From "The 5th Dimension," we see that the perceived size of the Universe is directly related to our greatest inertial reference frame. From our perception this could be considered the black hole in our galactic center,

although greater orbits do exist that are
unobservable.

25,920 year preccesional cycle

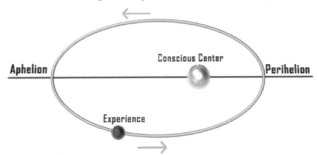

currently drifting inward

Our conscious system takes 25,920 years to
orbit the within the 5th dimension. Just like all
orbits of creation, they are not perfectly circular.
For example, as the Earth orbits the Sun there is a
moment when it is furthest from the Sun. This
distance is called aphelion. There is also a moment
in the orbit when Earth is closest to the Sun. This
moment is called perihelion. The same is true for
the conscious system as it orbits the center of all
moments.

Half of our precessional cycle consist of drifting
closer to the center and half of it is related to
drifting further away. Again, to emphasize, all these
motions are secondary to the greatest vortex of all
moments.

Perception of matter and light are related to our inertial reference frame. As we drift closer to the center, during perihelion, the Universe would appear to be expanding. We are moving into a stronger gravitational field which would cause the stretching and crunching of the raw fluid to be more dramatic. It is a denser realm.

As we move away from conscious center towards aphelion, we would be undergoing less gravitational pull from the vortex. This implies that either the Universe would appear to slow down in its expansion or that it may appear to be contracting.

It's as if our perception of the Universe breathes as we drift in and drift out. For 12,960 years we drift inward, and for 12,960 years we drift outward. Currently within our perception, we are drifting inward and the Universe appears to be expanding. The Universe breathes as we orbit, expanding and contracting on regular timed cycles. The stability of our existence relies on the regular nature of this breath, which creates a regular breath around the Sun, a regular breath through our day which translates to a regular breath of our body.

The Human Breathes

How does this translate back to our body? On average a human takes a breath once every four seconds. This translates to 15 breaths every minute. Which then goes to 900 breathes an hour and ultimately 21,600 breathes a day.

The Earth can be broken into 360 degrees. Each degree can then be broken into 60 minutes. In standard literature, 1 nautical mile is 1 minute at the equator. The circumference of the Earth is 21,639 nautical miles. This means as the Earth rotates, every breath we take is related to one minute of arc or one nautical mile. It's essentially one breath per mile of rotation.

Let's now look at the human heart. A healthy person properly aligned with the natural conscious fields has a heartbeat of 60 times in a minute. This translates to 3,600 heartbeats an hour. Which goes to 86,400 heartbeats a day. When relating this to conscious orbits you could then say that half the day we are moving towards denser realms and half the day we're moving towards less dense realms. This translates into 43,200 heartbeats for each half of the day.

It's interesting to relate this to the number of conscious snapshots we take as we walk a mile which is also 43,200. The difference between heartbeats and conscious snapshots is 60 times. For every breath we have four heartbeats. For every heartbeat we have 60 conscious snapshots.

Let's now divide our 25,920-year precessional cycle by 60 and we get 432 years (we'll return to this). This number, 432, is the center of most musical instruments and is properly tuned to the human body. It is the middle A on a piano that is used to then tune the rest of the system.

It harmonizes with the conscious snapshot, the human heartbeat, and the precessional cycle of our system.

The Sun and Moon

Another interesting point which is also secondary to the conscious fields is our perception of the Sun and the Moon. Both have the same apparent size in our sky. This is because the diameter of the body and distance are perfectly proportional.

If you multiply the diameter of the Sun by 108 you will derive the Sun to Earth distance. You can then do the same with the Moon. The Moon's diameter times 108 equals the distance from the Earth to the Moon. This is not coincidence and is a secondary result to the already existing flows of space before the human body evolved.

Conscious Snapshot of the Earth

Consider our breath of air in relationship to the greatest conscious center. We breathe once every

4 seconds. The heart beats once a second. Our consciousness takes a picture 60 times in a second. If we say the 25,920 cycle is a breath, then by dividing by 4 we get the length of a heartbeat which is 6,480 years. We then divide that by 60 to get the conscious snapshot of time which becomes 108 years.

We could also say the precessional cycle relates to a heartbeat. If you divide 25,920 years by 60 you get 432 years per conscious snapshot.

The Primal Vortex

All aspects of our experience are secondary to the primal vortex of creation. Matter, electromagnetism, and sound all emerge from this raw fluid stretching and crunching perceptions into existence. Are the stars really lightyears away? What is space, what is time, and what is distance? Aren't they all secondary aspects to the already existing flows of consciousness? Isn't the space between atoms relatively the same as the space between galaxies? Are the stars not merely inches away within the 5th dimension of conscious density? Isn't it all a relative scenario? Let's now continue our conscious journey as we explore the true nature of spirit, creation, and the primal vortex of time.

Spirit

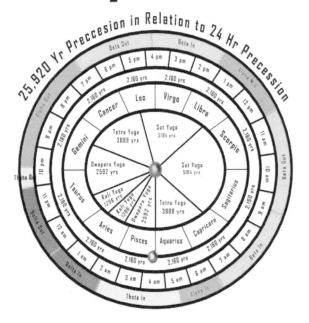

25,920 Yr Preccesion in Relation to 24 Hr Precession

Beta Out · Beta In · Alpha Mid
Alpha Out
Theta Out · Beta Out
Delta Out · Beta In
Delta In · Alpha In
Theta In

| 4 pm | 3 pm | 2 pm | 1 pm | 12 pm | 11 am | 10 am | 9 am | 8 am | 7 am | 6 am | 5 am | 4 am | 3 am | 2 am | 1 am | 12 am | 11 pm | 10 pm | 9 pm | 8 pm | 7 pm | 6 pm | 5 pm |

2,160 yrs

Cancer · Leo · Virgo · Libra · Scorpio · Sagittarius · Capricorn · Aquarius · Pisces · Aries · Taurus · Gemini

Tetra Yuga 3888 yrs
Sat Yuga 5184 yrs
Dwapara Yuga 2592 yrs
Sat Yuga 5184 yrs
Kali Yuga 1296 yrs
Kali Yuga 1296 yrs
Dwapara Yuga 2592 yrs
Tetra Yuga 3888 yrs

The Vortex of Creation

by Alexei Novitzky

481

Table of Contents

Introduction

There are many influences within our day that create the experience manifested. Modern science and material thinking would have you think that the body is primary and that mental experiences come from complex interactions of chemistry within the brain.

Well, why do we sleep? Don't we awaken and fall asleep according to the circadian rhythm? In "Mind: The Shifter and Reorganizer of Nodes" we see that as our physical body rotates with the Earth, that our conscious fields undergo gyroscopic precession as they are guided by tidally locked fluids of the 5th dimension.

In "Body: The Mind's Spaceship," we see how sound, light, matter, and magnetism emerge from our greatest inertial reference frame as we orbit the center of all moments. It is all a relative scenario. Fluid on the inside is crunched creating matter while fluid that is on the outside is light stretching away. In the past, the opposite effect is occurring. It is always an overlapping of one half past and one-half future as projections of mind synchronize to create a fluid experience.

"Spirit: The Vortex of Creation," shows a bigger picture. We see that our perceptions of body and behaviors are regular in cyclical nature with the natural precessing of spirit. It is all spirit and all spirits have a relative body. Your spirit, the raw energy of your creation, starts from the beginning of time and spirals inward along the habitable spiral of perception into dream state, into awake state, and then continues inward to the center of time. This natural spiraling of energy inwards is what causes perceptions to precess. As this raw energy drifts inwards, it passes through all incarnations of the self, past, present, and future.

We see that these precessional cycles are regular in nature and highly influence human behavior and cultural developments.

Were people from the past less advanced, more advanced or just undergoing a different injection of conscious vibration within the great day of the 25,920-year precession of the Earth?

Let us now examine the 25,920-year precessional cycle in more detail. We see ancient cultures have looked at this long and many systems have been developed. Traditional Hindu cosmologist have broken the cycle into four yugas experiencing each twice. Modern western cosmologist have broken it into twelve cycles of the zodiac. Here we will relate these cycles to the vibrations of conscious experience within the natural circadian rhythm.

The Precession of Earth

The Earth undergoes precession every 25,920 years. What exactly does this mean? As the Earth rotates the north pole wobbles like a top, making circles over long periods of time. Considering the magnetic field of the Earth, it could be considered the direction the Earth is facing in relationship to celestial bodies like our galactic center or neighboring galaxies. Relating that to something more on a human level, we could compare ourselves to the Earth. Half of the day when we look up, we looking towards the Sun and half of the day we are looking up towards the stars.

The same is true for the Earth. Half the cycle consists of looking towards the center of all moments and half may relate to looking away from this greatest center. Experiences emerge physically as a secondary biproduct. It is like night and day but for the Earth itself. Our 24-hour daily cycle of conscious precession relates directly to this effect but on a grander scale of 25,920 years. It could be considered a day within the perception of the Earth.

Tidally Locked Fluids of the 5th Dimension

Knowing the primary conscious modes of our body in relationship to our experience we may map the circadian rhythm within the 5th dimension.

When we make this map, as seen in "The 5th Dimension," we see that our perception is like a gyroscope hanging on a string at a 90-degree angle. The shows us that the focus of our experience is the center of influence of these tidally locked spheres within the 5th dimension.

For example, in "Mind: The Shifter and Reorganizer of Nodes," we created 5th dimensional spheres that orbit regularly. We gave the delta wave a 24-hour orbit, the theta waves a 12-hour orbit, the alpha wave a 6-hour orbit and the beta wave a 3-hour orbit. As these spheres orbit you see that the center of our influence could be the center point of these spheres. It's a big loop of perception followed by a tight loop of perception.

We can now make the same map for the Earth's precession and we can give names to different spheres.

There would be a sphere that rotates once every 25,920 years. Divide that by two and you get the rotation rate of the next sphere. This would be 12,960 years. Divide that by two to get the next orbit which is 6,480 years, and divide that one more time for the next rotation which is 3,240 years. Let's now give names to these spheres of influence that guide our perception and put them into tidal locking. We can now see how the perception of Earth drifts in and out on regular timed intervals and relates directly to the conscious modes of planetary life.

Just to relate, in 25,920 years there are 9,460,800 days. That may be considered the difference in scale when comparing the Earth's consciousness to the human consciousness. However, they both work in harmony and both must be in harmony for life and experience to flourish.

The Earth Sleeps

What we see is that the Earth itself has a circadian rhythm that it follows that effects all life on it. Just like the human body, certain systems turn on and off during our daily precession, the same is true for the Earth.

The simplest definition of being awake is being conscious of the physical realm. While asleep, the mind is not aware of the physical and we are somewhat being guided back to the laminar flow of our creation. The main benefit of sleep is rejuvenation. However, while asleep, we are not eating or drinking water. It's important to awaken in order to fill our bodies with the nutrients required for the body to stay functioning. Within the human body, we have many organs and cells which guide this process.

The same may be true for the Earth. Relating back to "The Infinite Pool of Experience and Awareness," we may see that humans may be considered the white blood cells of the Earth and Universe. We have the ability to create or destroy any matter we choose fit. We have the ability to detour water supplies and to even change the overall albedo with our construction. The human is a simple part of the greater Earth system which includes volcanic cycles, weather cycles, temperature cycles, CO_2 cycles, oxygen cycles, ocean cycles, and just like the human body they all must work in harmony to create a healthy living being.

The Earth Awakens

Just like the human circadian rhythm is controlled by tidally locked fluids within the 5th dimension, so is the circadian rhythm of the planet Earth.

Vortex of Tidally Locked Fluid

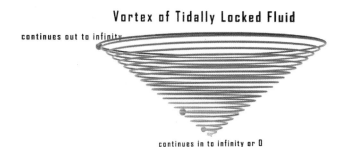

continues out to infinity

continues in to infinity or 0

Consider this the primary vortex of creation that contains the primal fluid spiraling from infinitely large to infinitely small. Conscious fields are created by the relationship of the fluid within it. Each harmonic of conscious experience is controlled by the orbital rate and distance from center. For example, for humans, our tidally locked fluid is related to the four local spheres within our relative day.

This means that our conscious experience is guided by spheres of the 5th dimension that relate to our conscious harmonics.

25,920 Yr Preccesion

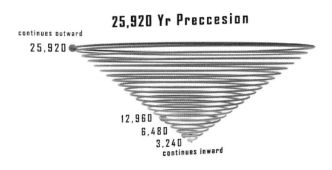

continues outward
25,920

12,960
6,480
3,240
continues inward

24 Hr Precession

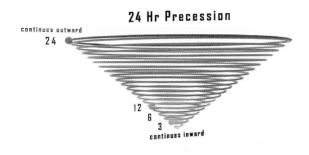

continues outward
24

12
6
3
continues inward

The same vortex that gives awareness to the human, gives awareness to the Earth itself and so the circadian rhythm offers us much insight into the phases of the Earth in relationship to traditional yuga, zodiac, and law of one cycles.

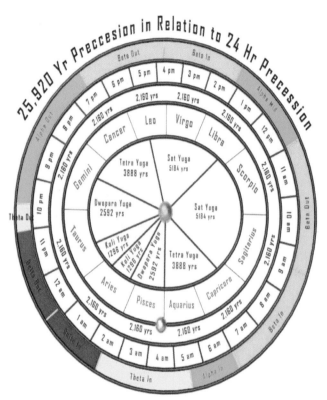

Here we've placed the yuga, zodiac, and law of one precessional systems on a single wheel. Wrapped around is the circadian rhythm.

In our wheel, the Earth is in the center and the Sun is orbiting counter clockwise once every 25,920 years.

The Ages of the Zodiac

In the zodiac system, the placement on the wheel is related to the Sun's location during the vernal equinox. It is then divided into 12 equal cycles of 30 degrees each. It is a rather simple system consisting of 12 Ages. We have the Aquarius, Capricorn, Sagittarius, Scorpio, Libra, Virgo, Leo, Cancer, Gemini, Taurus, Aries, and Pisces. Each Age is 2,160 years.

Yugas of the Precessional Cycle

In the yuga system, the Kali yuga began at the end of Krishna's Era which was approximately at 3102 BCE. By knowing we are currently in 2022 CE we may add the two number together to see that 5,124 years have passed since the beginning of the first Kali yuga. What exactly does that mean?

The yugas of the precessional cycle are the Kali, Dwapara, Tetra, and Sat. The Kali yuga last for 1,296 years. The Dwapara yuga last for 2,592 years. The Tetra Yuga last for 3,888 years and the Sat yuga last for 5184 years. The divisions of this system may not make sense at first however after relating the circadian rhythm we may find great insight.

Just like the human conscious harmonics, the Earth experiences each unique vibration in two different ways per orbit. It experiences once as an inward motion and once as an outward motion as we orbit the center of all moments. The end of Krishna's Era marks the beginning of Kali out.

If 5,124 years have passed since Krishna's Era then we may simply add to see where we are in this cycle. Each Kali yuga is 1,296 years long so Kali out plus Kali in equal 2,592 years. This would be the start of the Dwapara yuga. The Dwapara yuga last for 2,592 years. The total is 5,184 years. By subtracting 5,184 by 5,124 we may see that we are about sixty years from fully entering Tetra yuga. It is nearly the same moment as fully entering the age of Aquarius as seen in the Zodiac system.

The Law of One

The Law of One is a series of channeled works that discuss a similar concept. It is interesting how they speak of energy patterns that exist within each cycle and how they affect experience. In the Law of One teachings, we are in transition from what they call a yellow ray energy center into a green ray energy center.

The Wheel

Let's now take a closer look at our 25,920 precessional cycle and the various systems previously mentioned.

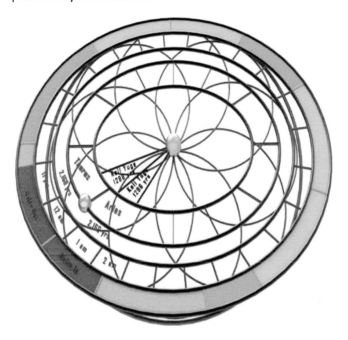

The Deltaverse

Now that we have aligned our wheel, we may relate the various systems to the circadian rhythm. Notice how we are in Sat yuga for half of the cycle. When relating to the circadian rhythm the only harmonic we are in for that long is the beta wave which is a turning point within our orbit of conscious density. This means within the conscious system we may orientate the midpoint of our beta experience to the midpoint of the Sat yugas. It is interesting to see that when we do this the various lengths of each yuga system seems to align perfectly in relationship to the relative length that each of our conscious harmonics vibrations last. Let's go step by step and relate.

From "Mind: The Shifter and Reorganizer of Nodes," we see that we experience each harmonic twice in two different ways. Once, we are drifting in towards the Noviverse, and once we are drifting out towards the Lowerverse. Our turning point is approximately 12:45 am. This moment of our circadian rhythm could be considered the turning point in relationship to the Kali yugas. In essence, this turning point near midnight is the turning point of the Earth's conscious experience.

At this moment on the wheel, we see that Kali out and Kali in relate directly to our delta out and delta in. The Age of Taurus would relate to Kali out and delta out. The Age of Aries would then relate to Kali in and delta in as we move towards denser vibrations.

These times, the ages of Taurus, the age of Aries, Kali in and Kali out would be equivalent of being in a deep sleep when relating to the circadian rhythm. This is a time when spiritual development is at its lowest.

The Thetaverse

As we continue to drift inwards, following the habitable spiral of perception, we see that a new harmonic is created once we hit a distance that is ¼ the diameter of the previous wave. Relating to the circadian rhythm, this is the moment we are dreaming, we have entered the theta wave of Earth harmony.

Here again we see how each yuga is related directly to a conscious harmonic. The theta wave may be directly related to the Dwapara yugas and yellow ray energy system. In this model, the theta out relates directly to Dwapara out, and the end of the Age of Gemini and the start of the Age of Taurus. Theta in relates directly to Dwapara in, and the Age of the Pisces.

The Alphaverse

As we continue to drift inward, we reach a moment when we are again at ¼ the diameter of the wave that is bigger and we reach our alpha state of Earth harmony. This is the moment when the Earth awakens. It is like going from the dream state of theta into the awake state of alpha.

It is interesting how this transition from theta to alpha seems to be highlighted in all other traditional systems as well. It is the moment when we transfer from Dwapara yuga to Tetra yuga and also the moment when we go from the Age of Pisces into the Age of Aquarius. This transition also symbolizes the transition from yellow ray energy centers to green ray energy centers.

As we drift inwards, alpha in relates to Tetra in, both the Ages of Aquarius and Capricorn, and also the green ray energy system.

As we drift outwards, alpha out relates to Tetra out, both the Ages of Cancer and Gemini, and the green ray energy system.

The Betaverse

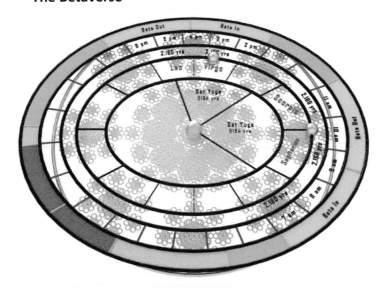

As we continue to drift inwards, at a distance of ¼ the previous wave, the beta wave of Earth consciousness is awakened. This is the moment of our most heightened states of being in all three aspects, mind, body, and spirit. The entire system, from the Earth to the human is fully awake. Historical records indicate this is the time we built the great pyramids of Egypt, the Sphinx, and countless other megalithic structures across the globe.

Beta in relates directly to Sat in, the Ages of Sagittarius and Scorpio, and the blue ray energy center.

Beta out relates directly to Sat out, the ages of Virgo and Leo and the blue ray energy center.

One thing to note is that in our updated model, which includes the circadian rhythm, is that we have added a section in green. Alpha mid, which is placed directly at the turning point of Sat in and Sat out, corresponds directly to the Age of Libra.

Why might we have added this dip? All conscious experience is related and stems from the same primal vortex of creation. As fluid rotates above it also rotates below and realms of experience overlap. All tidally locked in the great whirlpool of creation.

A Primal Vortex

Vortex of Tidally Locked Fluid

continues out to infinity

2.3 million yrs	Galactic Tunings
25,920 yr	Earth Tunings
24 hr	Human Tunings
2.4 x 10^-15 seconds	Atomic Tunings
	Subatomic Tunings

continues in to infinity or 0

All vibrations stem from a rotation or distortion of this greatest center. Just a note, this drawing is not to scale as the rotation rate of the Earth's great day is 9,460,800 times greater than our human experience. This spiral holds all experiences of all sizes, from infinitely large to infinitely small. All a function of a spiraling inward related to a Fibonacci spiral of inward drifting as we, the harmonizers of the 5th dimension, strive for harmony within this fluid.

Let's now take a closer look at this tidally locked vortex that contains all conscious experiences.

Tidally Locked Vortex of the 5th Dimension

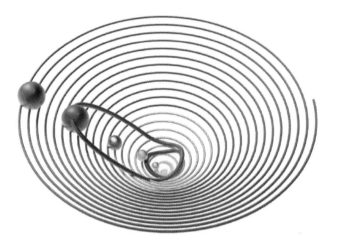

In the drawing above, each sphere represents a local sphere of influence of the 5th dimension which is relative to the scale of mind perceiving reality. It could be the mind of a human, the Earth, the Solar System, and even a galaxy. Either way, there are local spheres as this vortex stems from 0 to infinity. The purple route indicates the center of influence for the mind within the tidally locked fluid as the system orbits. The sphere on the route represents our maximum vibration of influence determined by the center of "mass" of the local system.

For example, for a human day of 24 hours the red sphere will orbit once every 24 hours. For the

Earth's day of 25,920 years, the local sphere would orbit every 25,920 years.

For the human, the yellow sphere would have a 12-hour orbit. The green sphere would have a 6-hour orbit, and the blue sphere would have a 3-hour orbit.

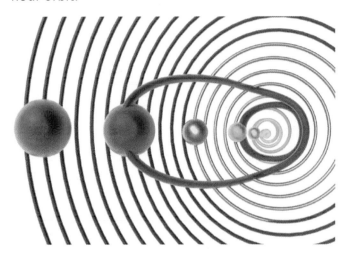

When comparing the vortex to Earth's precessional cycle, the yellow sphere would have a 12,960-year orbit. The green sphere would have a 6,480-year orbit, and the blue sphere would have a 3,240-year orbit.

This same system also applies to our 185-day alignment as well as our 2029-year alignment. It applies to every and all alignments within creation drifting inward as well. This means it also influences our hourly alignment as well as the one second alignment.

A Grand Clock

Let's now take a closer look at this system and relate our center of influence to the times and the circadian rhythm. For this, we will start at midnight.

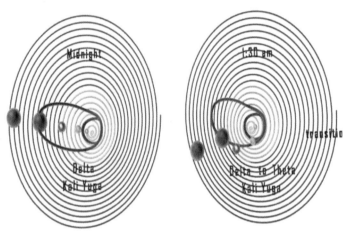

Starting at midnight you can see that all the spheres are aligned on the left side of the vortex. As the full 360-degree circle is made by the red sphere the inner spheres rotate accordingly in a 1 to 2 to 4 to 8 relationships. Each drawing represents a change of 22.5 degrees of arc for the red sphere, 45 degrees of arc for the yellow sphere, 90 degrees of arc for the green sphere, and 180 degrees of arc for the blue sphere. The sphere on purple path is red for both these drawings and symbolizes that is the main vibration of influence

502

during these modes of alignment. In the yuga system, this would represent the Kail in. In the Law of One, this would represent red ray energy centers. In the Zodiac, this would represent the Age of Aeries as we are currently on the half of the orbit that is drifting inwards. For simplicity, we will say midnight is the turning point of our orbit although it is closer to 12:45 am. Let's now rotate our clock by 22.5 degrees.

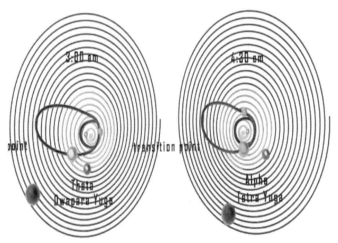

In the drawing relating to 3 am, we have now shifted from the delta harmonic to the theta inward harmonic and the sphere on the purple path is yellow as the center of our influence may be the center of "mass" of these 5th dimensional spheres. The red sphere is now 45 degrees from the starting point. The yellow sphere is 90 degrees from start. The green sphere is 180 degrees from start and the blue sphere has done a complete orbit. In the yuga system this could be considered Dwapara in. In the Law of One this would be yellow ray energy centers. In the Ages of the Zodiac, we would be in Pisces.

The drawing relating to 4:30 am shows the transition from theta brain harmony to alpha brain harmony as we continue to drift inward. This would be significant of the change from Dwapara in to Tetra in and the change from yellow ray energy centers to green ray energy centers. It also represents the shifting from the Age of Pisces to the Age of Aquarius. This is our current location on the clock in relationship to the 25,920-year precessional cycle. Let's rotate our clock 22.5 more degrees.

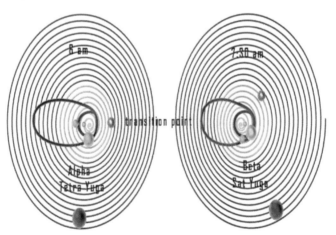

At 6 am, the red sphere has now rotated 90 degrees, the yellow sphere has done 180 degrees, the green sphere has made a complete rotation and the blue sphere has made two complete rotations. Notice how the green, blue, and yellow spheres are in a line and red is the only one offset. The sphere along the purple path is currently green symbolizing the alpha in brain state, the green ray energy system, the Tetra in, and the end of Aquarius and start of Capricorn. The transition from green to blue is approximately 7 am which is shown in the second drawing.

At 7:30 am, we are now in the Beta in brain harmony, the Sat in yuga, the Age of Capricorn, and the blue ray energy centers.

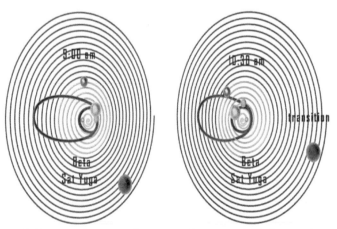

It is now 9 am and we continue to drift inward. The red sphere has rotated 135 degrees, the yellow sphere has done 315 degrees, the green sphere is at 180 degrees from 0 and the blue sphere is at 0. Again, the center of our influence is the center of "mass" of these tidally locked spheres and remains in the beta state, Sat yuga, blue ray energy center and we are now in the Age of Sagittarius.

In the drawing representing 10:30 am, we are now drifting back outward slightly and so we will call this our first Beta out. This relates to Sat in, the Age of Scorpio, and blue ray energy centers.

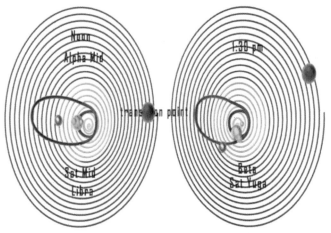

At noon, our red sphere has orbited 180 degrees, the yellow sphere has now made a complete circle. The green sphere has now orbited 2 times and is back at its starting point and the blue sphere has now orbited 4 times and is back at its starting point.

In essence, the only difference between midnight and noon is the location of the red sphere. The alignment of the yellow, green, and blue, pull us back outwards however the red sphere's location causes us to not fully drift back into the yellow and red centers. Our sphere along the purple path will be green during this time. This time relates to the transition from Sat in to Sat out, the Age of Libra, a dip into the green ray energy center, and may be a great time for a quick nap.

The next drawing represents 1:30 pm and shows how we reenter the Beta state before drifting back outwards. This would relate to Sat out, the transition from the Age of Libra to the Age of Virgo, and the blue ray energy centers.

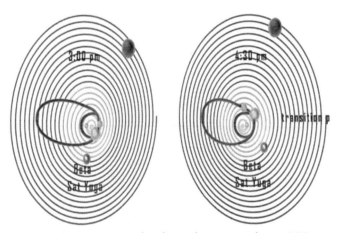

At 3 pm, our red sphere has now done 225 degrees of rotation. The yellow sphere is at 90 degrees. The green sphere is at 180 degrees, and the blue sphere is at 0. Our center of influence remains in the blue ray energy centers as we are now drifting outwards into less dense realms consisting of lower vibrations. Both these drawings represent Sat out, Beta out, and the Age of Virgo with transition to the Age of Leo.

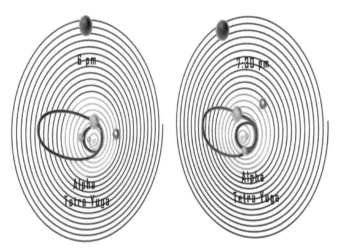

At 6 pm we are in transition from the blue to green spheres. One thing to note is that this is the same orientation as 6 am. The only difference is the location of the red sphere. This time relates to Alpha out, Tetra out, green ray energy centers, and the transition from the Age of Leo into the Age of Cancer. Our red sphere has done 270 degrees of rotation, the yellow is at 180 degrees, and the green and blue spheres are at 0 degrees.

At 7:30 pm, we remain in Alpha out, Tetra out, green ray energy centers, and are fully in the Age of Cancer.

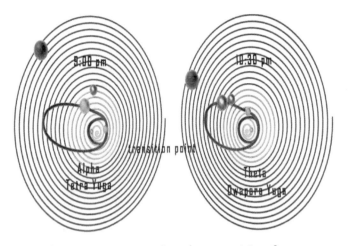

At 9 pm, we are nearing the transition from Alpha out into Theta out. This also symbolizes the transition from green ray energy centers into yellow ray energy centers and the switching from Tetra out into Dwapara out. This is also the age of Gemini. Our red sphere has done 315 degrees, the yellow sphere is at 270 degrees, the green sphere is at 180 degrees and the blue sphere is at 0 degrees. Our center of influence is in the green.

At 10:30 pm we have now transitioned from Alpha out into Theta out. We are now in the yellow ray energy centers, Dwapara out, and entering the Age of Taurus.

This is the moment when we begin to dream and the vibration of the Earth system slows dramatically. It is as if the Earth goes to sleep during this time.

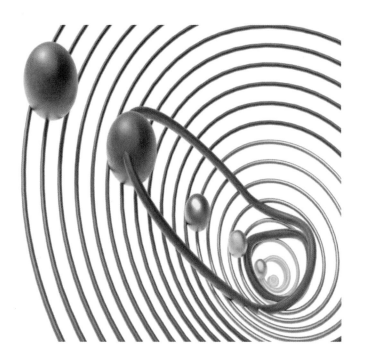

The orbit then begins again as the tidally locked fluid of the 5th dimension whirlpools inwards. For the human circadian rhythm, this takes 24 hours to complete. For the Earth's precession, it takes 25,920 years. We can now see how these systems are forever intertwined as all experiences are secondary and emerge from this vortex.

A Bouncing Orbit

One thing to note is that the path drawn out by the purple sphere is not a single ellipse. It consists of two ellipses. One big orbit and one tight orbit. The two orbits in combination are what gives us a full cycle of the yugas, ages of the zodiacs, and circadian rhythm.

Influences on Life

Just like the human and the individual cells that create the body undergo changes in function according to the circadian rhythm, so does the planet during this precessional cycles. This implies that humans, being the white blood cells of the Universe, will also undergo changes in function within the Earth system. We will return to this.

Distortions of Self

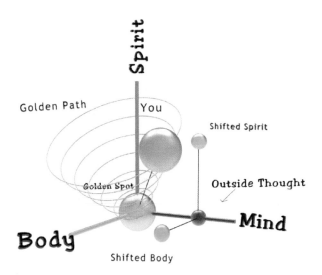

Distortions in mind, body, or spirit create delusions which are spiraling flows of space that act like habitats for beings to evolve within. They also cause us to misalign with the natural incoming flows of space and disconnect us from the greatest flow.

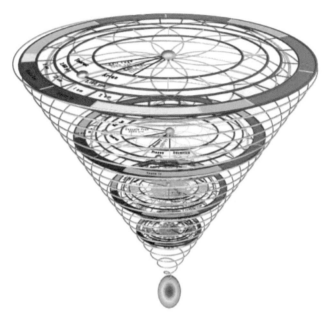

Our current delusions have solidified within the Theta state of Earth harmony. As we drift closer to the Alpha state of Earth consciousness, our personal bodies need to align with this energy as well. Not aligning with this flow could be comparable to running into a wall at light speed. This may result in spiraling deeper and deeper into personal delusions and will result in a great moment of turmoil. It is up to those who are connected to the laminar flow to use their knowledge of the mind, body, and spirit to help

guide spiraling minds towards this greatest
vibration.

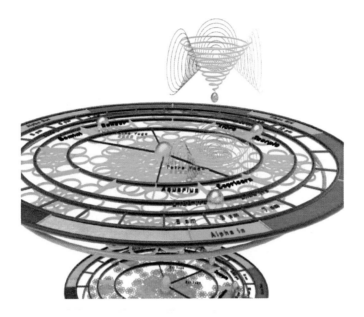

This drawing represents someone who is holding
postures of delusion while entering the Alpha state
of Earth harmony. The shape of the postures could
be considered one's ego. It is the postures they
hold in all three aspects; mind, body, and spirit.
The overall light-state harmony in relationship to
the green ray energy system may determine how
dramatic this will be for the individual. Postures
that do not align with this denser and higher
vibration will ultimately melt away through tight
spirals of delusion as they must harmonize with the
incoming flows of the Lowerverse.

Delusions Must Melt

As we enter the Alpha state of Earth harmony all delusions will melt away. This may be considered a convergent moment of conscious experience as we will all become connected to this new vibration. In essence, we will emerge into this new realm free of delusions and in tune with Earth harmonies. Individuals that refuse to let go of their postures will not be able to properly harmonize. They may become sick in all aspects of mind, body, and spirit.

Understanding this, we may take precautions for this upcoming time and begin the guiding process to ease the transition from yellow to green.

Recrystallization

    This drawing represents aligning your personal body within itself. We must start from small and work up to the greater flows. The first step is to align the chakra centers of your body. Once your body is in harmony with itself in all aspects; mind, body, and spirt we may then shift our attention to the greater bodies of our experience such as the Earth, Moon, and Sun.

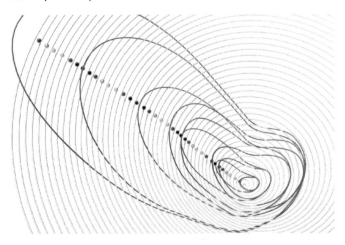

The Awakened Earth

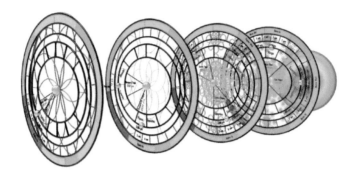

As recrystallization takes place, so does the sense of purpose within our experiences. We will see the Earth is alive. We will see the Earth needs bandages as for the last 10,000 years or so we have been dreaming and are finally awakening from this great sleep.

We will see how magnetic focal points of Earth may be amplified and strengthened by use of geometric structures focusing and reflecting healing energy across the Earth and cosmos. We will have a new purpose, one that is greater than the self and the idea of a soul will no longer be science fiction.

The perfect rotations of an aligned spirit lead to the perfect projections that allow for faster than light travel as we will traverse dimensions of space and time itself.

Moving into a Great Era

As the wheel of time turns so do all experiences and relationships. Concepts and ideologies that seemed practical and reasonable will no longer have any merit as ultimately, we are all intertwined with the greatest vortex of all moments.

The push of one, causes the pull of another as we all strive for harmony and bliss within creation. Through experience, through synchronization, and through love, we are the harmonizers of the 5th dimension.

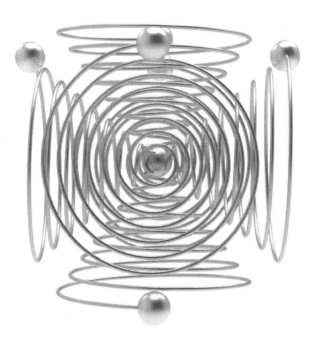

Tohu va-Vohu

61d323d8-e351-4bb1-a59a-5a0ecb3fa8e3R01